River Cottage

much more Veg

Hugh Fearnley-Whittingstall

Photography by Simon Wheeler

Illustrations by Mariko Jesse

BLOOMSBURY

LONDON · OXFORD · NEW YORK · NEW DELHI · SYDNEY

For Louisa, who loves raw peas and carrots,
and quite likes cooked cabbage and spinach.

Following the recipes

- All spoon measures are level unless otherwise stated:
  1 tsp = 5ml spoon;
  1 tbsp = 15ml spoon.
- All herbs are fresh unless otherwise suggested.
- Use freshly ground black pepper unless otherwise listed.
- All fruit and veg should be washed before you start cooking. Choose organic fruit and veg where possible.
- If using the zest of citrus fruit, choose unwaxed fruit.
- Oven timings are provided in the recipes for both conventional and fan-assisted ovens. These are intended as guidelines, with a description of the desired final colour or texture of the dish as a further guide. Individual ovens can deviate by 10°C or more either way from the actual setting, so it's important to get to know your oven and to use an oven thermometer to check the temperature.

- *For vegans* The recipes in this book are vegan, but always check that any prepared or processed ingredients you buy – such as sugar, stock cubes, wine, sauces, condiments, curry paste, fruit juice and vinegar – are suitable for vegans. Some brands may contain animal products or animal products may have been used during their manufacture – but there are always alternatives. Online suppliers such as planetorganic.com and healthysupplies.co.uk stock many vegan products. For guidance on choosing animal-free ingredients, contact vegansociety.com.
- *For coeliacs/those avoiding gluten* Barley and spelt contain gluten, so the recipes with these ingredients are not suitable. When you are buying naturally gluten-free grains, such as rice and oats, as well as prepared and processed products such as sauces, condiments, stock cubes and seasonings, always check that they are guaranteed gluten-free, as some may contain traces of gluten (justnatural.co.uk stock certified gluten-free grains). For general advice and guidance on choosing gluten-free ingredients, contact coeliac.org.uk.

THIS IS THE SECOND book I have written with the pleasingly simple aim of making vegetables delicious – irresistibly, satisfyingly so. I want to do this so that you eat more of them; more of the ones you already love, and more of those you're not quite sure about yet. My mission is to increase your veg consumption, and expand your veg horizons, to the absolute maximum. I think it should be fairly obvious why this is a good idea. But I do like an opportunity to be vocal on the topic, so here goes…

If I were to choose just one thing we could all do in order to be healthier and feel more energised, to have a better relationship with food and with our environment, it would be this: eat more veg.

This is true for all of us, which is why this book is for omnivores, vegetarians and vegans alike. Whoever we are and however we choose to eat, it is without doubt a very good idea to make vibrant, nutritious plant foods the basis of our diets.

These foods are incontrovertibly beneficial to our health: full of the vitamins, minerals, antioxidants, fibre and complex carbs that genuinely nourish us. Just as importantly, the more lovely fresh veg we eat – in both quantity and variety – the less space there is in our diets for other foods which are, shall we say, of more questionable value – or certainly less unequivocally virtuous! In particular, we can start to 'nudge out' some of those knee-jerk 'empty carbs' – the gap-filling bread and biccies that so often get us through the day.

More veg is good for the planet too: simple and inexpensive to produce, and vastly less demanding of energy and resources than animal-based foods. And if we eat more veg, we can also eat less meat and fish – or none

at all, if we choose. As many of you know, I do eat both (discerningly, I hope, with the welfare of our farm animals, and the environment, in mind). But you'll find none of either in these pages. I want this book to be wholly inclusive. And I think vegetables should be the most inclusive foods we eat – a bounty for all. I've been making a conscious effort for some years now to shift towards a veg-centric way of eating – and the recipes here are a testament to that exciting, satisfying culinary adventure.

I'm pretty sure most of us *know* that we should be consuming more vegetables (and fruits), so why aren't we? Perhaps it's because our culinary culture has not been particularly kind to veg. We've long eaten them, of course, but not often in the colourful, creative, *respectful* ways that other cuisines have come up with. There's been too much boiling going on: so many of us grew up viewing vegetables as something plain on the side of the plate, hidden under the gravy. That's no way to learn how exciting veg can be!

For much of my (semi-) professional cooking career, I also put veg mainly 'on the side', allowing well-chosen meat and fish to dominate my culinary thinking. I certainly wasn't a veg-dodger. But I had my favourites – raw peas from the pod, simply buttered greens, roast parsnips, barbecued courgettes and spring onions – and I didn't seek to ring the changes with any great conviction.

But as I began to grow more veg of my own at River Cottage, and dabble in a more worldly (often Asian-inspired) way with vegetables, I began to realise that I was hugely underestimating the power of veg to deliver pleasure as well as goodness to me and my family. That was when I decided that a stint as 'vegetarian' might do me – and my kitchen repertoire – some good. It was transformative. *River Cottage Veg Every Day* – the book and the TV series – was the result of that experiment. And in many ways this book is too.

The way that I cook has been recalibrated, forever. Vegetables are now the major force in my kitchen. They are my first port of call when tummies are rumbling. And I've taught myself a fair bit about how to make veg taste great, without too much kitchen faff. Now I want to share what I've learned with you. And so I've packed these pages with easy, appetising recipes that will take your enjoyment of veg to a whole new level.

I begin, all guns blazing, with two chapters of the kind of belly-filling veg-based main courses that ensure you won't miss the meat (or the fish, dairy, pasta or bread). These recipes use the saucepan, the frying pan and roasting tray to bring the very best out of veg. Augmented with grains, nuts and pulses, spiked with spices, herbs and aromatics, these are easy, hot, filling veg dishes that feel 'complete' and substantial.

Next you'll find pages rammed with big veg tray-roasts, hearty, healthy salads and beautiful, satisfying soups, followed by one of my favourite parts of the whole book – a chapter of easy and delicious ways to pack in a daily dose of completely raw veg. What better, easier way could there be to boost one's healthy eating credentials? These lovely dishes – raw veg sliced, slivered, grated, pulsed and puréed – represent the freshest of quick fixes. They are easily incorporated into, or added on to, your usual daily fare – a shot of raw goodness that ranks way better than popping vitamin pills.

I've also shared rafts of recipes for the super-tasty, smaller dishes – the tapas and mezze-style treats – that are such good vehicles for veg. Mixing and mingling a few of these dishes on the dinner table, along with some of the simple side dishes found in the final chapter, is one of my optimum ways to eat. And in the same chapter I take the idea of 'veg side dishes' and give them a hefty nudge towards centre stage. So often it's the simple addition of a little spice, a simple sprinkle, or a doddle of a dressing that makes a pile of greens or roots alluringly easy to eat.

I have plundered the vegetable kingdom for this book, using every root, shoot, bean, allium and vine-vegetable I can think of – often in ways I *hadn't* previously thought of. And fruits have become honorary vegetables for me too – in fact, I could have just called the book 'Much More Plants' but somehow it didn't have quite the same ring to it. I'll show you how everything from apples, plums and pears to summer berries can be liberated from the fruit bowl and take their place in salads, soups, tapas and savoury suppers.

As you might expect, beans and pulses are peppered generously throughout. And I've used nuts and seeds with abandon, allowing them to reveal a whole new spectrum of qualities – not just crunch, but creaminess and richness too. Grains such as oats, rice, barley and pearled spelt make a significant mark in these recipes, as well as 'grains' that are actually seeds, such as quinoa and buckwheat.

To enhance these fabulous raw materials, I've raided my spice cupboard and my herb garden, as well as turning to the classic seasonings which I always have to hand to give my veg a boost: salt, pepper, lemon juice, ginger and garlic. A few good, cold-pressed virgin oils have gone to lubricate all this, while a little vinegar, mustard and tamari give a nice piquant edge to many dishes.

While all the recipes here are delicious just as they're described, it nevertheless matters a lot to me that you shouldn't see them as strict prescriptions. They're organic – in the broadest sense – and you should feel free to make them your own, adding alternative ingredients or tinkering with the seasoning to suit your taste and to make best use of the foods you have to hand. To this end, you'll find a list of 'Swaps' on almost every page, suggesting various veg, fruit, herbs, spices, nuts and seeds that can take the place of those listed in the recipe itself.

You don't need to get hung up on quantities either. I never do. As well as specifying, say, '3 medium carrots' or 'half a cauliflower', I often give a weight for veg. But these figures are just a guide; don't ever feel you can't cook one of the recipes because you've got a little less of this ingredient or a little more of that. One of the great things about veg cookery is that it's wonderfully elastic – endlessly adaptable, totally tweak-able.

To make this book inclusive, there are quite a few things I've left out. You'll find no meat, fish, eggs or dairy products – not a scrap of butter, cheese or yoghurt. There's no honey either – because I want the book to be completely vegan-friendly – and there's only the odd pinch or spoonful of sugar here and there.

Perhaps more unexpectedly for a veg book, there's no bread, no pasta, no noodles, and no pastry. It's not that I don't like these things, or that I think we ought to give them all up entirely. But I do believe our culinary culture has become massively over-dependent on them. The latest nutritional research makes it increasingly clear that too much refined carbohydrate is harming our health and expanding our waistlines. So I think it's useful to have a cookbook that puts it to one side.

I've also avoided (without much effort) all refined flours, and many of the recipes in the book are suitable for coeliacs and those avoiding gluten. The exceptions are the recipes that contain barley or spelt – and you should check prepared goods such as condiments and stock cubes for wheat or gluten. I use oats, rice, quinoa and buckwheat too, which though naturally gluten-free can sometimes be 'contaminated' with gluten. However, gluten-free versions are available so these recipes are not off-limits. In the end I've found none of these 'restrictions' particularly limiting. Plants, and the grains, spices and oils that come from them, are the best building blocks for delicious, healthy meals. I still see meat and fish, eggs and butter, pasta and good bread as fine foods. I just think they should be consumed in moderation. It's the natural plant ingredients that best sustain us, and that should run rampant through our kitchens.

When it comes to kitchen kit for getting the most from veg, requirements are pretty modest. A couple of good knives will do you: one large, sharp cook's knife for most of the chopping, and a small paring knife for more precise jobs such as slicing the seeds out of squash or coring apple quarters. The only other essential bits of kit are a food processor, a blender, a pestle and mortar, and a few pieces of plus-sized cookware: a big frying pan, a big saucepan (a two-handled 'stockpot' is what I use most) and a big roasting dish – the largest that will go in your oven. Veg is bulky stuff – to create a hearty meal, you sometimes have to start with what seems like armfuls of raw produce. It's one of the things I love about veg-led cookery, actually, the generosity of it: the 'before' pile of voluptuous squash, lustrous greens and plump alliums that a bit of chopping, stirring and simmering will turn into the 'after' of a lovely dinner.

Since you are going to be eating Much More Veg (that's the plan, right?) it may be worth thinking about *how* you eat it – and therefore how you serve it. Plenty of the dishes in this book can be enjoyed in the 'conventional' way – one big dish on the table, and everyone gets a portion. But making more of veg naturally opens the door to a slightly different approach to meals – one that often feels easier and less restrictive than what we're generally used to. It's about laying out a few veg dishes, and passing them around; a colourful, sociable and life-enhancing way to eat. You may end up with a little more than you need on the table, but that's a good thing. Refrigerate your leftovers as soon as you've finished a meal, and they'll live to delight another day. This 'roll-over' approach to cooking has long been at the heart of my kitchen, and I love it.

In the end, when it comes to upping the veg in your life, my only rule is: have no rules. Fix it your way. Eat your gorgeous veg curry with a simple scoop of brown rice, or make it part of a spread with spicy potato rösti and dhal. Feast on a tray of roast veg just as it comes, or offer it up with a big green salad and a dish of herby spelt. Eat a raw soup for breakfast if you want to, or Bircher muesli for your supper.

Eat your veg any way you like – just eat much more of it!

Veg feasts

IF WE ARE TO EAT more veg, then we must welcome it into every part of our daily diet. We have to banish the concept of it as just 'the bit on the side' and instead celebrate the wonderful generosity and variety of the veg kingdom with big main-meal dishes that leave us feeling satisfied and fully refuelled. If you think that dishes based on vegetables might struggle to step into this role, I (heartily) beg to differ.

In fact, I've made it my mission to seek out and create recipes that utterly trounce the idea of veg as a mere supporting player. I've gone out of my way to dream up and develop veg-only dishes that are as gratifying and pleasing as any Sunday roast or meaty curry. Here are my latest offerings: bowlfuls, panfuls and platters of gorgeous, glorious veg-based fare, full of flavour, texture and substance, that will assuage robust appetites.

What makes a veg dish really satisfying? Quantity comes into it, of course, but that's by no means all the story. A good balance of flavours and textures is essential – otherwise, a dish can leave you feeling full, but somehow not fulfilled. Meals that merely sate hunger never satisfy in the same way as those that please the senses and the palate too.

The dishes in this chapter usually feature something starchy, be that spuds or other root vegetables, or grains like rice or spelt. I often add protein too, in the form of beans, pulses and/or nuts. That takes care of the belly-filling side of things. But along with these pleasing, ballast-providing elements, there must be other things to bring contrast, complexity, variety.

Full-flavoured veg such as aromatic fennel, earthy mushrooms, tangy tomatoes and sweet peppers come into their own in many of these dishes. And real 'kickers' like onions, garlic, chilli, herbs and vinegars will often help you to relish every mouthful. Less obvious ingredients can do this too, including bittersweet pomegranate molasses, pungent saffron, salty capers and smoky paprika.

Cooking methods are another way to ramp up flavour: you'll find lots of roasted and seared veg here, all carrying that lovely depth of character that caramelisation brings. And if you deploy a barbecue as an alternative to the frying pan, you will add the extra allure of wood smoke to that fusion of flavours.

Meat-free main meals often use dairy products and eggs as a way to add richness. But throughout this book I've chosen to show just how toothsome and satisfying you can make a dish using only plant-based ingredients. However, I've not shied away from using moderate amounts of beneficial fats such as those found in olive and rapeseed oils, coconut oil and coconut milk, as well as lovely, crunchy nuts, and even some antioxidant-rich avocado now and then. Fat always lends flavour and a pleasing mouth-feel to a dish, not to mention a feeling of satiety to whoever's eating it! You'll be selling your veg short if you leave it out.

And, while sometimes a trickle of good virgin oil is enough to perfect a veg dish, I frequently make sure my heartiest examples go beyond that to include a distinctly saucy element. Just as meat-based centrepieces need their gravy or their *jus*, so veg feasts benefit from the lubrication of a tangy dressing, soupy liquor, or a well-seasoned sauce – all things, as you'll see, that can be conjured up from the plant kingdom.

Some of the dishes here are enhanced by the addition of something simple on the side, such as a salad or one of the delicious dishes in my Spuds and grains chapter (pages 372–403). But many of them are one-pot winners that can be enjoyed without added extras. They will hold their own as delicious dinners, and demonstrate what I fervently believe, and want everyone to discover: that eating more veg need never mean feeling less satisfied.

Roast fennel, new potato and tomato stew

Serves 4

3 medium-large fennel bulbs (about 1kg in total)

600–700g new or waxy potatoes, scrubbed, cut into 2–3cm chunks

2 medium onions, roughly chopped

300g cherry tomatoes

3 garlic cloves, sliced

1–2 sprigs of rosemary (optional)

2 tbsp olive or rapeseed oil

700ml tomato passata

1 rounded tbsp harissa paste

400g tin chickpeas, drained and rinsed

75g pitted olives (about 100g stone-in)

Sea salt and black pepper

1 tbsp chopped preserved lemon, to finish

Laced with spicy-hot harissa paste and a sprinkling of salty preserved lemon, this rich vegetable stew has a tempting Moroccan feel to it. Eat it with a simple green salad, or add a bowlful of colourful, crunchy, Moroccan carrot blitz (page 284).

Preheat the oven to 190°C/Fan 170°C/Gas 5.

Trim the fennel bulbs of their bases, tops and tough outer layer, reserving any green feathery fronds attached to the stalks. Quarter the bulbs then cut each quarter into 2 or 3 wedges. Put these into a large roasting dish.

Add the potatoes, onions, cherry tomatoes and garlic. Throw in the rosemary if you have it, trickle over the oil, season with salt and pepper and stir everything together. Roast in the oven for 45 minutes, giving the veg a good stir after about 30 minutes.

Meanwhile, in a jug, combine the passata with 150ml water and stir in the harissa.

When the veg are tender and starting to brown, take the dish out of the oven and add the passata mixture. Stir it in well with a spatula, using the passata to deglaze the roasting dish, scraping up any nice bits of caramelised veg from the base and sides.

Add the chickpeas and olives then return the dish to the oven for 20 minutes or so, until the passata is bubbling and slightly reduced.

When the bubbling dish of veg comes out of the oven, taste it, then sprinkle with a little more salt and pepper if you think it needs it. Scatter over the preserved lemon, tear over any saved fennel fronds and then bring the dish to the table. Serve with more harissa if you like things spicy.

Swaps
Veg Use roughly chopped red, orange or yellow pepper (or all three!) as an alternative to fennel.
Pulses Instead of chickpeas, add white beans such as cannellini or butter beans.

Pepper, potato and chard stew with saffron

Serves 4

2 tbsp olive or rapeseed oil

1 tsp cumin seeds

1 large onion, quartered and thinly sliced

1 large (or 2 small) red pepper(s) (about 250g in total)

200g chard

500g new, waxy or salad potatoes, scrubbed

2 garlic cloves, finely grated or crushed

2 x 400g tins tomatoes

A large pinch of saffron strands

½ tsp hot smoked paprika

1 tsp sugar

Juice of ½ small lemon, or to taste

Sea salt and black pepper

TO FINISH

About 30g toasted flaked almonds

A handful of coriander leaves

Extra virgin olive or rapeseed oil

This is based on the lovely chachouka in *River Cottage Veg Every Day*. There are no eggs this time, but even more veg, with potatoes and chard adding to the rich pepper and tomato base. I really like the earthy, pungent tang of saffron in the dish, but the stew is still delicious without it.

Place a large flameproof casserole or small stockpot over a medium heat and add the oil. When it's hot, add the cumin seeds and let them sizzle for a minute or two. Add the onion with a pinch of salt, stir well, then cover and lower the heat. Let the onion sweat, stirring once or twice, for about 10 minutes.

In the meantime, quarter, deseed and thinly slice the pepper(s). Separate the chard stalks and leaves and cut both into 1cm thick slices. Cut the potatoes into bite-sized chunks.

When the onion is nice and soft, stir in the garlic, then add the red pepper, chard stalks and potatoes. Replace the lid and cook gently for about 20 minutes until the pepper is softened, stirring now and again to ensure nothing sticks and burns.

Add the tomatoes with their juice, crushing them with your hands as you do so. Add the saffron, smoked paprika, sugar and some more salt and pepper and stir well. Simmer gently, uncovered, for about 15 minutes, until the potatoes are tender, stirring regularly.

Toss in the chard leaves, cover the pan and cook for another 5 minutes, or until they have wilted. Stir the leaves into the stew. Take off the heat.

Add the lemon juice then taste the stew and adjust as necessary, with more salt, pepper and/or lemon. Serve scattered with the toasted almonds and coriander and trickled with extra virgin oil.

Swaps

Leaves Use spinach instead of chard – there's no need to cook the stalks separately, just wilt the spinach in at the end of cooking.
Herbs Finish the dish with mint or parsley rather than coriander.

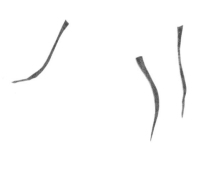

Roast cauliflower, almonds and barley with parsley and chilli

Serves 4

100g pearl barley or pearled spelt

1 medium-large cauliflower (800g–1kg untrimmed)

6 garlic cloves, peeled and roughly bashed

2 tbsp olive or rapeseed oil

75g blanched almonds

2 tbsp capers, rinsed and drained

½ lemon, to spritz

Sea salt and black pepper

FOR THE PARSLEY AND CHILLI DRESSING

1 medium-hot red chilli, deseeded (for less heat, if preferred) and finely chopped

A small bunch of flat-leaf parsley (about 25g), leaves picked from the stems and finely chopped

1 small garlic clove, finely chopped

2–3 tbsp extra virgin olive oil

Plump barley grains, earthy-sweet cauliflower and toasty almonds are all tied together here with a piquant parsley and chilli dressing to make a deliciously satisfying dish.

Start by cooking the barley or spelt. If you have time, soak the grain in cold water first, for 20–30 minutes. Either way, rinse it well in a sieve then tip into a saucepan, add a pinch of salt and cover with plenty of cold water (it will absorb a lot). Bring to the boil, lower the heat and simmer until tender: barley should take 35–40 minutes, spelt only about 20 minutes. Once cooked, drain in a sieve and set aside.

In the meantime, preheat the oven to 190°C/Fan 170°C/Gas 5.

Trim away the coarser leaves and stalk end of the cauliflower then roughly cut up the rest – it should still be in medium-large florets. Include the stalk and tender leaves too.

Put the cauliflower into a large roasting tin with the garlic, oil and some salt and pepper. Toss together, then roast for 20 minutes. Stir the cauliflower, then scatter over the almonds and capers and return to the oven for 15 minutes, until the cauliflower is tender and well browned in places and the almonds are golden brown. Scatter over the cooked grain and return to the oven for another 5 minutes.

While the veg is cooking, make the dressing: combine all the ingredients together in a bowl and season with salt and pepper.

Transfer the contents of the roasting tin to warmed serving bowls. Dot the parsley dressing over the cauliflower and grain, squeeze over some lemon juice, and serve straight away.

Swaps

Grains Use cooked wholegrain (or red or black) rice instead of barley or spelt.

Veg Replace some or all of the cauliflower with large broccoli florets. Or base the dish on root veg – chunks of celeriac, carrot and parsnip – giving them a bit longer in the oven to become tender before you add the almonds.

Red pepper and olive hash

Serves 3–4

500g floury potatoes, such as
King Edward or Maris Piper,
or 400g cold, cooked potato

2 medium red peppers (about
350g in total)

2 tbsp olive or rapeseed oil

1 tbsp capers, rinsed, drained and
chopped

100g pitted kalamata olives
(about 120g stone-in), chopped

2 garlic cloves, chopped

2 tsp chopped rosemary

2 tbsp chopped flat-leaf parsley

Sea salt and black pepper

It's worth boiling the potatoes especially in order to make this lovely spin on bubble and squeak, but it's also a good way to use up leftover cooked spuds or mash. You'll need about 400g cooked potato – but you could scale down the other ingredients if you have less.

If you are cooking the potatoes from scratch, peel and cut into large chunks (no smaller than an egg) then put them in a saucepan. Cover with water, add a little salt and bring to the boil. Lower the heat and simmer the potatoes for 15–20 minutes, until completely tender. Drain the potatoes and leave them to steam in a colander.

Meanwhile, halve the red peppers and remove the stalks, seeds and white membrane, then chop the flesh into roughly 1cm pieces.

Put a large, non-stick frying pan over a medium heat and add the oil. When it is hot, add the chopped peppers with some seasoning and fry quite briskly, so they start to soften, for about 10 minutes.

Meanwhile, tip the potatoes back into their saucepan and mash them roughly with a potato masher – it needn't be a super-smooth mash.

Add the chopped capers, olives, garlic and rosemary to the peppers, stir well and fry for a further 2–3 minutes.

Add the mashed potatoes to the pepper mixture in the pan, along with the chopped parsley and some salt and pepper. Mix together with a spatula, then form into a roughly round, flat cake. Fry the mixture until golden brown on both sides – as it cooks, flip it over in rough sections and squash them back down. Flip and squash, flip and squash, until nicely browned all over, adding a little more oil to the pan if necessary.

Serve the hash in big, rough wedges, with wilted greens, such as spinach and lettuce.

Swaps

Veg Chopped fennel is a lovely alternative to the red pepper. You can also add sweetcorn kernels, or broad beans (blanched and skinned), along with the capers and olives.
Roots Replace some of the potato with parsnip or celeriac.

Nutty gratin of greens and leeks

Serves 4

20g whole raw buckwheat (buckwheat 'groats')

20g flaked almonds

20g jumbo oats

2 tbsp olive or rapeseed oil

1 large onion, halved and sliced

1 large leek (about 300g), trimmed and cut into 5mm rounds

1 head of spring greens (about 250g), shredded into 1–2cm ribbons

75g cashew nuts, soaked in cold water for at least 3 hours

350ml hot veg stock (see page 190 for home-made)

1 tsp English mustard

Sea salt and black pepper

A creamy-textured, savoury sauce – made by blitzing cashews with mustard and sweated-down onions – ensures this is as good as any dairy-laden gratin. Serve it hot and bubbling for a really comforting meal. (Don't forget to put your cashews to soak a few hours ahead.)

Preheat the oven to 190°C/Fan 170°C/Gas 5.

Combine the buckwheat, almonds and oats in a bowl and set aside.

Heat the oil in a large frying pan over a medium-low heat. Add the onion with a pinch of salt and cover the pan. Cook for 5 minutes or so, to encourage the onion to soften and sweat, then remove the lid and cook for a further 15 minutes or so until very soft and golden.

Meanwhile, bring a large pan of water to the boil, add the leek and greens and simmer for about 5 minutes, until the leek is tender but not soft. (Alternatively, you can cook them in a steamer.) Drain thoroughly.

Drain the soaked cashews and put them into a blender. Add the hot stock and blitz until you have a smooth, thin liquid. Add the soft onions and mustard and blitz again to get a thin, savoury 'cream'. Season with salt and pepper to taste.

Spread the greens and leek mix in a shallow oven dish (about 1.5 litre capacity), season with salt and pepper and pour on the cashew cream. Scatter the buckwheat mix over the top and transfer the dish to the oven. Bake for about 20 minutes until golden and bubbling. Serve straight away, with mash or seaweed oven chips (page 380).

Swaps

Greens Replace the spring greens with other leafy veg, according to what is in season: try curly kale or Savoy cabbage.

Pea speltotto with lemon and hazelnuts

Serves 4

75g hazelnuts (skin on or off)

2 tbsp olive or rapeseed oil

1 large onion, chopped

4 garlic cloves, sliced

250g pearled spelt or pearl barley (soaked in cold water for 20 minutes if time)

400g frozen petits pois

400ml hot veg stock (see page 190 for home-made)

1 large lemon

Sea salt and black pepper

TO FINISH

Flat-leaf parsley, chopped (optional)

Extra virgin olive oil, to trickle

This lovely, loose-textured speltotto has a summery feel but, since it uses frozen petits pois, you can make it at any time of the year.

Bash the hazelnuts roughly using a pestle and mortar, or wrap them in a tea towel and hit with a rolling pin, to break up into chunks. Put the bashed nuts into a frying pan with 1 tbsp oil and some salt and fry gently for a few minutes, until golden, keeping an eye on them as they can go from golden to burnt very quickly. Tip onto a plate and set aside.

Heat 1 tbsp oil in a medium saucepan. Add the onion with a pinch of salt and fry gently for about 10 minutes, stirring often, until soft. Add the garlic and fry for a minute longer. Take off the heat for a moment.

Rinse the pearled spelt or barley thoroughly in a sieve then tip into a saucepan, cover with plenty of water (it will expand a lot) and add a pinch of salt. Bring to the boil, reduce the heat, cover and simmer until just tender. This will take around 20 minutes for spelt, more like 40 minutes for barley.

While the grain is cooking, return the pan of softened onion to the heat and add half of the petits pois and the hot stock. Bring to the boil and cook for 2 minutes. Take off the heat and use a stick blender or a jug blender to blitz the contents of the pan into a bright green liquid purée. If you've used a jug blender, return the purée to its saucepan.

When the grain is just tender, add the other half of the petits pois to it. Let it return to a simmer and cook for a couple of minutes until both the grain and peas are tender. Drain well.

Combine the drained spelt or barley and peas with the hot green pea purée (reheating it gently first if necessary). Add some salt and pepper and mix well.

Spoon the speltotto into warmed serving bowls. Finely grate the zest of the lemon over the bowls and scatter the toasted hazelnuts on top. Add a little parsley if you have some, then trickle with extra virgin oil. Halve the lemon and give each bowl a spritz of the juice. Add a final grinding of salt and pepper, then serve.

Swaps

Grain Use wholegrain rice instead of the spelt or barley.
Veg Replace half of the petits pois with baby broad beans, adding them to the simmering spelt.

Bashed potatoes and broad beans

Serves 2–3

400g new potatoes, scrubbed, halved if large

About 400g podded broad beans (1–1.2kg in the pod)

1 tbsp olive or rapeseed oil

1 medium onion, chopped

1 small garlic clove, chopped

Sea salt and black pepper

TO FINISH

Mixed herbs (flat-leaf parsley, chives, thyme, basil, chervil etc), roughly chopped

Marigold, chive, thyme, rocket or nasturtium flowers (optional)

Extra virgin olive, rapeseed or hempseed oil, to trickle

Crushed into a pan of sweet, garlicky fried onions, broad beans form a chunky, vibrant and satisfying mix – exceptionally good on bashed new potatoes with a scattering of summer herbs.

Put the potatoes into a saucepan, cover with cold water and add a pinch of salt. Bring to the boil then simmer for 12–15 minutes until they are tender enough to crush easily.

Scoop out the potatoes with a slotted spoon and drain in a colander. Add the broad beans to the simmering water and cook until tender (anywhere from 3–10 minutes depending on the age of the beans). Drain. As soon as they are cool enough to handle, slip the broad beans out of their skins (very small, young beans can be left with skins on).

Meanwhile, heat the oil in a small frying pan over a medium-low heat. Add the onion and sweat gently for 10 minutes or so, then add the garlic and cook for a couple of minutes more. Take off the heat.

Tip the warm beans into the pan of hot onion and add some salt and pepper. Use a potato masher to roughly bash and mix the beans into the onion. Taste and add more salt and pepper if required.

Now use the masher to very roughly crush the new potatoes. Divide between warmed plates, top with the crushed broad beans and scatter over the herbs, and edible flowers if you have some. Finish with a trickle of extra virgin oil.

Swaps

Veg Try peas instead of the broad beans (they don't need skinning, of course!).

Summer veg sauté

Serves 2

1 tbsp olive or rapeseed oil

150–200g small new potatoes, scrubbed

100–150g baby beetroot, scrubbed, trimmed and cut into small wedges

100–150g baby carrots, halved or quartered lengthways

100–150g small courgettes, sliced on the diagonal

About 100g podded peas and/or broad beans

4–6 spring onions, trimmed and sliced on the diagonal

A handful of spinach leaves, roughly torn

A squeeze of lemon juice

Sea salt and black pepper

TO FINISH

Chives and flat-leaf parsley, roughly chopped

Extra virgin olive or rapeseed oil, to trickle

A medley of young vegetables, sweated down in a frying pan then finished with lemon juice and herbs, is one of my favourite summer meals. It's a super-simple dish, with the veg added in stages – depending on the time they take to cook. Whether you're using veg from your own garden or from a market or shop, choose small, new season specimens.

Have all the veg prepared before you start. Put a large frying pan over a medium heat and add the oil. When it's hot, add the new potatoes and beetroot with some salt and pepper and sweat, tossing the veg once or twice, for 3–5 minutes, depending on age and size.

Add the baby carrots and cook for another 3–5 minutes, depending on their size, again tossing once or twice. Add the courgettes and cook for 3 minutes more. By this time, all the veg should feel reasonably tender, but certainly not soft, when prodded with the end of a small, sharp knife. If they still seem hard, give them a few minutes more.

Add the peas and/or broad beans and sliced spring onions and toss them with the other veg, then add about 4 tbsp water to the pan. Cover with a lid (or anything that will trap in the steam – a baking tray will do) and let the veg steam and sweat for 2 minutes.

Uncover the pan again and strew the spinach over the veg. Leave for a couple of minutes more, so the leaves start to wilt, then take the pan off the heat and give everything a good stir. Add a squeeze of lemon juice and season with more salt and pepper.

Transfer to a warmed serving dish if you like, or serve straight from the pan, finished with some chopped herbs and a swirl of good oil. Either serve it just as it comes or paired with Puy lentils.

Swaps

Veg Use young green beans or halved radishes in place of the baby carrots, and/or mangetout or sugarsnap peas instead of courgettes.
Leaves Replace the spinach with lettuce leaves or sorrel, or use a leafy mixture of all three.
Herbs Swap the chives and parsley with other soft herbs, such as basil, chervil or mint.

Bazzoffia

Serves 3–4

4 globe artichokes (cricket-ball sized or larger)

1 large lemon

2 tbsp olive or rapeseed oil

2 bunches of spring onions, trimmed and cut into 1cm slices

1 garlic clove, sliced

1 large (or 2 small) fennel bulb(s) (about 350g in total), trimmed and cut into 1cm pieces

100ml dry white wine

200ml veg stock (see page 190 for home-made) or water

150g peas or petits pois (fresh or frozen)

1 medium courgette (about 200g), trimmed and cut into 1cm cubes

A handful of broccoli florets, (100–150g in total), roughly chopped

1 large little gem lettuce, roughly shredded

Sea salt and black pepper

TO FINISH

Chopped flat-leaf parsley, basil, chives or mint (or a mixture)

Extra virgin olive or rapeseed oil, to trickle

This Italian dish of green summer veg, lightly braised in wine and stock, is based around delectable globe artichoke hearts. They take time to prepare – but they taste so good it's a job I'm happy to apply myself to every now and then. If you don't fancy it, or you can't get fresh artichokes, you can make this dish with good quality, roasted artichoke hearts, adding them at the end rather than the beginning.

First prepare the artichoke hearts. Squeeze the juice of half the lemon into a large bowl of cold water. As you work, periodically dip the artichokes in the lemony water to help stop discoloration.

Take an artichoke and use a large, sharp knife to cut off the stalk about 2cm from the base of the head (leaving a bit attached). Working around the artichoke, pull away the tough green leaves, until the heart is only surrounded by a couple of layers of pale yellow leaves. Cut off most of the top of the artichoke, leaving just the base of the leaves and the heart attached to the stalk, exposing the furry 'choke' at the centre. Use a sharp-edge teaspoon to scrape out all the little fibres of the choke.

Use a small, sharp paring knife to trim away the remnants of the green leaf bases, the fibrous outer layer of the stalk and anything else that doesn't look pale and tender. You'll be left with a small, goblet-shaped heart. Quarter it and drop into the lemony water. Repeat with the rest.

Heat the oil in a large flameproof casserole or wide frying pan over a medium heat. Add the spring onions and garlic with a pinch each of salt and pepper, reduce the heat and sweat gently for about 5 minutes.

Using a slotted spoon, lift the artichoke hearts out of the lemony water and add them to the pan with the fennel. Give it a good stir, then pour in the wine and stock or water, add a little more salt and pepper, and bring to a simmer. Cover and simmer for about 10 minutes, until the artichoke hearts are starting to feel tender, but not cooked through.

Add the peas, courgette and broccoli and scatter the lettuce on top. Cover and simmer for a further 15–20 minutes, stirring once or twice, or until everything is tender. Taste and add more salt and/or pepper and lemon juice, as needed. Sprinkle with the chopped herbs and trickle on some extra virgin oil, then serve alone or with new potatoes.

Swaps

Veg Add green or runner beans, broad beans, mangetout, sugar snaps and/or samphire instead of, or as well as, the peas/courgette/broccoli.
Leaves Use baby leaf spinach, watercress or rocket in place of lettuce.

Seared summer cabbage with rosemary, chilli and capers

Serves 4

750g new potatoes, scrubbed and cut into evenly sized chunks if large

1 pointed summer cabbage, such as hispi/sweetheart (about 600g)

1 tbsp olive or rapeseed oil

4 tbsp extra virgin olive, rapeseed or hempseed oil

1 tbsp baby capers, rinsed and drained (or larger capers, roughly chopped)

1 garlic clove, finely chopped

1 tbsp chopped rosemary

A pinch of dried chilli flakes

Sea salt and black pepper

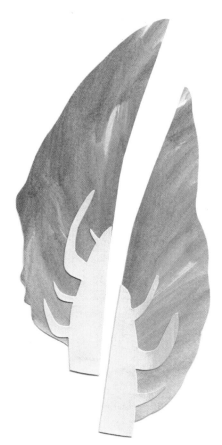

This is summer food at its most hearty and comforting. Wedges of pointed cabbage are fried until deliciously browned and sweetened, a generous scattering of garlic, chilli, chopped rosemary and capers seasons the dish, and a pile of crushed new potatoes makes the whole thing substantial.

Put the potatoes into a saucepan, cover with cold water and add a pinch of salt. Bring to the boil then simmer for 12–15 minutes until completely tender – soft enough to 'bash' easily. Drain well then return to the pan to keep hot.

Meanwhile, remove the outer couple of leaves from the cabbage and trim the stalk if it is long or grubby. Slice the cabbage in half, going down through the centre, then slice each half into 4 wedges. Don't worry if some of the leaves come free – they can all go into the pan.

Heat the olive or rapeseed oil in a large, non-stick frying pan, about 30cm, over a medium-high heat. (Or use two smaller pans, or cook in two batches.) Add the cabbage wedges, along with any loose leaves, and sprinkle over some salt and pepper. Fry for about 15 minutes, turning the cabbage wedges with tongs a few times – make sure you get lots of golden brown colour on each cut surface. Turn the heat down a little if the cabbage starts to blacken too much, but don't be afraid of plenty of colour! Sprinkle on a little more salt and pepper as you go.

Add 2 tbsp extra virgin oil and some salt and pepper to the hot new potatoes and use a potato masher or fork to very roughly mash them.

When the cabbage is nicely coloured, the outer leaves are tender and the stalk at the centre just yields to the tip of a knife (it should still be quite firm), throw the capers, garlic, rosemary and chilli flakes into the pan. Cook for another minute or so, turning the cabbage so it picks up the flavourings, then take the pan off the heat.

Divide the bashed potatoes between warmed plates. Add a couple of cabbage wedges to each. Add 2 tbsp more extra virgin oil to the still-warm cabbage pan and stir with a spatula, warming the oil and scraping up any seasonings and flavourings still in the pan.

Trickle the flavoursome oil over the plates of potato and cabbage and serve straight away. The cabbage will still be crunchy at the core, while the leaves will be wonderfully soft and wilted – enjoy it all!

Courgette, corn and cannellini bean stew

Serves 3–4

4 large, flavourful, ripe tomatoes (300–350g in total)

2 tbsp olive oil

1 large onion, chopped

1 large garlic clove, finely grated or crushed

2 cobs of corn, kernels sliced off

200g chard, cut into thin ribbons (stalks and leaves)

400g tin cannellini beans, drained and rinsed

1 medium courgette, or 4–5 baby courgettes, sliced very thinly, plus 2–3 courgette flowers if available

Sea salt and black pepper

TO FINISH

Flat-leaf parsley, roughly chopped

Extra virgin olive oil, to trickle

Here's a beautiful bowlful of summer flavours. The ingredients are cooked only lightly – with the courgettes staying almost raw – so they remain *al dente* and fresh-tasting. I like to finish the stew with ribbons of courgette flower, but don't worry if you can't find any of these delicate blooms – the dish is still wonderful without them.

First peel the tomatoes: cut a little cross in the base of each tomato, just through the skin to the flesh. Put all the tomatoes into a large bowl and cover with boiling water. After 2 minutes, test one to see if the skin will peel away easily (from the cuts). If it does, take all the tomatoes out of the water. If not, leave them for another minute or two. Peel off the skins, quarter the tomatoes and scoop out the seeds and surrounding juicy jelly into a sieve over a bowl. Chop the tomato flesh roughly and set aside. Press the seeds and juicy bits in the sieve to extract as much juice as possible. Keep the juice; discard the seeds.

Heat the oil in a large saucepan or small stockpot over a medium-low heat. Add the onion and garlic and cook gently for 7–8 minutes until soft. Add the chopped tomato flesh and cook for a further 5 minutes, stirring, so that the tomato starts to break down.

Add the sweetcorn kernels, chard, cannellini beans, the reserved tomato juice and enough water to almost, but not quite, cover the veg (start with about 300ml and add more if needed). Cook for a further few minutes, stirring once or twice, until the veg are just tender.

Add the sliced courgette and take the pan off the heat. Leave to stand for 5 minutes, stirring once or twice, then season the stew with salt and pepper to taste. If you have any courgette flowers, slice them thinly and scatter over the stew, along with the parsley. Trickle over some extra virgin olive oil and serve.

Swaps

Veg Replace the sweetcorn with peas or young broad beans.
Leaves As an alternative to the chard, use torn spinach leaves or finely ribboned kale.
Pulses Use tinned chickpeas in place of the white beans.
Herbs Try finishing the dish with chives and/or mint – and a few little chive flowers too, if you have them – rather than parsley.

Roast sweet potatoes with guacamole

Serves 4

1kg sweet potatoes

2 tbsp olive or rapeseed oil

Sea salt and black pepper

FOR THE GUACAMOLE

200g cherry tomatoes, cut into quarters

4–5 plump spring onions, trimmed and thinly sliced

1 medium-hot red chilli, deseeded and finely chopped

A small bunch of coriander (25g), leaves picked from the stems

Juice of ½ lime, or more to taste

2 large or 3 medium ripe avocados

2 tbsp extra virgin olive oil, plus extra to finish

The rich flavour of sweet potato is fantastic offset with this chunky, bashed-up version of guacamole, which is tangy with tomatoes, lime juice, spring onion and chilli. Together, they make a colourful, fresh-flavoured centrepiece for the table.

Preheat the oven to 200°C/Fan 180°C/Gas 6.

Peel the sweet potatoes then slice into discs, 5–8mm thick. Put them on a large baking tray, trickle over the oil and sprinkle with salt and pepper then mix with your hands, making sure all the sweet potato gets coated with oil. Spread the potato slices out as evenly as you can on the tray.

Roast for 30 minutes, until the potatoes are tender, then use a spatula to turn them over carefully (they'll be quite soft). Give them another 20–30 minutes, until the potatoes are browning in places.

When the sweet potatoes are nearly done, make the guacamole: put the tomatoes, spring onions and chilli into a bowl and add the coriander leaves, keeping back a few to finish the dish. Add the lime juice and some salt and pepper and toss to mix.

Halve and stone the avocados. Scoop out the flesh with a teaspoon and drop it into the bowl with the tomato mixture. Add the olive oil then use a fork to roughly mash and crush the avocado into the tomato mixture. Taste and add more salt, pepper and lime juice if needed.

Transfer the roasted sweet potatoes to a warmed large serving plate and spread them out in a shallow layer. Heap the guacamole in the centre. Give everything a final trickle of oil, sprinkle on the reserved coriander leaves, and serve.

Note

Avocados are a tricky topic at the moment – our growing appetite for them has led to deforestation and excessive use of both chemical pesticides and irrigation water in some of the regions where they are grown. Fairtrade and/or organic avocados are the best options.

Roast tomatoes and red rice with orange and almonds

Serves 4

200g Camargue red rice

650g cherry tomatoes, or other flavourful tomatoes

300g shallots, halved or quartered, depending on size (or roughly chopped onions)

4 garlic cloves, sliced

½ medium orange, cut into 1–2cm pieces (skin, pith and all)

2–3 sprigs of thyme, leaves picked

2 tsp sweet smoked paprika

1 tbsp sugar

3 tbsp olive or rapeseed oil

2 tsp balsamic vinegar

75g blanched almonds

Sea salt and black pepper

TO FINISH

Extra virgin olive or rapeseed oil, to trickle

Flat-leaf parsley, roughly chopped

This dish is all about the tomatoes and the rich, sweet, tangy liquor they create when roasted with oranges, shallots, paprika and a touch of balsamic vinegar. The little pieces of orange soften and caramelise as they roast and you can eat them, skin and all.

Preheat the oven to 190°C/Fan 170°C/Gas 5. Put the rice to soak in cold water.

Halve the cherry tomatoes (or cut larger tomatoes into bite-sized pieces) and place them in a medium roasting dish (which will hold all the ingredients quite snugly). Add the shallots, garlic, pieces of orange, thyme, smoked paprika, sugar and some salt and pepper. Trickle over the oil and balsamic vinegar and stir well. Roast for 30 minutes.

Meanwhile, drain the rice, put it into a saucepan and cover with plenty of water. Bring to the boil, reduce the heat and simmer until the rice is tender – probably 25–30 minutes but it depends on the variety of rice. When the rice is done, drain it well.

After 30 minutes' roasting, you should have a dish full of collapsed tomatoes and golden shallots in bubbling juice. Give everything a gentle stir, then scatter the whole almonds over the top and return to the oven for 10 minutes, to brown the nuts a little.

Tip the hot rice into the dish of juicy, roasted tomatoes and shallots. Stir it all together then taste and add more salt and pepper if needed.

Transfer to a warmed serving dish, trickle with a little extra virgin oil and sprinkle with parsley. Serve with wilted greens or something raw, such as a green salad or mushrooms with olives (page 263).

Swaps

Rice Use any wholegrain rice in place of the red rice.

Citrus You can replace the orange pieces with chopped preserved lemon rind for a sharper, saltier taste.

Herbs Finish with a scattering of chopped coriander or chives rather than parsley.

Celery, potato, barley and bean stew

Serves 4

100g pearl barley or pearled spelt

2 tbsp olive or rapeseed oil

1 head of celery, 3–4 most fibrous outer stems removed

2 medium onions, chopped

2 garlic cloves, chopped

1–2 bay leaves

1–2 sprigs of rosemary

100ml dry white wine

500ml veg stock (see page 190 for home-made) or water

300g potatoes (any kind)

400g tin white beans, such as cannellini, drained and rinsed

Sea salt and black pepper

TO FINISH

2 tbsp roughly chopped flat-leaf parsley

Extra virgin olive oil, to trickle

Hot and hearty, this has something of a peasant-food feel about it – inexpensive vegetables, very simply cooked, brought together at the end with some lovely virgin olive oil.

Put the barley or spelt in a bowl, cover with cold water and leave to soak while you start on the veg.

Heat the oil in a flameproof casserole or small stockpot over a medium heat. Slice the head of celery across into 1cm slices and toss them into the pan. Add the onions, garlic and some salt and pepper and stir well. When everything is sizzling nicely, cover, turn down the heat and let the veg sweat for about 10 minutes, stirring once or twice.

Drain the barley or spelt in a sieve and rinse well under the cold tap. Add to the celery and onions with the bay leaves and rosemary. Pour in the wine and stock or water and bring to a simmer. Put the lid on and cook gently for 20 minutes for pearl barley, just 5–10 minutes for spelt.

Meanwhile, peel or scrub the potatoes and cut into 1–2cm chunks.

Add the chunked potatoes and drained white beans to the pan and stir well. Put the lid back on, return to a simmer and cook for another 15–20 minutes, until the potatoes and barley or spelt are tender. Taste the stew and season with more salt and pepper as needed.

Serve scattered with the parsley and some more black pepper, and generously trickled with a good, peppery olive oil.

Swaps

Celery Use a couple of fennel bulbs, chopped, instead of the celery.
Roots Replace some or all of the potatoes with cubed celeriac.

Aubergine and tomato gratin

Serves 4

2 fairly large aubergines (about 700g in total), trimmed

4 tbsp olive oil, plus a little extra to finish

A small bunch of basil (25g), leaves picked from the stems and roughly torn

4–5 sprigs of thyme, leaves picked from the stems

About 30g flaked almonds

Sea salt and black pepper

FOR THE TOMATO SAUCE

2 x 400g tins tomatoes

3 garlic cloves, sliced

75g cashew nuts

1 tbsp olive oil

2 bay leaves

A pinch of sugar

Serve this hearty bake with a green salad on the side, or precede it with a delicious raw dish, such as fennel, melon and basil (page 249).

To make the sauce (which you can do ahead), put the tomatoes into a medium saucepan. If you're using whole plum tomatoes, crush them in your hands as you add them, removing any stalky end bits. Add the garlic, cashews, oil, bay leaves and a little salt and pepper. Bring to a simmer and cook, uncovered, for about 20 minutes, stirring regularly.

Remove the bay leaves. Add the sugar and blitz to a purée, using a stick blender or a jug blender. Stir in about 50ml water to thin the purée to the texture of lightly whipped cream. Taste and adjust the seasoning. (If making ahead, cool then refrigerate; reheat gently before using.)

Preheat the oven to 180°C/Fan 160°C/Gas 4. Cut the aubergines lengthways into 5mm thick slices. Heat up a griddle pan (or a barbecue) or preheat your grill. Measure 4 tbsp olive oil into a small bowl and use to brush the aubergine slices on both sides. Griddle or grill the aubergine slices, in batches if necessary, for 2–3 minutes each side, until tender and marked with brown patches or grill stripes, seasoning with salt and pepper as you go.

Layer one third of the aubergine slices over the base of an oven dish (about 2 litre capacity). Scatter over one third of the basil and thyme leaves. Dollop one-third of the tomato sauce over the top and carefully spread it out over the aubergines. Repeat until you have used up all the aubergines, herbs and sauce. Scatter over the flaked almonds and add a final trickle of oil.

Bake in the oven for 30–35 minutes, until bubbling and lightly coloured on top. Let it stand for 10–15 minutes before serving.

Swaps
Veg Use grilled slices of courgette or roasted slices of squash in place of the aubergine.

Parsnip, sprout and chestnut hotpot with cider

Serves 4

100g pearl barley or pearled spelt

250g shallots or baby onions

300g Brussels sprouts

400g parsnips

2 tbsp olive or rapeseed oil

150g cooked, peeled chestnuts

150ml medium-dry cider

2 bay leaves, torn

A couple of sprigs of thyme

750ml hot veg stock (see page 190 for home-made)

Sea salt and black pepper

Extra virgin olive or rapeseed oil, to finish

A steaming bowl of this hotpot is exactly what I want on a bleak, grey day. I wouldn't normally cook Brussels sprouts for this long but combined with all the other tender earthy veg, some nutty pearl barley and delicious cooking liquor, it works a treat.

Put the pearl barley or spelt into a bowl, cover with cold water and leave to soak while you prepare the veg.

Peel the shallots or onions and, if they are larger than a walnut, cut them in half. Trim the stalk ends of the Brussels sprouts and remove any dirty or damaged outer leaves. Peel and trim the parsnips and cut them into 2–3cm chunks.

Place a flameproof casserole or small stockpot over a medium heat and add the oil. When it's hot, add the shallots, Brussels sprouts, parsnips, chestnuts and some salt and pepper. Fry for 15 minutes or more, stirring only occasionally, so that you get some nice golden brown colour on the veg. This really adds to the flavour of the dish.

Meanwhile, drain the pearl barley or spelt in a sieve and rinse it well under the cold tap.

When the veg are nicely coloured, add the cider to the dish and cook, stirring and scraping the bottom of the pan to deglaze it, for a couple of minutes, until the liquor has reduced to almost nothing. Add the rinsed pearl barley or spelt, throw in the bay leaves and thyme then pour in the hot stock.

Stir well, bring to a simmer then turn the heat down low and cover the pan. Let the stew simmer for 35–40 minutes, until the barley or spelt is tender (spelt will cook a little more quickly). Taste and add more salt and pepper if needed.

Spoon into warmed bowls and add a trickle of extra virgin oil. Serve with greens, such as blitzed kale with lemon and garlic (page 362).

Swaps

Roots Add celeriac, potato or carrots (or any combination of these) in place of the parsnips.

Alliums Use red or brown onions, roughly chopped, as an alternative to the shallots.

Booze If you don't have cider to hand, white wine works just as well.

Red cabbage, celeriac and apple braise

Serves 4

1 small (or ½ large) red cabbage (600–700g in total)

2 medium eating apples, such as Cox's or russets

½ large celeriac (300–400g)

2 tbsp olive or rapeseed oil

1 large onion, chopped

100ml red wine

2 garlic cloves, finely grated or crushed

A pinch of dried chilli flakes

75ml cider vinegar or red wine vinegar

2 tsp sugar

50g raisins

400g tin dark-coloured beans such as carlin peas or red kidney beans

Sea salt and black pepper

TO FINISH

75g walnuts, roughly chopped or broken

2–3 tbsp roughly chopped flat-leaf parsley

Extra virgin olive or rapeseed oil

This is inspired by those classic sweet-and-sour braised red cabbage dishes that work so well as an accompaniment. But with celeriac, pulses and nuts — enriched with wine and spiked with a little chilli — this is a meal in itself.

Remove the outer couple of leaves from the cabbage if they are damaged or dirty. Quarter the cabbage, trim out the white heart, then cut each quarter into 5–8mm slices. Quarter and core the apples and cut into roughly 1.5cm pieces. Set aside.

Cut off the rough outer layer from the celeriac, then slice 1cm thick and cut each slice into chunky batons, about 1cm wide and 4–5cm long. Set aside, separate from the cabbage and apple.

Heat the oil in a large flameproof casserole or small stockpot over a medium heat. Add the onion and celeriac batons, with a pinch of salt, and fry gently, stirring from time to time, for about 8 minutes.

Pour in the wine, then once it is bubbling, add the garlic, chilli flakes, vinegar, sugar and 100ml water. Stir well to combine. When it is simmering, add the cabbage, apple and raisins. Season with salt and pepper and stir well again.

Put a lid on the dish, reduce the heat and let it simmer away gently for about 45 minutes–1 hour, stirring from time to time, until the celeriac is tender and the cabbage is yielding but still has a bit of bite.

Add the beans, stir and simmer for another 10 minutes. Taste and add more salt and pepper if needed.

Transfer to serving bowls, or leave in the casserole. Scatter the walnuts and parsley over the top, give it a trickle of extra virgin oil, then serve.

Swaps

Brassicas Use white rather than red cabbage.
Roots Replace the celeriac with 2 or 3 fat beetroot.
Fruit Try firm, slightly under-ripe pears as an alternative to the apples.

Rooty spelt bake

Serves 4

150g pearled spelt or pearl barley

500g Jerusalem artichokes

2 large leeks (600–700g in total)

1 celeriac (about 600g)

2 garlic cloves, sliced

A few sprigs of thyme

2 bay leaves, torn in half

3 tbsp olive or rapeseed oil

1 tbsp chopped rosemary

Sea salt and black pepper

This is a lovely, one-pot winter supper – simple, earthy and hearty. The veg cook in their own steam with a handful of seasonings and aromatics, becoming beautifully tender and producing a flavourful, savoury liquor. Seasoned cooked spelt goes on top at the end.

Preheat the oven to 190°C/Fan 170°C/Gas 5. Put the spelt or barley to soak in cold water while you prepare the veg.

Peel the artichokes and cut into roughly 1cm slices. Trim the leeks and slice 1cm thick. Peel the celeriac and cut into 1cm chunks. Put all the veg into a large oven dish (about 3 litres capacity) and add the garlic and some salt and pepper. Toss the veg together, then even everything out in the dish.

Tuck the thyme sprigs and bay leaves in among the veg. Trickle over 100ml water, then 2 tbsp oil. Cover the dish tightly with foil and bake for 50–60 minutes until the veg are completely tender.

As soon as you've put the dish of veg into the oven, rinse the spelt or barley well in a sieve under the cold tap. Tip it into a saucepan, cover with plenty of cold water and add a pinch of salt. Bring to the boil, cover and simmer the grain until tender: about 20 minutes for spelt, 35–40 minutes for barley. Drain well, then combine with 1 tbsp oil, some salt and pepper, and the chopped rosemary.

When the veg are tender, take the dish out of the oven and turn the setting up to 200°C/Fan 180°C/Gas 6. Scatter the seasoned spelt or barley over the top of the veg (it should mostly, but not completely, cover it) and return to the oven for 10–15 minutes, until the grains are lightly coloured.

Serve the bake just as it comes, or with wilted kale or spring greens.

Swaps

Roots Replace some or all of the Jerusalem artichokes with potatoes; a fairly firm, maincrop variety such as Desiree works well.

Boston bean and squash stew

Serves 4–6

200g dried 'black badgers' (carlin peas) or black turtle beans, soaked overnight

2 tbsp olive or rapeseed oil

2 medium onions, chopped

1 medium-hot green or red chilli, deseeded (for less heat, if preferred) and sliced

2 tsp sugar

2 tbsp molasses

2 tbsp English mustard

About 850g squash (such as a small butternut or onion squash, or ½ large Crown Prince), peeled, deseeded and cut into bite-sized chunks

1 litre hot veg stock (see page 190 for home-made)

400g tin tomatoes

1 tbsp cocoa or cacao powder

1 garlic bulb, halved crossways

2 bay leaves

A couple of sprigs of thyme

Sea salt and black pepper

Traditional Boston baked beans, slow-cooked in a rich, molasses-flavoured liquor, always include a good hunk of pork or bacon. But I've used other ingredients (tomatoes, cocoa, onions, cloves) to create a deep, delicious and savoury flavour in this Boston-bean-inspired hearty hotpot. You can eat it just as it comes or partner it with rice and/or greens, or a green salad – in which case, it will serve six. Don't forget to soak the beans the night before (or use tinned ones – see below). I like British-grown little 'black badger' peas (available from hodmedods.co.uk), but any bean works well.

Drain the soaked beans and put them into a saucepan. Cover with plenty of fresh water, bring to a vigorous boil, then reduce the heat, cover the pan and leave the beans to simmer for an hour or so while you prepare the rest of the stew. Check them every now and then to see if the simmering water needs topping up.

Heat the oil in a large flameproof casserole or small stockpot over a medium heat. Add the onions and chilli with some salt and pepper and fry gently for about 10 minutes until nice and soft. Take the pan off the heat for a moment and add the sugar, molasses and mustard, stirring well to form a thick, dark paste.

Add the chunks of squash to the onion mixture and pour on the hot stock. Add the tinned tomatoes with their juice, crushing them first in your hands to break them down a bit. Add the cocoa, garlic, bay leaves and thyme. Return the pan to the heat and bring to the boil, then reduce the heat to a gentle simmer and cook, uncovered, until the squash is tender – probably 30–40 minutes, depending on the variety.

When the squash is cooked, test the simmering beans. If they are tender and easily crushable, drain them and add to the stew. If they're still a little firm, simmer them a bit longer, turning the heat off under the stew while you do so.

Once the beans are added, simmer the stew for a few more minutes to ensure everything is piping hot. Pick out the thyme stems. Taste and add more salt or pepper if needed, then serve in big steaming bowlfuls.

Swaps

Pulses To save time, replace the dried beans with two 400g tins black beans (or any other tinned beans you like), adding them once the squash is cooked.

Veg Replace the squash with a mix of root vegetables, such as chunks of carrot, parsnip and potato.

Seared chicory, chickpeas and olives

Serves 2–3

2 tbsp olive or rapeseed oil

4 heads of chicory, quartered lengthways

2 garlic cloves, sliced

400g tin chickpeas, drained and rinsed

75g pitted green olives, thickly sliced (about 100g stone-in)

Finely grated zest of 1 medium orange, plus some of its juice

2 tbsp chopped flat-leaf parsley, plus extra to finish

Sea salt and black pepper

This delicious warm salad is freshened with a hint of orange and a scattering of flat-leaf parsley. If you happen to have a barbecue on the go, sear the chicory on that, for added smoky savour, and heat the chickpeas and flavourings separately.

Heat the oil in a large, non-stick frying pan over a medium-high heat. Add the quartered chicory heads and season with salt and pepper. Sear the chicory, tossing every now and again, for about 5 minutes, until well coloured on all sides.

Add the sliced garlic, chickpeas, olives, orange zest and chopped parsley and toss together. Cook for 2–3 minutes, tossing again a few more times.

Remove from the heat and give the salad a good squeeze of orange juice. Toss again, then taste and add more salt or pepper if required.

Heap the chicory and chickpeas onto serving plates and scatter some more parsley over the top. Serve straight away.

Swaps

Leaves As an alternative to chicory, use radicchio (a relative of chicory), or quartered little gem lettuce.
Pulses Use tinned white beans or pre-cooked Puy lentils instead of the chickpeas.
Herbs Replace the parsley with mint.

Charred radicchio and shallots

Serves 4

250g echalion (banana) shallots

3 tbsp olive or rapeseed oil

2 radicchio (200–300g each)

Several sprigs of thyme

200ml coconut milk

200ml tomato passata

1 garlic clove, finely grated or crushed

Sea salt and black pepper

I love the delicious bitterness of radicchio, and this bubbling bake is a wonderful way to enjoy it. The veg is sauced with a combination of tomato passata and coconut milk – which doesn't make it taste coconutty, just rich and savoury.

Preheat the oven to 190°C/Fan 170°C/Gas 5. Have ready a shallow oven dish (2–2.5 litre capacity) that will hold all the veg fairly snugly in a single layer. Preheat a griddle pan or grill.

Peel the shallots and trim them but keep the root ends intact. Slice each shallot in half lengthways. Put them into a large bowl, add 1 tbsp oil and some salt and pepper and mix well.

Griddle or grill the shallots for 3–4 minutes on each side, until they are starting to soften and are marked with griddle stripes, or browned from the grill. (You could also do this on a barbecue.)

Meanwhile, quarter the radicchio and place in the bowl. Add another 2 tbsp oil and some salt and pepper and use your fingers to work the oil and seasoning into the radicchio quarters.

As the shallots are done, transfer them to the oven dish. Add the oiled radicchio pieces to the griddle or grill pan and cook for 2–3 minutes on each of their cut surfaces, again until browned.

Add the radicchio to the dish with the shallots and tuck the thyme sprigs in amongst the veg.

Put the coconut milk and tomato passata into a saucepan and add the garlic and some salt and pepper. Bring gently to the boil, stirring to amalgamate the coconut and passata. Taste to ensure the mixture is well seasoned.

Pour the hot tomato/coconut mixture all over the veg. Transfer to the oven and bake for 20–25 minutes until the sauce is bubbling, the shallots are tender and the top is nicely charred. Serve straight away, with a grainy side dish, such as one of those from Spuds and grains (see pages 390–403).

Swaps

Leaves Use chicory in place of the radicchio.
Alliums Replace the echalion (banana) shallots with fat spring onions or wedges of red onion.

Baked big mushrooms with dressed Puy lentils

Serves 4

8–12 large, open cap mushrooms (i.e. 2–3 per person)

Olive oil, for brushing

Sea salt and black pepper

FOR THE LENTIL MIX

75g Puy lentils

1 small garlic clove, chopped

1 small shallot, chopped

1 tbsp capers, rinsed, drained and chopped

2 tbsp chopped flat-leaf parsley, chives or chervil

½ tsp English mustard

Finely grated zest and juice of ½ lemon

50ml extra virgin olive oil

Hot, juicy baked mushrooms are delicious topped with Puy lentils and a piquant, lemony dressing.

Preheat the oven to 190°C/Fan 170°C/Gas 5.

Remove and discard the stalks from the mushrooms then place them, gill side up, on a large baking tray (one with an edge, to hold the juices). Pour a little olive oil into a small bowl and use to brush each mushroom lightly. Season the mushrooms with salt and pepper. Bake in the oven for 15–20 minutes until dark, tender and juicy.

Meanwhile, put the lentils into a saucepan, cover with cold water and bring to the boil. Lower the heat a little and simmer for 10–15 minutes, until tender but still with a bit of bite.

Drain the lentils and return them to the hot pan. Immediately add all the other ingredients for the lentil mix, and some salt and pepper. Stir well.

The cooked mushrooms will have released lots of juice in the oven. Pour most of this off into a jug – don't discard it.

Transfer the mushrooms to a warmed serving platter and spoon the dressed lentils on top of them. Trickle the reserved mushroom cooking juice over the lentil-topped mushrooms, then serve. Eat with crushed potatoes or something from Spuds and grains (pages 372–403).

Swaps

Veg Spoon the lentil mix onto barbecued or griddled veg, such as thickly sliced fennel or courgettes, or quartered lettuces.

Spicy suppers

THE MARRIAGE OF vegetables with spices is such a natural and happy one that it's been easy to devote a whole chapter to it. With their heat, aroma and intensity of flavour, spicy veg dishes are often deeply satisfying and comforting, making this chapter the natural successor to my opening Veg feasts.

Where vegetables are concerned, spices play many welcome roles: they give edge and definition to mild, starchy roots; they bring depth and piquancy to peppers, aubergines and tomatoes; and they warm up the cool, grassy tones of greens and beans. Pungent seasonings can so often be the thing that takes a recipe up a notch, making it really special – even celebratory. A vibrantly spiced dish has such complexity of flavour that it tends to feel like more than the sum of its parts. I find it particularly exciting when such a dish is composed entirely of vegetable ingredients – including the spices themselves, of course. What a ringing endorsement of the potential of plants!

I've got to say that when I'm on the hunt for big, crowd-pleasing veg dishes, recipes with a South Asian slant come to mind perhaps more often than any other single genre. Maybe that's not surprising: after all, the Indian subcontinent, where spices are so liberally and so skilfully used, is home to probably the finest vegetarian cooking in the world. You'll find several curries in this chapter, rich with coriander, cumin, cardamom, chilli, ginger and turmeric, that look to India for their inspiration.

But it's not only Asian-style spicing that's represented here. Other spice-centric culinary cultures – from Mexico, with its dried chillies and nutty moles, to the fruity, fragrant spicing of Morocco – yield great inspiration for the vegetable cook and I've plundered many of them for ideas.

If you're chilli-shy, please don't skim over these recipes thinking there'll be nothing here for you. 'Spicy' certainly doesn't have to mean 'fiery'. In fact, it doesn't have to mean hot at all. Chilli heat is a component of many of these recipes, but it's one to be tinkered with at your own discretion. If you don't like chilli at all, leave it out – the dish will still work. If you love a whisper of heat, use a pinch of dried chilli flakes or a medium-hot fresh chilli, deseeded. Or if, like me, you're a bit of a chilli fiend, keep your chillies with their seeds and membranes (where most of the heat resides) intact, or even boost the heat by using hotter varieties, such as bird's eye or habaneros, if you choose.

Dry spices give the best account of themselves in a dish if they've been freshly ground. This is particularly true of fragrant seeds like cumin, coriander, cardamom and fennel – and the reason why I think a sturdy pestle and mortar, or little electric spice grinder, is invaluable. The flavour of ready-ground spices diminishes easily – often in a rather uneven way, so that a jar of powdered spice might retain pungency or bitterness or heat while losing all its perfume or floral tones.

But, just as using a decent ready-made stock can be a corner worth cutting when you're busy, so opting for a good proprietary spice blend can be a good time-saver. With the exception of turmeric, I don't use dry ground spices or curry powders very often these days, but 'wet' curry pastes, and blends such as harissa, which tend to be more richly aromatic, have earned their place in my kitchen.

You'll see curry paste as an option in some of the recipes here, though I'd urge you to also have a go at the simple home-made curry paste on page 95. Perfect when a bit of impromptu soup-making or leftovers cooking is on the cards, it's delicious, punchy and incredibly useful.

Spiced veg dishes fit exceptionally well into a 'mix-and-match' way of eating, and many of the recipes in this chapter pair up very well with each other – the lovely onion-topped tomato dhal on page 102, for instance, goes with almost everything else! Or put a couple of these aromatic beauties together and add a rice or grain dish from my Spuds and grains chapter and you're in for yet another fine feast.

Fragrant veg stoup

2 tbsp rapeseed oil

300g well-flavoured mushrooms, such as chestnut or portobello, thickly sliced

2 medium leeks (350–400g in total), trimmed, split in half lengthways and thinly sliced

2 medium carrots (about 200g in total), peeled and cut into thin batons

2 garlic cloves, sliced

A thumb-sized piece of ginger, peeled and finely sliced

1 medium-hot green chilli, sliced (seeds and all, if you like it hot)

1 tbsp coriander seeds, roughly bashed

2 nuggets of fresh turmeric root, each 4–5cm, peeled and finely sliced, or 1 tsp ground turmeric

400ml tin coconut milk

250ml veg stock (see page 190 for home-made)

50ml Chinese rice wine, mirin or dry sherry

About 300g purple sprouting broccoli

2 tbsp tamari

Sea salt and black pepper

½ lime, to finish

A 'stoup' is a comforting dish somewhere between a stew and a soup. Showcasing purple sprouting broccoli, ably supported by leeks, carrots and mushrooms, this one is creamy with coconut milk, and there are plenty of aromatics – garlic, ginger, turmeric and citrusy coriander seeds. You could serve it with rice, like a curry, but I like to eat it with a spoon from a soup bowl.

Heat the oil in a flameproof casserole or stockpot over a medium-high heat. Add the sliced mushrooms and fry 'hard' for 5–8 minutes, stirring from time to time, until they have plenty of colour and any liquid they release has evaporated.

Add the leeks and carrots to the mushrooms, along with the garlic, ginger, chilli and coriander seeds. Add some salt and pepper, cover the pan, turn down the heat and let everything sweat for about 10 minutes, stirring once or twice.

Add the turmeric, coconut milk, stock and rice wine to the pan and stir well. (If the coconut milk has separated in the tin, you can amalgamate it now over the heat.) Bring up to a simmer and cook gently, uncovered, for about 5 minutes while you prepare the purple sprouting broccoli.

Trim or snap off any tough, fibrous ends from the broccoli then cut into 3–4cm lengths. Make sure you include all the lovely green leaves.

Add the broccoli to the stew and cook for 4–5 minutes, stirring once or twice, until it is just tender, but not soft. Take off the heat.

Stir the tamari into the stew, then taste and add a little more salt or pepper if necessary. Ladle into warmed bowls and spritz with a little lime juice to serve.

Swaps

Alliums Replace the leeks with sliced onion, spring onion or shallots.
Veg Outside the sprouting broccoli season (December–April), use ordinary broccoli (aka calabrese).

Roast PSB and tofu with chilli miso dressing

Serves 3–4

400g plain tofu

400g purple sprouting broccoli

2 tbsp rapeseed oil

Sea salt and black pepper

FOR THE CHILLI MISO DRESSING

1 tbsp white miso paste or shiro miso paste (see page 270)

2 tbsp rapeseed oil

1 garlic clove, finely grated or crushed

1 hot red chilli, such as a bird's eye, finely chopped (seeds and all, if you like it hot)

This is a fantastically flavourful way to eat tofu – roasted so it starts to brown, then doused in an assertive miso dressing. I make the dressing chilli-hot because it's such a great contrast to the mild tofu and earthy broccoli, but if you prefer less heat, remove the seeds and membranes from the chilli before chopping it.

Preheat the oven to 200°C/Fan 180°C/Gas 6.

Take the tofu from its pack, pouring away any liquid. Wrap the block(s) in a clean tea towel and press quite firmly to get rid of a little more excess liquid. Then unwrap the tofu and cut it into 2cm cubes.

Snap off any tough or fibrous ends from the purple sprouting broccoli. Trim and save any leaves attached to these tough bits of stalk before discarding them. Cut the broccoli stems into 3–4cm lengths.

Put the broccoli (including any stray leaves) and tofu into a large roasting tray. Trickle over the oil, season with salt and pepper and toss gently, taking care not to break up the tofu. Roast in the oven for 25 minutes, giving everything a gentle stir halfway through cooking.

Meanwhile, to make the dressing, in a bowl, whisk the ingredients together thoroughly. Don't worry if they don't emulsify completely.

Take the roasting tray from the oven and leave to cool slightly for a few minutes, then spoon over the miso dressing. Use a spatula to mix the dressing through the hot broccoli and tofu.

Serve straight away, piping hot, or leave to cool and eat at room temperature. Either way, add plain rice or one of the rice dishes from Spuds and grains (see pages 398–403).

Swaps

Veg Replace the PSB with pak choi: use 5 or 6 heads and split each lengthways into 4–6 wedges.

Summer veg coconut curry

Serves 4

1 tbsp virgin coconut oil

4 large shallots, or 1 medium onion, chopped

1 tbsp freshly grated ginger

4 garlic cloves, finely grated or crushed

2 lemongrass stems, tough outer layers removed, thinly sliced

2 bird's eye chillies (or to taste, deseeded for less heat, if preferred), sliced into thin rounds

Finely grated zest of 1 lime and the juice of ½ lime, or more to taste

400ml tin coconut milk

200ml veg stock (see page 190 for home-made) or water

1 tsp ground turmeric (or 1 tbsp freshly grated turmeric root)

A pinch of sugar

250g new potatoes, scrubbed and cut into small-bite size pieces

150g green beans, trimmed and halved

100g peas (fresh or frozen)

2 little gem lettuces, quartered lengthways

A large bunch of coriander (about 50g), leaves and tender stems chopped

Sea salt and black pepper

New potatoes, lettuce, green beans and peas are spiced with ginger, chillies, turmeric and lemongrass to make a creamy, fragrant curry.

Place a flameproof casserole or small stockpot, ideally non-stick, over a medium heat and add the coconut oil. Once melted, add the shallot or onion. When sizzling, lower the heat, cover the pan and sweat, stirring often, for 5–10 minutes until softened. Add the ginger, garlic, lemongrass, chillies and lime zest and cook, stirring regularly to stop the mixture sticking and burning, for another 5 minutes.

Add the coconut milk, veg stock or water, turmeric, sugar and a pinch of salt. Bring up to a gentle simmer and cook for 5 minutes.

Add the potatoes to the pan and simmer for 10 minutes or until barely tender, stirring a few times to stop anything sticking. Now add the green beans and peas and simmer for 5–7 minutes, or until the beans are just tender. Add a splash more water if it seems overly thick.

Add the lettuce quarters and cook gently for a further 2–3 minutes, stirring often, just until the lettuce has wilted. Remove from the heat. Stir in the lime juice and most of the coriander. Taste and add more lime and/or salt and pepper if you think it needs it.

Scatter the remaining chopped coriander over the curry and serve with rice or quinoa.

Swaps

Peas Use young broad beans instead of, or as well as, the peas.
Beans Replace the green beans with 150g young, tender runner beans, destringed and sliced.
Leaves Use spinach in place of lettuce.
Aromatics To save time, substitute 2 tbsp Thai green curry paste for the shallot, ginger, garlic, lemongrass, chilli and lime, cooking it for a couple of minutes before adding the coconut milk.

Barbecued veg curry

Serves 3–4

2 tbsp curry paste, home-made (see page 95) or your favourite ready-made one

2 tbsp rapeseed oil

About 300g baby leeks or large salad onions, trimmed (halved lengthways if more than 1cm in diameter)

200g green beans, stalk ends trimmed

3 medium courgettes (about 500g in total), trimmed

2 medium aubergines (about 500g in total), trimmed

FOR THE DRESSING

1 tbsp cumin seeds, ideally lightly toasted

1 tbsp coriander seeds, ideally lightly toasted

A pinch of dried chilli flakes

A pinch of flaky sea salt

Finely grated zest of 1 lemon

2 tbsp chopped mint

2 tbsp chopped coriander

2 tbsp rapeseed oil

1 tbsp lemon juice

In this lovely 'dry' curry, earthy spices, lemon and herbs enhance the wonderful flavours created by charring vegetables over a barbecue (or under a grill). It takes a little time to marinate and grill all the veg, but it's well worth it.

You can cook this on a barbecue, under a hot grill, or in a ridged grill pan on the hob. Whichever you choose, get it nice and hot before starting to cook.

To prepare the dressing, using a large pestle and mortar, pound the cumin and coriander seeds, chilli flakes, sea salt, lemon zest and herbs together to a coarse mix. (Or, you can whiz the spices and salt briefly in a grinder, then combine them with the herbs.) Stir in the oil and lemon juice to make a loose, chunky dressing. Taste, adding more salt or lemon if needed, then transfer to a large serving bowl and set aside.

In a large bowl, mix the curry paste and oil together. Add the baby leeks or salad onions and green beans to this spicy marinade and use a pastry brush to brush it lightly all over them.

Lift the veg from the bowl with tongs (making sure you leave a fair amount of marinade in it), and place on the barbecue/under the grill/in the pan to cook. They'll need 3–4 minutes on each side to become tender (though not soft) and temptingly charred. As they are done, take them off the grill and put them straight into the bowl of dressing, tossing them in it so they soak up the flavours while still hot.

While the leeks or onions and beans are cooking, slice the courgettes lengthways into thin slices, about 3mm thick. Slice the aubergines to a similar thickness. Put both into the bowl with the remaining marinade and brush it all over them.

As soon as there's space on the barbecue/grill/pan, start cooking the courgettes and aubergines too, for 3–4 minutes each side until tender and marked with dark brown char lines, transferring them to the bowl of cooked veg and dressing, and tossing them to combine, as you go.

When all the veg are cooked, dressed and still fairly hot, bring the dish to the table. Serve with rice and/or dhal.

Swaps

Spices For a Middle Eastern variation, replace the curry paste with harissa and the lemon zest with 1 tbsp chopped preserved lemon.
Veg Try carrots, thinly sliced lengthways, instead of green beans. Deseeded quarters of red pepper are good in place of the courgettes.

Aubergine and pak choi stir-fry

Serves 4

2 medium aubergines (about 500g in total), trimmed

About 150g spring onions, trimmed

About 200g pak choi (or tat soi)

2 tbsp rapeseed oil

A spritz of lime juice, to taste

FOR THE SAUCE

2 tbsp tamari

2 tbsp Chinese rice wine, mirin or dry sherry

1 tbsp rice vinegar

2 tsp sugar

1 tsp Chinese five-spice powder

2 garlic cloves, grated

1 thumb-sized piece of ginger, grated

1 medium-hot chilli, deseeded and chopped

In this quick and simple stir-fry, sliced aubergine is cooked in an aromatic sauce until silky and intense, with pak choi contributing crunch and freshness.

For the sauce, mix all the ingredients together in a bowl, stir in 2 tbsp water and set aside.

Cut the aubergines in half lengthways and then slice about 5mm thick. Cut the spring onions into 5mm thick slices on the diagonal. Separate the pak choi leaves from the stems and cut both into slices about 2cm thick.

Heat the oil in a large wok over a high heat. Add the aubergine pieces and stir-fry for 5–10 minutes until tender and browned. You may think there's not enough oil, but as the pieces soften, the oil gets distributed. Add the spring onions and fry for a minute or two.

Tip the sauce into the wok. Cook, stirring frequently, for a couple of minutes, then add the pak choi stems and cook for another couple of minutes. Stir in the pak choi leaves so that they just start to wilt, then remove from the heat.

Give the stir-fry a spritz of lime juice and serve with rice.

Swaps

Aubergines Replace these with courgettes.
Greens Instead of pak choi, use finely sliced kale or spring greens, adding either veg with the spring onions; or try lettuce or spinach, wilted in at the end.

Squash and chickpea patties

Serves 3–4

500g squash, such as ½ medium butternut or a chunk of Crown Prince

400g tin chickpeas, drained and rinsed

A bunch of spring onions, trimmed and sliced

1 tsp coriander seeds

1 tsp cumin seeds

A pinch of dried chilli flakes (optional)

1 tsp tamari

50g mixed seeds, such as sunflower, pumpkin and sesame

Olive or rapeseed oil, for frying

Sea salt and black pepper

These lightly spiced, seed-encrusted patties are lovely with a dollop of dhal or hummus; you could serve them with some wholegrain basmati rice or a green salad too. The squash is steamed first so it becomes tender but not soft or soggy.

Peel and deseed the squash then cut into 2–3cm pieces. Put these into a steamer basket and place over a pan of simmering water. Cover the pan and steam for around 30 minutes, until the squash is tender but not mushy, topping up the simmering water if necessary. (Alternatively, use a proprietary steamer.)

Tip the tender squash into a large bowl and mash, using a potato masher – keep it quite rough and textured, rather than completely smooth. Leave to cool completely.

Tip the drained chickpeas into a bowl and use a fork to mash them roughly – again, keep them quite coarse and chunky. Add to the squash with the sliced spring onions.

Using a pestle and mortar, bash the coriander and cumin seeds with the chilli flakes, if using, and a pinch each of salt and pepper to a coarse powder. Add this spice mix to the squash, trickle over the tamari and mix everything together. Taste and add more salt or pepper if needed.

Put the mixed seeds on a plate. Divide the squash mixture into 6 equal portions. Form one into a ball, then flatten it into a patty, about 1.5cm deep. Place on the plate of seeds and pat a scant layer of seeds over the top and base of the patty. Shape and coat the rest of the patties in the same way.

Heat a large, non-stick frying pan over a medium heat and add a thin film of oil. Add the patties and cook for about 10 minutes, turning them carefully a couple of times, until golden brown on both sides. Serve straight away.

Swaps

Veg Replace the squash with steamed parsnip or beetroot.
Pulses Use white beans such as cannellini instead of the chickpeas.
Spices When time is short, use about 2 tsp good ready-made curry paste instead of the whole spices.

Two-tray spicy roast veg

Serves 4

1kg flavoursome tomatoes

4 garlic cloves, thickly sliced

3cm piece of ginger, thinly sliced

3 tbsp rapeseed oil

2 medium aubergines (about 500g in total), trimmed

500g squash, such as ½ medium butternut or a chunk of Crown Prince, peeled and deseeded

2 medium onions, each cut into 8 wedges

1 medium-hot red chilli, deseeded (for less heat, if preferred) and sliced

1 cinnamon stick, broken in half

6 cardamom pods, bashed to split open

1 tsp nigella (black onion/kalonji) seeds

2 tsp fennel seeds

2 tsp cumin seeds

2 tsp coriander seeds

About 200g chard, leaves separated from stems

Sea salt and black pepper

TO FINISH

Coriander leaves, chopped

1 lemon or lime, halved, to spritz

Jam-packed with goodness, this is a great dish to slam in the oven while you get on with something else. One tray of roast veg forms the 'bulk' of the curry; a second tray of sweet, roasted tomatoes forms the saucy element. Mix the two together and dinner's done.

Preheat the oven to 190°C/Fan 170°C/Gas 5.

Halve the tomatoes and place in a single layer in a large roasting tray. Scatter the garlic and ginger on top of the tomatoes (not onto the tray, where it would burn), trickle over 1 tbsp oil and sprinkle with salt and pepper. Set aside while you prepare the other veg.

Cut the aubergines into 2–3cm cubes and the squash into bite-sized chunks. Put both veg into a second large roasting tray with the onions, chilli, cinnamon, cardamom pods and nigella seeds. Using a pestle and mortar, bash the fennel, cumin and coriander seeds roughly (they needn't be finely ground) then add to the tray, along with some salt and pepper and 2 tbsp oil. Stir well to mix everything together.

Put both trays into the oven, placing the veg tray on a higher shelf than the tomatoes, and roast for 30 minutes. Roughly chop the chard stems and add to the veg tray. Give this tray a good stir (there is no need to stir the tomatoes) and roast for a further 30 minutes. Meanwhile, shred the chard leaves.

After the full hour, take the tomatoes out of the oven; they should be blistered, wrinkled, juicy and browned in places. The tray of veg should be tender and nicely coloured. Add the prepared chard leaves to the veg, give it a stir and return this tray to the oven, with the heat turned off, for 5–10 minutes to wilt the leaves.

Take the tray of hot veg from the oven, add the tomatoes to it, scraping in all the lovely pan juices, and mix well. Taste and add more salt and pepper if needed. Scatter with coriander and add a spritz of lemon or lime juice. Serve with rice and dhal for a really sustaining meal.

Swaps

Spices To save time, replace the chilli, cinnamon, cardamom, nigella, fennel, cumin and coriander seeds with 2–3 tbsp good ready-made curry paste.

Aubergines Use courgettes in place of the aubergines.

Squash Try bite-sized chunks of root veg, such as carrots, potatoes and parsnips instead.

Leaves Replace the chard with spinach (no need to separate leaves from stems), adding it for the last 5 minutes.

Beet and chard stir-fry with chilli, ginger and lime

Serves 2

300g small, young beetroot, plus leaves if attached

300g chard

200g spring onions, trimmed

1 tbsp rapeseed oil

1 hot green chilli, deseeded (for less heat, if preferred), thinly sliced

2 tsp freshly grated ginger

Juice of ½ lime, or more to taste

Sea salt

Tamari, to serve (optional)

This really simple stir-fry is colourful and fresh flavoured. Prep your veg before you start – it doesn't take long, and then the cooking is done in minutes. If you've got a bunch of beetroot with leaves still attached, use these in the stir-fry too.

Peel and trim the beetroot, reserving the leaves if attached. Halve each beetroot, then cut into 2–3mm slices. Separate the chard stalks from the leaves, then slice the stalks into roughly 1cm pieces. Slice the chard leaves into 2cm thick ribbons; do the same with any beetroot leaves. Slice the spring onions, about 1cm thick.

Heat the oil in a large wok over a fairly high heat. Add the beetroot slices with a pinch of salt and stir-fry for about 5 minutes. Keep a close eye on the beetroot – you'll see it quickly starts to colour at the edges, which is what you want, but don't let it burn.

When the beetroot is starting to brown, add the chard stalks and spring onions to the pan. Stir-fry for about 3 minutes.

Add the chilli and ginger and stir-fry for about 30 seconds. Toss in the chard/beetroot leaves and stir-fry for another minute or so, just until they wilt. Take off the heat and add the lime juice and a little more salt.

Taste the veg to check the seasoning, then serve with plain rice. Have some tamari on the table for a little extra seasoning, if you like.

Swaps

Roots Use thinly sliced carrots or kohlrabi in place of beetroot. *Leaves* Instead of chard, use spinach – there is no need to separate the stalks, just wilt it all in at the end.

Roast spiced brassicas with split pea purée

Serves 4–6

2 tsp coriander seeds

2 tsp cumin seeds

2 tsp fennel seeds

2 tsp caraway seeds (optional)

A pinch of flaky sea salt

A pinch of dried chilli flakes

2 tsp ground turmeric

2 tsp sweet smoked paprika

1 large head of broccoli (about 500g), stalk end trimmed

1 medium cauliflower (about 800g), stalk end trimmed

2 tbsp rapeseed oil, plus extra to finish

150g kale leaves

Sea salt and black pepper

FOR THE SPLIT PEA PURÉE

200g yellow split peas

3 garlic cloves, peeled but left whole

1 tbsp tahini

50ml rapeseed oil

1 tsp cumin seeds, roughly bashed

Juice of ½ lemon, or more to taste

I love the full flavours and varied textures in this delicious, hearty dish, which comes from Charlie James, former head chef at the River Cottage Canteen in Bristol. The crispy kale is a particular treat.

Start with the split pea purée. Put the split peas and garlic cloves into a saucepan with 750ml water. Bring to the boil, lower the heat and simmer, uncovered, for about 40 minutes until the split peas are completely tender and most of the water is absorbed. If there is more than a few tablespoonfuls of water left in the pan, pour some of it off.

Tip the peas, garlic and residual water into a food processor. Add the tahini, oil, cumin, lemon juice and some salt and pepper. Blitz to a purée. It might seem quite liquid at first, but will soon start to thicken up. (If it stays a bit thin, return to the pan and simmer briefly before serving.)

While the peas are cooking, preheat the oven to 190°C/Fan 170°C/ Gas 5. Using a pestle and mortar, bash the coriander, cumin, fennel and caraway seeds, if using, with the flaky salt and chilli flakes to break them down a bit. Add the turmeric, smoked paprika and some pepper and stir well.

Cut the broccoli into large florets, splitting the stalks if they are thick. Remove any tough outer leaves from the cauliflower, keeping the tender inner leaves attached, then split into quarters, down through the stalk. Cut each quarter into 3 wedges, keeping the stalk attached.

Put the broccoli and cauliflower into a large roasting tray, trickle over 1 tbsp oil and toss the veg in it. Scatter over the spice mix and mix with your hands to coat all the veg. Roast for 30 minutes, stirring halfway through cooking, until the veg are tender and starting to brown.

Meanwhile, strip the kale leaves off their central stalks and tear the leaves into rough pieces. Put them into a large bowl with 1 tbsp oil and some salt and pepper and toss well so they are all coated in oil. After 30 minutes' roasting, take the tray of broccoli and cauliflower from the oven, scatter the oiled kale leaves over the veg and return to the oven for 10–15 minutes, or until most of the kale is slightly crisp.

If the split pea purée has cooled down, warm it up gently in a pan, with a splash of boiling water from the kettle if necessary. To serve, spoon the purée onto a warmed serving platter or plates and arrange the roasted veg on top, scattering over any bits of toasty spice mix still in the roasting dish. Give it a final trickle of rapeseed oil before serving.

Red pepper, courgette and white bean chilli

Serves 4

3 medium courgettes (about 450g in total), trimmed and cut into 1cm slices

2 medium onions, cut into slim wedges

2 large (or 3 small) red peppers (350–400g in total), halved, cored, deseeded and roughly chopped

3 tbsp olive or rapeseed oil

½ tbsp cumin seeds

½ tbsp coriander seeds

3 garlic cloves, sliced

1 hot red chilli, deseeded (for less heat, if preferred) and chopped, or a good pinch of dried chilli flakes

400g plum tomatoes, skinned and roughly chopped, or a 400g tin tomatoes

400g tin white beans, such as cannellini or butter beans, drained and rinsed

Sea salt and black pepper

TO SERVE

Avocado, sliced

Lime juice

Coriander leaves

The veg for this simple chilli is roasted to intensify its flavour before being added to a simmering, spiced tomato sauce.

Preheat the oven to 190°C/Fan 170°C/Gas 5.

Put the courgettes, onions and peppers into a large roasting tray. Trickle over 2 tbsp oil, season with salt and pepper and toss well. Roast for 40 minutes, or until the veg are tender and starting to colour, stirring halfway through.

Meanwhile, using a pestle and mortar, bash the cumin and coriander seeds roughly. Heat another 1 tbsp oil in a large saucepan over a medium-low heat. Add the sliced garlic, chilli, the bashed cumin and coriander and a pinch of salt. Fry gently for a few minutes until the garlic just starts to colour.

Tip the tomatoes into the pan (if using tinned tomatoes, crush them in your hands as you add them). Pour in 400ml water, bring to a simmer and cook gently for about 25 minutes until the spicy tomato mixture is reduced and thickened.

Take the roasted veg from the oven and add it to the simmering tomato sauce. Add the white beans and simmer for another 10 minutes or so, then taste and add more salt or pepper if necessary.

Serve the chilli with avocado dressed with lime juice, salt, pepper and coriander leaves. A simple rice dish, such as brown rice with onions (page 400) makes this really substantial.

Swaps

Veg Roast other veg alongside or instead of the courgettes and red peppers – try fennel, aubergine, carrot or mushrooms.
Pulses Use tinned black beans or kidney beans instead of white beans.

Spicy squash and bean mole

Serves 4

1 squash, such as a butternut or harlequin (about 1kg)

3 tbsp olive or rapeseed oil

1 dried chipotle chilli, stem removed

100g cashew nuts

1 large onion, roughly chopped

1 celery stem, thinly sliced

300g large, ripe tomatoes (4–5), halved

4 garlic cloves, peeled but left whole

½ tsp black peppercorns

1 star anise

½ cinnamon stick

2 tsp cocoa or cacao powder

A pinch of cayenne pepper or chilli powder (optional)

400g tin beans, such as cannellini or kidney beans, drained

Sea salt and black pepper

TO FINISH

1 lime, halved, to spritz

Pumpkin seeds

Coriander leaves

A hot chipotle chilli – a smoked, dried jalapeño – gives heat and smoky flavour to this rich, satisfying dish. I favour 'morita' chipotles, which are a little hotter than 'meco' chipotles, but take your pick! (Try southdevonchillifarm.co.uk for mail order chipotles.) If you can't get hold of chipotles, a good pinch of dried chilli flakes works too.

Preheat the oven to 190°C/Fan 170°C/Gas 5.

Cut the squash into fairly slim wedges, no more than 3–4cm at the outside edge (no need to remove the skin). Scoop out the seeds. Put the squash wedges into a large roasting dish. Trickle over 1 tbsp oil and use your hands or a brush to distribute the oil over the squash flesh. Season with salt and pepper. Roast for 20 minutes.

Meanwhile, roughly chop the chilli and place in a bowl with the cashews, onion, celery, tomatoes, garlic and spices. Trickle over 2 tbsp oil, add some salt and stir well.

Take the tray from the oven, push the squash to one end and tip the tomato mix into the space. Return to the oven for about 40 minutes until the tomatoes are soft and bubbling, the onion is cooked, the cashews are nicely coloured and the squash is tender, stirring the tomato mix halfway through. Take out the squash pieces and set aside.

Pour 400ml boiling water into the dish and stir well with the tomato mix to lift any nice, caramelised residue off the base of the dish. Now tip the entire contents of the dish into a blender, add the cocoa and purée thoroughly until thick and smooth (you don't want pieces of dried spice or tomato skin remaining in the mix). Taste the sauce. Add more salt if necessary and, if you'd like a little more heat, some cayenne or chilli powder.

Use a knife or spoon to scoop the cooked squash off its skin in large chunks. Put these back in the roasting tray and add the beans. Tip on the thick mole sauce from the blender and stir well. Return to the oven for 10–15 minutes until bubbling and piping hot.

Serve spritzed with lime juice and scattered with pumpkin seeds and coriander, with plain rice on the side.

Swaps

Squash Replace this with chunks of root veg – try a combination of carrot, celeriac, parsnip and potato – roasted in a separate tray rather than alongside the tomato.

Turnip and red lentil chilli

Serves 4–6

2 tbsp rapeseed oil

1 large onion, chopped

2 celery stems, chopped

2 garlic cloves, finely grated or crushed

1 tsp cumin seeds

1 tsp chipotle chilli powder or dried chilli flakes

1 tsp dried oregano

350g turnips, trimmed but not peeled, cut into 1cm cubes

150g red lentils, well rinsed

600ml tomato passata

2 tsp sugar

Sea salt and black pepper

TO FINISH

½ lemon, to spritz

Sprigs of coriander

If you've ever been unsure what to do with turnips, your troubles are over. They are wonderful in a veggie chilli, giving texture and a delicious peppery quality. This warming dish has a reasonable level of heat, but won't blow your head off; adjust the quantity of chilli if you fancy something hotter or cooler!

Heat the oil in a large saucepan over a medium heat. Add the onion, celery, garlic, cumin, chilli powder or flakes, oregano, a grinding of pepper and a couple of good pinches of salt. Stir well, turn the heat down a little and cover. Cook for about 8 minutes, stirring once or twice, until softened.

Add the diced turnips and red lentils, then stir in the passata, sugar and 300ml water. Bring up to a simmer, cover and cook gently, stirring from time to time to ensure nothing sticks, for about 30 minutes. When done, the chilli should be thick, the lentils tender and the turnip also tender but not soft. Check the seasoning, adding more salt and pepper if needed.

Serve piping hot, spritzed with lemon juice and finished with coriander, with quinoa or another grainy side dish from Spuds and grains (see pages 390–403) on the side. Plus a cold beer!

Swaps

Roots Use peeled, diced swede or parsnips instead of turnips.
Pulses If you feel your chilli *must* include beans, add a 400g tin black beans or kidney beans, drained and rinsed, towards the end of cooking (retaining the lentils in the mix).

Mushroom and spinach spelteree

Serves 3–4

- 125g pearled spelt or pearl barley
- 1 tbsp cumin seeds
- 1 tbsp coriander seeds
- 1 tsp fenugreek seeds (optional)
- 2 tbsp rapeseed oil
- 1 large onion, quartered and sliced
- 250g chestnut or open cap mushrooms, cut into bite-sized pieces
- 1 tbsp grated ginger
- 2 garlic cloves, finely grated or crushed
- 1 medium-hot red or green chilli, deseeded (for less heat, if preferred) and chopped .
- 200ml coconut milk
- 150g spinach, any tough stalks removed
- Finely grated zest of 1 lemon and the juice of ½ lemon
- Sea salt and black pepper
- Coriander leaves, to finish

Creamy coconut milk and chunky grains of pearled spelt make this veg-packed dish rich and satisfying. It makes a lovely main meal for three people – but serves four or more if you add a dish of dhal too.

Soak the pearled spelt or barley in cold water for 20–30 minutes, if you have time. Soaked or not, rinse the grain thoroughly in a sieve then tip into a saucepan. Cover with plenty of water (it will expand a lot) and add a pinch of salt. Bring to the boil, lower the heat and put the lid on. Simmer until tender: about 20 minutes for spelt, 40 minutes for barley. When the grain is tender, drain and return it to the pan to keep warm.

Meanwhile, use a pestle and mortar or spice grinder to pound or grind the cumin, coriander and fenugreek seeds, if using. It doesn't matter if the cumin and coriander stay quite coarse but the fenugreek should be broken down to a powder.

Heat the oil in a large frying pan over a medium heat. Add the onion with a pinch of salt and fry for about 10 minutes, until soft, letting it colour just a little, but not brown.

Add the mushroom pieces and fry with the onion for about 5 minutes until tender and lightly coloured. Keep stirring so that the liquid released by the mushrooms can evaporate.

Add the pounded spices and cook, stirring, for a minute or two. Add the grated ginger, garlic and chilli and stir briefly, then pour in the coconut milk. Stir well, making sure the coconut milk is fully amalgamated and mixing it with the veg. Scrape up any bits of caramelised veg or spice adhering to the base.

Bring the coconut milk to a simmer and let it bubble gently for a couple of minutes to reduce a little. Then add the spinach, a handful at a time, stirring it in as it wilts.

Take the pan off the heat and stir in the lemon zest and juice. Add the cooked spelt or barley to the pan and stir well. Taste and add more salt and pepper if needed, then spoon into warmed dishes, scatter with coriander, and serve.

Swaps

Spices Instead of the whole spices, use 2 tbsp good ready-made curry paste.

Leaves Replace the spinach with chard: separate the leaves from the stalks and cook the stalks (chopped) along with the onion before adding the shredded leaves at the end.

Roast swede vegeree

Serves 4

2 medium onions, roughly chopped

1 medium swede (600–700g), peeled and cut into 1–2cm cubes

2 tbsp rapeseed oil

200g wholegrain basmati rice

4 tbsp curry paste, home-made (see page 95) or your favourite ready-made one

200ml coconut milk

200g spinach, well washed and roughly chopped

Sea salt and black pepper

Coriander leaves, to finish (optional)

Swede is a much overlooked vegetable but its assertive flavour is wonderful when seasoned with plenty of spice – as in this easy, warming one-pan dish.

Preheat the oven to 190°C/Fan 170°C/Gas 5.

Put the onions and swede into a large roasting dish. Trickle over the oil, add salt and pepper, stir well and roast for about 40 minutes, stirring once, until tender and lightly coloured.

Meanwhile, cook the rice in plenty of boiling salted water until just tender; it will probably take 25–30 minutes, but check the packet guidelines. When it's done, drain well and keep warm, in its saucepan.

Once the swede and onions are cooked, add the curry paste and coconut milk to the roasting dish and stir well. Toss in the spinach and stir again. Return to the oven for about 10 minutes until everything is bubbling and the spinach is wilted. Tip in the cooked rice, stir well then serve, scattered with coriander if you like.

Swaps

Roots Try cubed parsnip or turnip, or a mix of carrot and potato, in place of the swede.

Leaves Use chard or shredded kale instead of the spinach.

Roast squash and chickpeas with spicy apricot sauce

Serves 4

1kg squash, such as a medium butternut or ½ Crown Prince

2 tbsp olive oil

400g tin chickpeas, drained and rinsed

Sea salt and black pepper

FOR THE SPICY APRICOT SAUCE

2 tbsp olive oil

About 125g shallots, halved and sliced

75g unsulphured dried apricots, roughly chopped

½ tsp cumin seeds

2 tsp freshly grated ginger

2 garlic cloves, grated or crushed

½ tsp dried chilli flakes

400g tin tomatoes

1 tsp sugar

2 tbsp coarsely chopped preserved lemon (skin and flesh, but no pips)

4 tbsp chopped coriander

½ lemon, to spritz

This is a sort of deconstructed veggie tagine: chunky squash, nutty chickpeas and a rich tomato sauce, combining sweet, sour, salty and spicy elements. It's quicker to cook than an authentic tagine and I like having the separate elements on my plate, so I can mix and mingle the flavours as I choose.

Preheat the oven to 200°C/Fan 180°C/Gas 6.

Cut the squash into slim wedges, 3–4cm wide at the outer edge. Put them into a roasting dish, trickle over 1 tbsp oil and brush it all over the squash. Season with salt and pepper. Roast in the oven for 45 minutes, or until the squash is tender and browned.

Meanwhile, toss the drained chickpeas with another 1 tbsp oil and some salt and pepper; set aside.

Also, while the squash is in the oven, make the sauce. Heat the oil in a small-medium frying pan over a medium heat. Add the shallots with a pinch of salt. Once sizzling, turn the heat down and cook for about 8 minutes until the shallots are softened, stirring once or twice.

Add the apricots and cumin and stir over the heat for a couple of minutes. Add the ginger, garlic, chilli flakes and a twist of black pepper and cook for a minute or two longer. Now tip in the tinned tomatoes with their juice. If using whole plum tomatoes, crush them with your hands as they go in, and remove any white stalky bits. Add the sugar.

Bring to a brisk simmer and cook for about 5 minutes, stirring a few times, until the sauce is thick and pulpy. Take off the heat, stir in the chopped preserved lemon and about 3 tbsp of the chopped coriander. Taste and add more salt as needed. Set aside.

When the squash is tender, add the seasoned chickpeas to the roasting dish and return to the oven for 5–10 minutes until they are hot. Meanwhile, reheat the sauce if necessary.

Place the squash wedges on a warmed platter or individual plates with the chickpeas. Spoon on the hot sauce and finish with the remaining coriander. Give each plate a little squeeze of lemon juice, then serve.

Swaps
Squash You can replace the squash with pretty much any veg you like – try roasted root veg, fennel, or aubergines and courgettes.

Roast curry-spiced cauliflower

Serves 4

1 medium cauliflower, about 800g (900g max), at room temperature

3 tbsp curry paste, home-made (see below) or your favourite ready-made one

2 tbsp rapeseed oil

Sea salt and black pepper

Cauliflower and spices always pair well. Here a fragrant curry paste is rubbed all over a whole cauliflower, which is then roasted until tender. It is deliciously spicy and intense on the outside, yet mild and sweet in the middle. Serve with rice, dhal or one of the grain dishes from Spuds and grains (see pages 390–403).

Preheat the oven to 200°C/Fan 180°C/Gas 6. Tear off two long sheets of foil – each long enough to go around the cauliflower with plenty of overlap. Place one of these in a roasting tin, with the ends overhanging the edges of the tin. Lay the second piece of foil on top, at right angles so the ends of that piece hang over the other two sides of the tin.

Take the outermost leaves off the cauliflower but leave half a dozen or so of the inner leaves still attached. Stand the cauliflower in the middle of the foil. Take a dollop of curry paste at a time and rub it all over the surface, over the leaves, and into any nooks and crannies around the base of the stalk. There should be no white bits of cauliflower visible.

Fold up the edges of the foil slightly. Trickle the rapeseed oil all over the cauliflower, then pour 75ml water onto the foil around the base (not over the cauliflower), making sure it doesn't escape into the tin. Bring the foil up around the cauliflower, leaving some space inside – don't wrap it tightly. Crimp the edges together firmly, creating a secure but baggy parcel. Transfer to the oven and roast for 1 hour.

Unwrap the cauliflower and test it by pressing a small, sharp knife in through the base; it should go in without too much resistance. If it is still very firm, put it back in the oven for 10–15 minutes and test again.

When the cauliflower is tender, cut it into chunky pieces and divide between warmed plates. Spoon any spicy juices from the foil parcel over the cauliflower and sprinkle with a little salt and pepper.

Curry paste

Put 2 tbsp each cumin and coriander seeds in a dry frying pan and toast briefly over a medium heat, tossing a few times, until fragrant (watch constantly so that they don't burn). Let cool. Using a pestle and mortar, pound the cooled toasted spices with 1 tsp dried chilli flakes to a coarse powder (give it some welly – to break up the seeds as much as you can). Add 2 tbsp ground turmeric, 10 finely grated garlic cloves, 2 tbsp finely grated ginger, 2 tbsp tomato purée, the juice of 1 lemon, ½ tsp fine salt and 1 tsp sugar. Stir well and your paste is ready. Use straight away or store in a sealed container in the fridge for up to 2 weeks, or in the freezer for longer.

Sweet potato, pineapple and red pepper pot

Serves 3–4

2 medium-large red peppers (about 400g in total)

500g sweet potatoes

400g peeled and cored pineapple flesh, (yield from 1 small-medium ripe pineapple ('eyes' removed)

2 medium onions, roughly chopped

4 garlic cloves, peeled and bashed

1 medium-hot red chilli, halved, deseeded (for less heat, if preferred) and sliced

3–4 sprigs of thyme

2–3 bay leaves

1 cinnamon stick

1 tsp ground allspice

2 tbsp olive or rapeseed oil

200ml hot veg stock (see page 190 for home-made)

1 tbsp cider vinegar

1 tbsp tamari

A pinch of cayenne pepper (optional)

Sea salt and black pepper

1 lime, halved, to spritz

With something of a Caribbean feel, this has a delicious sweet-sour quality – the roasted pineapple is particularly tasty! All the fruit, veg and seasonings are roasted together, then a portion of them is blitzed to make a thick, spicy sauce.

Preheat the oven to 190°C/Fan 170°C/Gas 5.

Halve, core and deseed the peppers, then chop into 2–3cm pieces. Peel the sweet potatoes and cut into roughly 2–3cm chunks. Cut the pineapple flesh into 3–4cm chunks.

Put the chopped veg, including the onions, the pineapple, garlic, chilli, herbs and spices into a large roasting dish. Add the oil and some salt and pepper and stir to combine everything. Roast for 1 hour, stirring about halfway through.

Spoon one-third of the contents of the roasting tray into a blender, making sure you don't include any bay leaves, thyme sprigs or the cinnamon stick. Add the hot stock, cider vinegar and tamari and blitz to a thick, smooth purée.

Tip this purée back into the roasting tray and stir it gently into the roasted fruit and veg. Taste and add more salt if needed, along with a pinch of cayenne pepper if you'd like to spice it up a little. If necessary, you can reheat the dish gently in a large pan for a couple of minutes.

Serve spritzed with lime juice, with rice or quinoa on the side.

Swaps

Veg Replace the sweet potatoes with squash – butternut works well.

New potatoes and lentils with coriander and tamarind sauce

Serves 4

750g new potatoes or waxy salad potatoes, cut into bite-sized chunks

150g Puy lentils

2 tbsp extra virgin olive or rapeseed oil

Sea salt and black pepper

FOR THE CORIANDER AND TAMARIND SAUCE

A very large bunch (about 200g) coriander, leaves and tender stalks roughly chopped

1–2 garlic cloves, to taste, grated

2 hot green chillies, deseeded (for less heat, if preferred), roughly chopped

2 tsp freshly grated ginger

2 tbsp tamarind paste

100g cashew nuts

2 tbsp olive or rapeseed oil

½ tsp freshly ground fenugreek seed (optional)

1 tsp sugar

TO SERVE

2 limes, quartered, to spritz

Tamarind has a wonderful, fresh, lemony quality that really enhances earthy potatoes and lentils. In this sauce, it's mingled with fragrant coriander, garlic and lots of hot green chilli. I also like to add a touch of bitter, spicy fenugreek if I have some to hand. A handful of cashew nuts makes the sauce thick and creamy. This zingy green sauce is also delicious served unheated as a fresh chutney with curries, biryanis and dhals.

For the sauce, put all the ingredients into a blender with a good pinch of salt and 200ml water. Blitz until smooth, then taste and add more salt if needed. Set aside.

Put the potatoes into a large saucepan, cover with cold water, add salt and bring to the boil then simmer for 12–15 minutes, until tender.

While the potatoes are cooking, put the lentils into a second saucepan, cover with cold water, bring to the boil and cook for 12–15 minutes, until tender.

Drain the cooked potatoes and return them to the hot pan. When the lentils are cooked, drain and add them to the hot potatoes. Add the virgin oil and some salt and pepper and turn gently together, using a large spoon. Divide between warmed individual dishes and sprinkle with a little more salt and pepper.

Tip the coriander sauce into a pan and heat gently for just a couple of minutes, stirring a couple of times, until steaming hot. Spoon the hot sauce over the hot veg. Give each portion a squeeze of lime juice and serve, with more lime wedges on the table.

Swaps

Pulses For a really fresh-tasting dish, replace these with lightly cooked peas or petits pois, or green beans.

Red cabbage and cashew biryani

Serves 5–6

2 tbsp virgin coconut or rapeseed oil

1 onion, halved and thinly sliced

3 garlic cloves, sliced

1 medium-large leek (200–250g), halved and thinly sliced

¼ red cabbage (about 300g), cored and shredded

400ml tin coconut milk

250g white basmati rice, rinsed and drained

125g cashew nuts

100g raisins

Sea salt

FOR THE SPICE MIX

2 tsp coriander seeds

2 tsp cumin seeds

1 tsp dried chilli flakes

1 tsp black mustard seeds

1 tsp black peppercorns

4 cardamom pods, seeds extracted

1 tbsp ground turmeric

OR

3 tbsp ready-made mild-medium curry paste

TO FINISH

2 mild red chillies, deseeded and sliced

Chopped coriander (optional)

You can grind your own spices for this generous, all-in-one rice dish, or use a good ready-made curry paste for an easy option.

Preheat the oven to 180°C/Fan 160°C/Gas 4. Have ready a large, wide, flameproof casserole with a well-fitting lid.

If preparing your own spice mix, put the casserole over a medium heat, add all the whole spices and toast them gently for 2–3 minutes until fragrant. Take off the heat and grind the spices coarsely using a pestle and mortar or spice grinder. Mix with the turmeric and set aside.

Return the casserole to a medium heat and add the oil. When hot, add the onion, garlic, leek and cabbage. Cook gently, stirring regularly, for about 10 minutes, until the veg are softened and reduced in volume. Add the freshly prepared spice mix, or bought curry paste, and cook for another couple of minutes, stirring a few times.

Meanwhile, heat the coconut milk gently in a saucepan with 300ml water until smoothly amalgamated.

Add the rice, cashews and raisins to the veg. Add 1 tsp salt, or if using a ready-made paste that already includes salt, just ½ tsp. Stir well so that everything is thoroughly combined.

Pour on the warm diluted coconut milk and stir well. Make sure the ingredients are level in the dish, then bring up to a simmer. Cover the casserole and cook in the oven for 20 minutes. Take it out of the oven and check that the rice is tender (if not, give it another 5 minutes). Then cover the dish again and leave it to stand for 5–10 minutes.

Remove the lid and fluff up the rice a little with a fork. Scatter over some red chilli and coriander, if using, then serve. This is really good with a spoonful of chutney on the side. Use your favourite mango chutney or make up a half quantity of the coriander and tamarind sauce on page 98 and serve it raw and unheated as a chutney.

Swaps

Brassicas Use white cabbage or a firm green winter cabbage instead of red cabbage.

Nuts Use whole, skin-on almonds rather than the cashews.

Dried fruit Add chopped dried apricots in place of the raisins.

Tomato dhal

Serves 4–6

1 tbsp rapeseed oil

1 bay leaf

2 garlic cloves, finely grated or crushed

2 tsp ground turmeric

2 tsp ground coriander

400g tin tomatoes

200g red lentils

Sea salt

FOR THE ONION TARKA

2 tbsp rapeseed oil

1 bay leaf

1 black cardamom pod, or 3 green cardamom pods, bashed to split open

1 tsp black mustard seeds

1 tsp cumin seeds

A good pinch of dried chilli flakes

1 large or 2 small onions (ideally red), halved and finely sliced

A filling protein-rich lentil dhal is delicious with nothing more than a steaming bowl of rice, but also pairs well with spiced veg dishes such as spiced cabbage with sunflower seeds (page 364), or curries like the ones on pages 71 and 77. This tomato dhal is finished with a lovely onion tarka (fried spice mix) – a finishing touch that makes the dish extra special but is by no means essential.

Heat the oil in a fairly large saucepan over a medium-low heat. Add the bay leaf, garlic, turmeric and coriander and stir well. Let the mixture fry gently for a couple of minutes, making sure the garlic doesn't burn. Add the tomatoes, crushing them with your hands as they go in, and stir to mix with the spices. Bring to a brisk simmer and cook, uncovered, for 10 minutes, to reduce and intensify the tomatoes.

Meanwhile, rinse the lentils well in a sieve under a running cold tap. Add the lentils to the tomato mixture with ½ tsp salt. Pour in 800ml water, Bring back to a simmer and stir well. Simmer fairly briskly, uncovered, for 20–30 minutes, until the lentils are completely tender and the dhal is thick, stirring often to stop it sticking. Stir with a whisk towards the end of the cooking time, to help break the lentils down.

Once the dhal is cooked, let it stand off the heat for at least 10 minutes (it will thicken a little more), then taste and add more salt if required.

To make the tarka, heat the oil in a frying pan over a medium-high heat. Add the bay leaf and spices and cook for a couple of minutes, stirring now and then, until the mustard seeds begin to pop. Toss in the onions, lower the heat a little and cook, stirring often, for about 10 minutes, until they are soft and lightly browned. Season with a little salt.

Pour the dhal into a serving dish, top with the onion tarka and serve.

Brown rice khichri

Serves 4

150g wholegrain basmati rice

2 tbsp rapeseed oil

2 bay leaves

6 green cardamom pods, bashed to split open

1 black cardamom pod, bashed (optional)

1 dried chilli, such as a habanero (hot) or a guajillo (medium), or a pinch of dried chilli flakes

1 tsp cumin seeds

1 tsp black mustard seeds

1 large onion, chopped

2 garlic cloves, chopped

150g red lentils

1 tsp ground turmeric

Sea salt

TO FINISH

1 medium-hot red or green chilli, deseeded and sliced (optional)

Sliced spring onion or finely chopped red onion (optional)

This simple Indian dish of rice and lentils has countless variations – some plain, some gently spiced like this one. It's usually made with white rice but this version uses wholegrain. You can eat it alone as a warming supper, or combine it with veg – I like it with simply cooked greens. It's also excellent with curried potato rösti (page 378) or the dhal on the previous page.

Put the rice into a bowl, cover with boiling water and leave to soak for 15–20 minutes.

Meanwhile, heat the oil in a large saucepan or small stockpot over a medium heat. When the oil is hot, add the bay leaves, cardamom pods (including the black one, if using), chilli, cumin and mustard seeds. Fry for a minute or so, until the bay leaves are lightly coloured and the mustard seeds start to pop. Add the onion and garlic, reduce the heat a little and fry for about 7 minutes, until the onion is softened.

Drain the rice and add it to the pan with the lentils, turmeric and 1 tsp salt. Pour in 900ml cold water and stir well. Bring to a simmer then cover and reduce the heat. Cook at a gentle simmer for 25–30 minutes, leaving it alone for the first 20 minutes, then stirring once or twice in the latter stages to ensure it doesn't stick.

When it is done, the khichri should have a risotto-like consistency, the rice should be just tender and the lentils soft and broken down. If you find the rice is still a bit nutty after 30 minutes, add a splash of boiling water and cook for a little longer.

Take the pan off the heat, and leave the khichri to stand, covered, for 10 minutes, then give it another good stir and it's ready to serve. I like it sprinkled with a little fresh chilli and raw onion. You can also spoon a little of your favourite spicy pickle or chutney alongside.

Roast veg

HERE'S A SWEEPING statement for you: if you love a vegetable, you'll love it more roasted. Or at the very least, love it differently – and that's not a bad way of looking at it, as roasting is a truly transformative cooking method.

This is also why, if you *don't* love a vegetable, roasting is the first thing you should try in order to improve your relationship. It is no accident that, while I have corralled all my latest favourite 'tray-roast' veg dishes into this chapter, veg-roasting finds its way into recipes throughout the book, as the first step to many delicious suppers, salads and soups.

There is no easier way to bring out all the lovely, sweet, multi-layered qualities of vegetables than to toss them with some oil, salt and pepper and slam them into a hot oven. And it is so easy – that is *all* you have to do (though, as you'll see, a few herbs and spices don't go amiss). The oven's heat takes care of the rest, setting in motion the chain of complex molecular changes we call 'caramelisation'. When exposed to fierce, dry heat, the natural sugars in the veg become concentrated and, when they reach specific temperatures, they break down into different molecules. These new molecules then react with each other to form new, aromatic compounds. It's the same process that occurs when you burn pure sugar to make caramel.

That's the science. The resulting transmogrification of taste is somewhat more magical. The emerging toasty, bittersweet caramel flavours (manifested visually as golden-to-brown-to-almost-black, crispy-sticky chewy corners and edges) combine with the natural aromatics of the veg in question – often also intensified by heat. The results are heady, sophisticated and delicious. To think that for generations we barely roasted any vegetables except the spud and, occasionally, the parsnip... Thank goodness we're wising up.

Alongside the time-honoured spuds and parsnips, many keen cooks have already discovered the pleasing roastability of almost all root vegetables, including carrots, beetroot, celeriac and turnips. The alliums – onions, shallots, garlic – have also entered the canon. Perhaps, like me, roasting is now your default preparation for squash too – I like skin-on wedges, roasted with shallots, rosemary and a pinch of dried chilli flakes.

If that's where you're at with roasting veg, great, but I say, let's go further. I've proved to my own satisfaction that you can successfully roast almost any veg, or indeed fruit. Now I want to prove it to yours. So you'll find here a roasted version of Greek salad – roasted cucumber is surprisingly good! And you'll find peas and parsley, leafy greens and lettuce – as well as plums, oranges and grapes – all given the hot-blast-in-the-oven treatment. They all work, they're all delicious.

To maximise the benefits of roasting, use the largest oven tray you have. The veg should start off in a more or less single layer to allow the heat to penetrate, drive off moisture and start the browning process. If crammed together or piled up, vegetables tend to steam in their own juices and may cook through without caramelising at all. If necessary, use two smaller roasting trays or oven dishes. A quick stir, around halfway through cooking, is always a good idea too, tumbling the veg with its seasonings and introducing any as yet un-coloured surfaces to the hot surface of the tray.

Most of the recipes in this chapter, served up solo, will feed two or three as a main course, and have enough flavour and variety to stand alone in this way. If you add an additional salad, some greens or grains, they'll do for four or more. Alternatively, you can serve them in smaller portions, with a selection of other dishes, as mezze.

Even if you cook more than you need initially, leftover roasted veg is a very useful commodity to have standing by – ripe for a simple reheat, or for throwing into all manner of improvised suppers. And the spirit of improvisation is one to carry throughout your veg-roasting adventure. These recipes are just jumping-off points – as the 'Swaps' show. You will, I am sure, have many delicious landings.

Roast new potatoes and courgettes with dill

Serves 3–4

750g new or waxy potatoes, scrubbed and cut into large bite-sized chunks

2 tbsp olive or rapeseed oil

750g courgettes, trimmed and cut into bite-sized chunks

2 garlic cloves, chopped

1 lemon

A bunch of dill (about 30g), fronds picked

A handful of flat-leaf parsley leaves, roughly chopped

Sea salt and black pepper

Extra virgin olive oil, to finish

Dill is often reserved for fish but it has the most fantastically veg-friendly flavour – fresh and aniseedy. It's beautiful against the sweet, caramelised tones of roasted potatoes and courgettes.

Preheat the oven to 190°C/Fan 170°C/Gas 5.

Put the potatoes into a large roasting tray. Add the oil and some salt and pepper, stir well and roast for about 30 minutes, or until the potatoes are just tender.

Take the tray from the oven and add the courgettes and garlic. Finely grate the zest of the lemon over the veg. Stir well and return to the oven for 30 minutes or until the potatoes are golden and the courgettes are soft and caramelised.

Squeeze the juice of half the lemon over the hot veg. Scatter over the dill and parsley and stir them in.

Serve straight away, with a sprinkling more salt and pepper and a trickle of extra virgin oil. To feed four, add simply cooked Puy lentils.

Swaps

Herbs Instead of dill, try other slightly aniseedy herbs such as fennel, tarragon or chervil.

Veg Use aubergines or peppers in place of, or as well as, courgettes.

Roast new potatoes, lettuce and spring onions with lemon and bay

Serves 2–4

500g new or waxy potatoes, scrubbed

6–8 bay leaves, torn

6–8 garlic cloves, peeled and bashed

1 large lemon

2 tbsp olive or rapeseed oil

2 little gem lettuces

200g spring onions, trimmed

Sea salt and black pepper

This trayful of roasted summer veg includes whole wedges of lemon, which take on a lovely, bittersweet, caramelised quality in the oven. As their juices escape into the tray of bay-scented veg, they season it deliciously – you might not want to eat the actual lemon rinds, but you can if you like!

Preheat the oven to 190°C/Fan 170°C/Gas 5.

Cut the potatoes into large chunks and put them into a large roasting tray. Add the bay leaves and bashed garlic. Cut the lemon lengthways into 8 slim wedges, removing the pips. Add the lemon wedges to the tray. Trickle over 1 tbsp oil and season with salt and pepper. Toss everything together and roast in the oven for about 30 minutes, until the potatoes are just tender.

Meanwhile, cut each lettuce into quarters. Rinse and dry if necessary then put into a large bowl. Add the spring onions too. Trickle over another 1 tbsp oil, season with salt and pepper and mix well with your hands so all the veg are coated with oil and seasoning.

Take the tray of just-tender potatoes from the oven and stir well to help distribute the bubbling, lemony juices then add the lettuce and onions, nestling them in among the spuds. Return to the oven for another 20 minutes, or until the lettuce is wilted and browned at the edges.

Serve straight away. It's delicious with something piquant on the side – a blob of harissa or pesto, perhaps, or seaweed tapenade (page 314). To serve four, add a 400g tin of chickpeas or white beans – drain, rinse, dress with a little oil, season and toss in with the hot veg.

Swaps

Alliums Baby leeks make a lovely alternative to spring onions.
Leaves In the colder months, use chicory or radicchio rather than little gem lettuce.
Citrus Add orange rather then lemon wedges to the potatoes, along with a pinch of cumin seeds, to bring an extra layer of warm flavour.

Green garlic and carrots with preserved lemon

Serves 2–4

4 green garlic bulbs (about 300g in total), halved lengthways

About 300g small carrots, halved lengthways

½ large or 2 small preserved lemons

2 tbsp olive or rapeseed oil

1 tbsp chopped lovage (or use 1 tbsp each chopped flat-leaf parsley and celery leaves, or 2 tbsp chopped parsley)

Sea salt and black pepper

Green or 'wet' garlic is in season from May to July. It's a slightly immature version of the dried garlic we are used to: similar in shape but plump, juicy and mild, with the individual cloves inside the bulb only just formed. You can use the whole bulb, slicing it like a leek or an onion, or you can roast it on its own or with other veg, as here. Salty, caramelised bits of preserved lemon go very well with it.

Preheat the oven to 190°C/Fan 170°C/Gas 5.

Put the green garlic bulbs into a large roasting dish with the carrots. Remove any pips from the preserved lemon and roughly chop the flesh and rind. Scatter the lemon over the garlic and carrots.

Trickle the oil over the veg, season with salt and pepper and stir well. Cover the dish with foil and roast for 40 minutes, stirring the veg halfway through cooking.

Test the veg by pressing the tip of a sharp knife into the thickest part of a garlic bulb and a carrot. If they are not quite tender, replace the foil and give them another 5–10 minutes.

When the veg are done, lift off the foil, scatter over the lovage (or other herbs) and return the dish to the oven for 5 minutes.

Stir well and serve. You can eat all of the garlic, or scoop the soft inner flesh away from the slightly chewy outer layer. To feed four, serve with tartare hash (page 388).

Swaps

Alliums When green garlic is not in season, baby leeks or halved shallots are delicious alternatives; add a little ordinary garlic too, roughly chopped.

Roots Slim wedges of beetroot or long, tapering wedges of parsnip stand in well for the carrots.

Citrus If preserved lemon is not to hand, use the finely grated zest of a large lemon instead.

Roast fennel, peas and parsley

Serves 2–4

2 large or 3–4 smaller fennel bulbs (about 700g in total)

2 tbsp olive or rapeseed oil

A large bunch of flat-leaf parsley (about 100g)

200g frozen petits pois

4 garlic cloves, sliced

A generous spritz of lemon juice

Sea salt and black pepper

This is a lovely, easy tray-roast with a delightful mix of textures: soft, caramelised fennel, wilted parsley and sweet, nubbly little peas (which can go into the tray straight from the freezer).

Preheat the oven to 190°C/Fan 170°C/Gas 5.

Trim off the tops and bases of the fennel bulbs, reserving any fresh-looking frondy bits. Remove the outer layer of each bulb if it looks damaged or fibrous. Quarter the fennel bulbs, then slice each quarter into 2 or 3 wedges.

Put the fennel wedges into a large roasting tray, trickle over the oil, season with salt and pepper and stir well. Roast for 30 minutes or until the fennel is tender to the tip of a knife and taking on some nice golden brown colour, stirring halfway through cooking.

Meanwhile, chop off the tougher stalks from the bunch of parsley (save these for stock-making). Chop the leaves and tender, upper stalks very roughly – just 2 or 3 cuts across the bunch is fine.

When the fennel is tender, add the parsley, peas and garlic to the roasting tray. Stir well, making sure the parsley is well coated in oil. Return to the oven for 15 minutes, until the parsley is wilted.

Give the whole thing a generous spritz of lemon juice, add more salt or pepper if required and scatter over any reserved fronds of fennel. Serve hot, warm or at room temperature.

To serve four, add a side dish such as Berber barley (page 396), brown rice with onions (page 400) or smashed new potatoes with coriander seeds and bay (page 377).

Swaps

Peas A 400g tin of chickpeas or any other pulse, drained and rinsed, can replace the peas.
Leaves Instead of parsley, add a few handfuls of spinach or sliced chard leaves.

Roast beetroot, tomatoes and plums

Serves 2–4

600–700g small-medium beetroot, scrubbed and cut into 2–4 pieces each

2 tbsp olive or rapeseed oil

1 tsp cumin seeds

500g plums, halved (or quartered if very large) and stones removed

500g medium tomatoes, halved

2 garlic cloves, sliced

A few sprigs of rosemary

A few sprigs of thyme

Sea salt and black pepper

Beautifully colourful, lusciously juicy and fragrant with herbs, this is a delicious summer tray-roast.

Preheat the oven to 190°C/Fan 170°C/Gas 5.

Put the beetroot wedges into a large roasting dish. Add 1 tbsp oil, the cumin seeds and some salt and pepper and toss together. Roast for 30 minutes or until just tender.

Take the dish from the oven and add the plums, tomatoes, garlic, another 1 tbsp oil and a little more salt and pepper. Toss with the beetroot then tuck in the rosemary and thyme. Return to the oven for 30–40 minutes until everything is tender and bubbling.

To feed four, serve with quinoa, or another grainy dish that will soak up the lovely juices.

Swaps
Roots Use a combination of carrots and waxy salad potatoes in place of the beetroot.

Roasted Greek salad

Serves 2–4

1 medium cucumber (about 400g)

750g ripe tomatoes, any size or shape (a mix is good)

1 medium or 2 small onions (ideally red), halved and sliced

1 garlic clove, finely chopped

2 tbsp chopped oregano, or 2 tsp dried oregano

2 tbsp olive oil

1 tbsp red wine vinegar

100g kalamata olives

Sea salt and black pepper

This recipe takes all the ingredients from a classic Greek salad – except the feta cheese – and roasts them in a hot oven. This drives off the moisture and concentrates all those lovely summery flavours.

Preheat the oven to 210°C/190°C/Gas 6–7.

Cut the cucumber in half across the middle, then cut each half into quarters lengthways. Slice each quarter into 2cm chunks and place in a large roasting tray that will hold all the ingredients in a single layer.

Cut the tomatoes into large-bite-sized chunks (you can leave cherry tomatoes whole or cut them in half). Add them to the cucumber with the onion, garlic and oregano, trickle over the olive oil and wine vinegar and season with salt and pepper. Stir well.

Roast in the hot oven for about 40 minutes until the veg are wrinkled and browned, juicy and bubbling. Scatter over the olives and return to the oven for 10 minutes.

Leave to cool slightly, then taste and add a little more salt or pepper if required. Serve warm or at room temperature. To feed four, add herby spelt and lentils (page 394) or crushed new potatoes.

Roast cabbage, carrots and onions with vinaigrette

Serves 3–4

1 medium Savoy cabbage (700–900g)

3 tbsp olive or rapeseed oil

3–4 generous sprigs of thyme, leaves picked from the stems

2 medium onions (ideally red)

250g carrots, scrubbed or peeled

Sea salt and black pepper

FOR THE VINAIGRETTE

2 tbsp extra virgin olive oil

1 tbsp cider vinegar

½ tsp English mustard

A scrap of garlic (about ¼ clove), finely grated or crushed

A classic, sharp vinaigrette is just what you need to balance the natural sweetness of these roasted winter veg.

Preheat the oven to 190°C/Fan 170°C/Gas 5.

Remove any damaged or dirty outer leaves from the cabbage and trim the stalk end. Quarter the cabbage then cut each quarter in half again, to give you 8 wedges, each held together by a section of core (any leaves that come loose as you cut the cabbage can still be included).

Put the cabbage wedges into a large bowl and trickle over 2 tbsp oil. Add about a quarter of the thyme leaves and some salt and pepper. Massage the cabbage with your hands to distribute the oil and seasonings, then transfer to a large roasting tray.

Cut the onions into 8–12 wedges each and put them into the bowl. Halve the carrots lengthways or cut them into chunky batons and add to the onions. Trickle over another 1 tbsp oil, add another quarter of the thyme and some more salt and pepper and mix well. Add these veg to the roasting tray, tucking them in between the cabbage wedges.

Roast for 30 minutes, then take the tray out of the oven and use tongs to turn the cabbage wedges over. Return the tray to the oven for another 30 minutes or until the cabbage is wilted and browned and the other veg are soft and caramelised.

Meanwhile, to make the vinaigrette, whisk all the ingredients together and season with salt and pepper.

Trickle the vinaigrette over the roasted veg, scatter with the remaining thyme and add a final shake of salt and pepper. It's now ready to serve. This is delicious with bay mash (page 382) or tartare hash (page 388).

Swaps

Leaves In place of Savoy, use wedges of pointed summer cabbage. Or try radicchio or chicory, adding them to the carrot and onion about 20 minutes before the end of cooking.
Alliums Use halved shallots or trimmed whole spring onions instead of onion.
Roots Replace the carrot with parsnip, celeriac or potato.

Squash, sweetcorn and plums with rosemary and fennel seeds

Serves 2–4

1kg squash, such as 1 butternut or ½ Crown Prince

2 medium onions (ideally red), sliced into slim wedges

3 tbsp olive or rapeseed oil

2 tsp fennel seeds

2 tsp coriander seeds

1 tbsp roughly chopped rosemary

2 dried chipotle or ancho chillies (or a good pinch of dried chilli flakes)

2 large cobs of corn, husks and silk removed

6 ripe medium plums (about 250g in total), halved and stoned

Flaky sea salt and black pepper

The squash and corn really take up the flavours of the fennel and coriander seeds in this dish, while the plums contribute a sweet-tart flavour that works deliciously with the squash.

Preheat the oven to 190°C/Fan 170°C/Gas 5.

Halve the squash, scoop out the seeds, then slice it into slim wedges (no need to remove the skin). Put the squash wedges into a large roasting tray (suitable to use on the hob). Add the onion wedges and trickle over 2 tbsp oil.

Using a pestle and mortar, roughly pound the fennel and coriander seeds with the rosemary, a pinch of flaky sea salt and some ground black pepper. Sprinkle the mix over the squash and onions and toss the whole lot together.

Chop the chillies into a few pieces each and add to the tray (or sprinkle over the dried chilli flakes). Roast in the oven for 30 minutes.

Meanwhile, cut each corn cob into about 6 sections (the core of a corn cob is very tough, so use a sharp, heavy knife). Put these into a bowl with the halved plums. Add a further 1 tbsp oil and some more salt and pepper and toss together with your hands.

After 30 minutes, take the roasting tray out of the oven, add the corn and plums and stir together with the squash and onions. Roast in the oven for another 30 minutes, or until the squash is completely tender.

Use tongs to transfer the squash and sweetcorn to a warmed serving dish. Put the roasting tray containing the plums, onions and spices over a low heat on the hob. Add 3 tbsp water and stir to deglaze the tray for a minute or two, scraping up the onion, sticky plums and spices and amalgamating them into a rough sauce.

Spoon this sauce over the hot squash and corn and serve straight away. To feed four, add a big, crisp salad.

Swaps

Fruit Swap the plums for wedges of apple.
Spices Try cumin or caraway seeds in place of the fennel seeds.

Roast squash and walnuts, two ways

In this dish, roasted squash and the lovely flavouring ingredients it's cooked with are served up both whole and puréed. Butternut, with its relatively moist flesh, is a great squash to use here because it purées so easily; Crown Prince and acorn also work well.

Preheat the oven to 190°C/Fan 170°C/Gas 5.

Cut the squash in half. Scoop out the seeds from both halves, then remove the peel from just one half (the peeled bits are the ones you'll be puréeing later). Cut all the squash into wedges, about 3cm wide at their outer edge. Put these into a large roasting dish.

Scatter the onion over the squash, followed by the garlic, chilli and rosemary. Trickle over the olive oil, season with salt and pepper and toss everything together. Roast for 45 minutes. Scatter the walnuts over the veg and return to the oven for about 8 minutes until the walnuts are nicely coloured.

Pick out the peeled squash pieces and put them into a large measuring jug that you can get a stick blender in to, or into a food processor. Add about half of the roasted onion, garlic, chilli, rosemary and walnuts. Add the balsamic vinegar then use a stick blender or the processor to blitz these ingredients to a thick, coarse purée. Taste and add more salt and pepper if needed.

Dollop the squash purée onto warmed serving plates and place the roasted squash wedges on top, adding all the roasted flavourings and walnuts from the roasting tray.

Scatter over the rocket leaves and add a sprinkling of salt and pepper and a few more drops of balsamic vinegar. Serve straight away, with a fluffy grain, such as quinoa.

Swaps

Leaves Replace the rocket with peppery watercress or flat-leaf parsley.

Serves 4

1kg squash, such as a medium butternut or acorn squash, or ½ Crown Prince

1 medium onion, halved and sliced

4 garlic cloves, peeled but left whole

1 medium-hot red chilli, deseeded and roughly chopped

A large sprig of rosemary, leaves picked from the stems

3 tbsp olive oil

100g walnuts

1 tbsp balsamic vinegar, plus a little extra to finish

About 100g rocket

Sea salt and black pepper

Roast spiced beetroot, radicchio and orange

Serves 2–4

1 tsp fennel seeds

1 tsp coriander seeds

1 tsp sweet smoked paprika

A pinch of dried chilli flakes

1 tbsp chopped rosemary (optional)

1 large orange

About 500g small-medium beetroot, scrubbed and each cut into 8 wedges

3 tbsp olive or rapeseed oil

2 medium-large onions (ideally red), peeled and each cut into 8 wedges

8 garlic cloves, peeled but left whole

2 radicchio (about 300g each), quartered lengthways, still attached at the root

Sea salt and black pepper

Bitter radicchio and sweet beetroot both taste wonderful with the fennel, paprika, garlic and chilli used to season this dish. The orange wedges, roasted with the veg, can be squeezed over everything at the end.

Preheat the oven to 190°C/Fan 170°C/Gas 5.

Using a pestle and mortar, crush the fennel and coriander seeds to a coarse powder. Add the smoked paprika, chilli and rosemary, if using. Finely grate the zest of the orange onto the spice mix, add some salt and pepper and stir well.

Put the beetroot wedges into a large roasting tray. Add 2 tbsp oil and toss the beetroot in it, then add the spice mix and stir so that the veg are well coated with spices. Cover the tray with foil and roast in the oven for 30 minutes.

Meanwhile, slice the zested orange into 8 wedges.

Take the tray from the oven, add the orange wedges, onion wedges and garlic cloves, and stir so that everything gets a coating of spicy, beetrooty juice. Cover again with the foil and return to the oven for 30 minutes or until the beetroot is tender to the point of a knife.

Meanwhile, put the radicchio quarters into a bowl, trickle over the remaining 1 tbsp oil and sprinkle with some salt and pepper. Use your hands to turn the radicchio in the oil and seasoning to coat all over.

Take the roasting tray from the oven and remove the foil. Add the seasoned radicchio, rubbing the cut surfaces into the spicy pan mix. Now roast, uncovered, for another 15–20 minutes or until the radicchio leaves are wilted and the stalk is tender.

Serve the roast veg hot, warm or cold, squeezing the juice from the caramelised oranges over them as you go. To feed four, serve with Puy lentils or lightly spicy buckwheat (page 391).

Swaps

Roots Try parsnip or celeriac instead of beetroot.
Leaves Replace the radicchio with 2 or 3 heads of chicory.
Citrus Swap a large lemon for the orange.

Roast potatoes and grapes with bay and star anise

Serves 3–4

1kg potatoes (any kind)

2 medium onions, halved and sliced root to tip

2 tbsp olive or rapeseed oil

300g grapes

75ml red wine

4 large bay leaves, each torn into 3–4 pieces

2 star anise

Sea salt and black pepper

This is a lovely way to put a different spin on roast spuds. The fruit, herbs and wine – together with the unique, spicy-sweet note of star anise – take them in a tempting new direction.

Preheat the oven to 190°C/Fan 170°C/Gas 5.

Scrub the potatoes but don't peel them. Cut into large, bite-sized chunks and put them into a large roasting tray. Add the sliced onions. Trickle over the oil, season with salt and pepper and stir well. Roast for 30 minutes.

Take the tray out of the oven. Add the grapes, red wine, torn bay leaves and whole star anise. Stir everything well then return to the oven for another 30 minutes or so, until the potatoes are golden, the onions caramelised, and the grapes juicy and wrinkled.

Stir everything well again to make sure the herby, spicy flavours are mingled in, then check the seasoning, adding more salt and pepper if required. Serve hot or warm. To feed four, add blitzed kale with lemon and garlic (page 362).

Swaps

Roots Rather than spuds alone, try a mixed root medley of potatoes, carrots and parsnips.
Fruit Replace the grapes with apple wedges.

Roast potatoes, swede, apples and kale

Serves 4

850g potatoes (any kind), scrubbed but not peeled, cut into 3–4cm chunks

1 large onion, halved and sliced

½ large swede (about 400g), peeled and cut into 2–3cm cubes

2 medium eating apples, cored and each cut into 12 wedges

4 garlic cloves, peeled and bashed

4 bay leaves, torn

A couple of generous sprigs of thyme, roughly torn up

3 tbsp olive or rapeseed oil

200g kale or cavolo nero

Sea salt and black pepper

The contrast between earthy, starchy roast roots, sweet apple and crisp, oven-darkened kale is delectable. This is a meal in itself, needing no more than a blob of mustard or tangy fruit ketchup.

Preheat the oven to 190°C/Fan 170°C/Gas 5.

Put the potatoes, onion, swede and apple wedges into a large roasting tray. Add the garlic, herbs, some salt and pepper and 2 tbsp of the oil. Stir well.

Roast in the oven for 50–60 minutes, until everything is completely tender and starting to colour, giving the veg a good stir about halfway through cooking.

Meanwhile, tear the kale leaves off the stalks, ripping the leaves into large pieces as you go. Put these into a large bowl, add another 1 tbsp oil and some salt and pepper and mix well with your hands so all the kale leaves are coated with oil and seasoning.

Add the kale to the tray of cooked veg, arranging it in a layer on top of the veg, and return to the oven for 10 minutes.

Stir the kale into the veg, then give the dish a final 5 minutes in the oven, to ensure the kale is done – it should be deliciously crispy but still a little chewy in places. Serve straight away.

Swaps

Roots Use parsnip instead of swede – it works equally well.
Brassicas Use purple sprouting broccoli or small cauliflower florets in place of the kale. They will take 20–25 minutes (rather than 10), so you can reduce the first stage of cooking to 40–45 minutes.

Roast turnips, shallots and dates with watercress

Serves 3–4

1kg baby turnips

300g shallots

4–5 bay leaves, roughly torn

3 tbsp olive or rapeseed oil

100g pitted dates, halved

8 garlic cloves, peeled

200g watercress

Sea salt and black pepper

This is a really successful combination of flavours: earthy, sweet and peppery, with the dates adding a touch of sweetness. I prefer a relatively firm date for this, such as a deglet nour, rather than the really soft and fudgy medjool type.

Preheat the oven to 190°C/Fan 170°C/Gas 5.

Trim the turnips. If they are golf-ball-sized or smaller, cut them in half. If they are larger, quarter them. Put the turnips into a large roasting tray. Halve the shallots if they are larger than a walnut. Add them to the tray with the bay leaves, 2 tbsp oil and some salt and pepper. Mix well and roast in the oven for 30 minutes.

Meanwhile, put the halved dates into a bowl. Smash the garlic cloves with the flat of a large knife, so that they break into 2 or 3 pieces each. Add to the dates with 1 tbsp oil and some salt and pepper. Mix well.

Spoon the dates and garlic, and any oil from the bowl, over the roasted turnips and shallots. Mix well and return to the oven for 15 minutes.

Roughly tear up the watercress, add it to the tray and mix it in, then return to the oven for a final 5 minutes, until wilted. Serve straight away – I like this just as it comes.

Swaps

Roots Try chunks of parsnip or celeriac instead of baby turnips.
Alliums Use onions or spring onions in place of the shallots.
Leaves Rocket works well as an alternative to watercress, or go for a less peppery leaf such as spinach or lettuce.

Celeriac, toasted buckwheat and parsley

Serves 3–4

50g whole raw buckwheat (buckwheat 'groats')

1 large or 2 small celeriac (about 900g in total)

2 tbsp olive oil

A small bunch of flat-leaf parsley (about 25g), roughly chopped

Sea salt and black pepper

FOR THE DRESSING

A scrap of garlic (about ¼ clove), finely grated or crushed

1 tsp English mustard

1 tsp sugar

1 tbsp lemon juice

3 tbsp extra virgin olive oil

Buckwheat – which is actually a seed, rather than a grain – is usually served cooked. But you can toast the whole seeds, or 'groats', and eat them just as they come. They're nutty, mild and deliciously crunchy – a lovely counterpoint to tender, roasted celeriac.

Preheat the oven to 180°C/Fan 160°C/Gas 4.

Spread the buckwheat out in a large roasting tray and toast in the oven for 8–10 minutes or until golden brown and smelling nicely nutty. Tip into a bowl and set aside. (Alternatively, you could use ready-roasted buckwheat, or *kasha*.) Turn the oven up to 190°C/Fan 170°C/Gas 5.

Prepare the celeriac: slice off the rough skin, cut the flesh into roughly 2cm slices, then cut each slice into bite-sized wedges.

Put the celeriac into the roasting tray vacated by the buckwheat. Add the oil and some salt and pepper and toss together. Roast for about 40 minutes until the celeriac is golden brown and tender, stirring halfway through cooking.

Meanwhile, to make the dressing, whisk all the ingredients together in a bowl with some salt and pepper.

Let the roasted celeriac cool slightly, for 5 minutes or so, then add the dressing and most of the chopped parsley and stir together. Transfer to a serving bowl.

Scatter the crunchy, toasted buckwheat over the top and finish with the remaining parsley, a pinch of flaky salt and a final grinding of pepper. Serve with a green salad. To feed four, serve Puy lentils on the side too.

Swaps

Seeds Replace the buckwheat with another seed, such as pumpkin or sunflower. Toast these in the oven for a little less time.
Roots Use parsnip instead of the celeriac, or a mixture of roots, such as potato, carrot and parsnip.

Roast squash, sweet potato, chilli and kale

Serves 3–4

About 500g butternut or other squash

About 500g sweet potatoes

4–6 garlic cloves, peeled

3–4 tbsp olive or rapeseed oil

4–6 mild-medium red chillies (at least 8cm long)

½ tsp sweet smoked paprika

300g kale or cavolo nero

Sea salt and black pepper

Richly coloured and nicely spicy, this is a winter warmer in every sense. The chillies go into the dish in large pieces, so choose some that aren't too incendiary. If you can only get hold of very hot chillies, use just one or two, deseed them and chop roughly before adding.

Preheat the oven to 190°C/Fan 170°C/Gas 5.

There is no need to peel the squash or sweet potatoes, just give them a wash. Cut the sweet potatoes into large bite-sized chunks and the squash into slim wedges, removing the seeds. Put these into a large roasting tray.

Set aside 1 whole garlic clove. Cut the rest into 2 or 3 chunky pieces each and add to the roasting tray. Add 1 tbsp oil and some salt and pepper and stir well. Roast for 30 minutes.

Meanwhile, halve the chillies lengthways, trim out all the seeds and white membranes and reserve these.

After 30 minutes, take the veg from the oven, add the chilli halves, stir them into the veg and return to the oven for 15 minutes.

Roughly chop the reserved chilli seeds and membrane and put into a very small pan. Finely chop the reserved garlic clove and add this too. Add 2 tbsp oil and the smoked paprika. Heat until everything is frying gently then remove from the heat and set aside to infuse.

Strip the kale leaves from their stalks, tear them into large pieces and put into a large bowl. Add a trickle of oil and some salt and pepper and massage all over the kale leaves with your hands, crushing and squeezing the leaves as you go (this helps to reduce the volume a bit).

Add the kale to the tray of veg and chilli. Stir it in so that at least some of the veg and chilli is on top of the kale. Roast, uncovered, for another 15–20 minutes, until the kale is wilted and a little crisp in places.

Strain the chilli-infused oil through a small sieve or colander over the veg. Add a sprinkle more salt and serve straight away. To feed four, add a couple of chopped avocados or a bowl of hummus.

Swaps

Roots Use all sweet potatoes or all squash rather than half of each. Or for an earthier-tasting dish, swap the sweet potato for ordinary spuds.

Roast cauliflower with Puy lentil purée

Serves 4

1 medium cauliflower, about 800g (900g max), at room temperature

2 tbsp olive or rapeseed oil

Sea salt and black pepper

FOR THE PUY LENTIL PURÉE

200g Puy lentils

1 large garlic clove, peeled but left whole

500ml veg stock (see page 190 for home-made)

TO FINISH

Extra virgin olive or rapeseed oil, to trickle

As with a piece of roast meat, a big roast cauliflower offers several different flavours and textures. There are salty, burnt leaves, a sweet, golden brown surface, tender inner curds and a still-nutty base. All are delicious sauced with a rough, savoury purée of Puy lentils. And both elements of the dish are very easy to prepare.

Preheat the oven to 200°C/Fan 180°C/Gas 6.

Take the outer few leaves off the cauliflower but leave half a dozen or so of the inner leaves still attached.

Rub the cauliflower with the oil, working it into the nooks and crannies and all over the leaves. Don't worry if some of the leaf stems snap, just keep them with the cauliflower. Season the cauliflower all over with salt and pepper. Put the prepared cauliflower in a roasting dish and roast for an hour.

When the cauliflower has been cooking for about half an hour, put the lentils into a saucepan with the peeled garlic clove and veg stock. Bring to a simmer then cover the pan and simmer gently for about 15 minutes until the lentils are tender.

Test the cauliflower by pressing a small, sharp knife into the core, going in at the base, which is the thickest, toughest part. It won't be soft but the knife should go in without too much resistance. If it seems very firm still, put it back in the oven for 10–15 minutes then test again.

When the lentils are tender, use a stick blender to blitz them in the pan with the garlic and stock – you want a fairly thick but still spoonable purée, with a little texture. If it's very thick, add a little hot water. Taste the purée and add salt and pepper if needed. Keep warm.

To serve, cut the hot roasted cauliflower into quarters and place on warmed plates. Spoon over the Puy lentil purée, give each portion a trickle of extra virgin oil, a sprinkling more salt and pepper, and serve.

Some leaves may be too blackened to eat, but the leaf stems will be deliciously bittersweet. Most of the cauliflower will be nicely *al dente* and the thickest part of the base will still be fairly firm – I pick this up with my hands and eat it when all the rest has been devoured.

Roast sprouts, celeriac and prunes

Serves 3–4

1 medium celeriac (about 600g)

3 tbsp olive or rapeseed oil

A few sprigs of thyme, roughly torn

500g Brussels sprouts

150g pitted prunes, halved

6 garlic cloves, peeled and bashed

1 tbsp balsamic (or red wine) vinegar

Sea salt and black pepper

Sweet, sticky prunes partner Brussels sprouts beautifully, and a little balsamic vinegar and garlic further enhance the flavours of the winter veg in this dish.

Preheat the oven to 190°C/Fan 170°C/Gas 5.

Prepare the celeriac: slice off the rough skin, cut the flesh into roughly 2cm slices then cut each slice into bite-sized chunks.

Put the celeriac chunks into a large roasting tray. Add 2 tbsp oil, the thyme and some salt and pepper and toss together. Roast in the oven for 20–25 minutes.

Meanwhile, peel away any dirty or damaged outer leaves from the sprouts, trim the stems if necessary, then cut each sprout in half. Put the sprouts into a bowl with the halved prunes and the bashed garlic cloves. Add 1 tbsp oil, the vinegar, some salt and pepper and toss together well.

Take the celeriac out of the oven and give it a good stir, then scatter over the sprouts and prunes, along with any vinegary juice from the bowl. Return to the oven for another 20–25 minutes, until both the celeriac and sprouts are tender and golden brown in places.

Serve straight away. For four people, add nutty, seedy, herby hummus (page 306).

Swaps
Roots Use parsnip, potato or carrot – or any combination thereof – in place of the celeriac.

Big salads

I LIKE THE WORD 'salad', and I like the way its meaning has expanded down the years. It's no longer just a few green leaves and a dressing. These days, in my way of thinking, a salad is quite often lunch, or indeed supper; it can even be breakfast. Importantly, it can denote a complete dish that is wholly satisfying, and not just something on the side. The dishes in this chapter are positioned very much at this hale and hearty end of the salad spectrum.

This crop of recipes is eclectic – shouting out the virtues of a whole range of vegetables, fruits, nuts, seeds, grains, herbs and spices. Flavours are big, dressings are tangy and tasty, colours are bright, and the techniques I've deployed to get my veg into salad-ready form vary from massaging and grating to roasting, char-grilling and simmering. If there's one thing that ties these dishes together, it's their generosity. They may be salads but they're not 'skinny' – they have substance and variety and you can enjoy them just as they come, without extra bulk. Devour them greedily for lunch or supper and you'll feel satisfied but not weighed down.

These salads will also sit well in the mix-and-match world of my mezze and tapas (pages 304–71), or alongside some of my starchy sides (pages 376–403). In these sharing-plate scenarios recipes that serve two generously will, of course, stretch to three, four or more.

I don't think a salad is ever really a salad without a well-seasoned dressing of some kind – it's the thing that turns an assembly of ingredients into a dish – and I've not stinted on these. Good, unrefined oils are my most frequent choice as the base. An extra virgin olive oil or cold-pressed rapeseed oil brings its own character: peppery, grassy and fragrant, in the former case; delicate, floral and nutty in the latter. Also, importantly, it carries the flavours of seasonings, spices and citrus throughout the salad, allowing them to touch every ingredient in a way they wouldn't if added 'dry'. But these luscious oils are not the only way to lubricate and caress your ingredients into salad perfection, and you'll find recipes here in which nut butter, puréed fruit and tangy pomegranate molasses step into the role.

Another thing that defines a salad, in my view, is the inclusion of at least one raw element in the mix. These dishes illustrate that. The first few recipes in this chapter are completely raw, but they are so hearty and satisfying that I feel they belong here.

Further on, there are dishes combining cooked veg with uncooked, where I've deliberately used the heat of roasted roots to wilt crisp leaves, or let the juices from raw tomatoes soak into the buttery warm flesh of boiled new potatoes. It's a technique I love – flavours marry so well when a little bit of heat is involved, even if the finished dish is eaten once it has cooled down to room temperature. In fact, especially if it's eaten at room temperature – that's when our palates can detect and savour the greatest breadth and depth of tastes and aromas in the food we eat. A great salad generally tastes *really* great when served unchilled.

This, along with the fact that many of these salads are just as good the next day as they are when freshly made, means they are lunchbox shoo-ins – just perfect for packing up and taking to work or school. They can be made the evening before and will positively benefit from a little time spent sitting in their bowl or box. Fridging overnight will keep them fresh, and the few hours before lunch will bring them back to that palate-pleasing ambience. They may lose their crisp good looks, as dressings mingle with leaves and cooked veg cools, but they'll taste all the better for it.

Chicory with orange, cashews and pomegranate

Serves 2–3

2 medium oranges

2 heads of chicory (ideally red), separated into leaves

½ pomegranate

FOR THE CASHEW MIX

150g cashew nuts

Finely grated zest of 1 orange

1 tbsp pomegranate molasses

¼–½ garlic clove, finely grated or crushed

Sea salt and black pepper

TO FINISH

Extra virgin olive or rapeseed oil

This stunning-looking salad is simple to make, and utterly delicious. A shot of pomegranate molasses (now widely available) brings a sweet-tangy flavour that complements the mild cashews and bitter chicory exceptionally well. Red chicory looks particularly eye-catching but white/yellow chicory tastes just as good.

To make the cashew mix, put all the ingredients into a food processor, adding a good pinch of salt and a grinding of pepper. Blitz until finely chopped and well mixed – the pomegranate molasses is very sticky, so you'll need to scrape down the sides of the processor quite firmly once or twice to make sure everything gets amalgamated. The final mix should not hold together in one lump, but should have a slight stickiness, with the nuts forming clumps here and there.

Cut a slice from the top and base of each orange. Stand one orange on a board and use a sharp knife to cut away the peel and pith, working around the fruit in sections. Once you have a whole, peel-less fruit, slice it horizontally into 5–10mm slices. Repeat with the other orange.

Spread the orange slices out over a large serving plate or individual plates. Arrange the chicory leaves over the orange and scatter the cashew mix on top.

Hold the pomegranate half, cut side down, over the plate and whack the skin side with a wooden spoon so that the seeds drop out. Give the pomegranate a bit of a squeeze now and then to help loosen the seeds and the beautiful pink juice. Finish with a trickle of oil.

This is delicious with a bowl of pea hummus alongside (page 304).

Swaps

Leaves Substitute radicchio for the chicory, or use crisp cos lettuce leaves or little gems.
Fruit Swap the orange slices for slim wedges of apple (keep the orange zest in the cashew mix though!), or use apple and orange.

Mango, spinach and buckwheat salad

Serves 2

50g raisins

A little apple juice (optional)

2 large, ripe mangoes

Juice of 1–2 limes

A pinch of dried chilli flakes

A pinch of ground allspice (optional)

50g baby leaf spinach

Sea salt and black pepper

TO FINISH

50g whole toasted buckwheat 'groats' (kasha)

Coriander leaves

This gorgeous raw salad is full of refreshing, sweet mango flavour, cut through with plenty of lime, chilli and coriander. A topping of crunchy, toasted whole buckwheat rounds it off a treat. You can toast your own buckwheat for this (see the recipe on page 136) or buy it ready toasted/roasted, when it is also sometimes called *kasha*.

If you have time, put the raisins into a small bowl and add enough apple juice to cover them. Leave for a few hours, or overnight, to plump up.

To prepare the mangoes, first slice off the two plump sections of flesh either side of the stone (i.e. the 'cheeks'). Hold one 'cheek' skin side down and use a small, sharp knife to make three equally spaced long cuts in the flesh, as far as, but not all the way through, the skin. Now work the tip of the knife all around the edge of the cheek, between the skin and flesh. (You should find this releases the two outermost slices.) Push the mango skin inside out, as it were, which will make the central two slices stand proud, and slice them away from the skin. Cut these larger slices in half lengthways again. Repeat with the other mango cheeks, so you have a pile of long, slender mango slices. Set aside.

Now turn to the remaining mango flesh still attached to the stones. Use the small knife to cut the skin away from the flesh, then cut the flesh off the stone in chunks and slivers. Put these bits of mango flesh into a jug blender, or into a jug that's big enough to take a stick blender.

To the mango in the blender/jug, add the juice of 1 lime, the chilli flakes, allspice if using, and some salt and pepper. Blitz to a smooth purée, adding some juice from the second lime if necessary to achieve a thick but pourable consistency. Taste and add more seasoning if necessary – bearing in mind this is the dressing for the salad and the mango's fruity sweetness needs to be tempered by the lime juice, salt and chilli.

To assemble, spread the spinach leaves out on individual plates and arrange the slices of mango over the top. Drain the raisins (if soaked) and scatter over the salad, then trickle over the mango dressing. Finish with the toasted buckwheat and coriander.

Swaps

Leaves Any delicate baby salad leaves can take the place of spinach.
Seeds Use lightly toasted pumpkin, sunflower or sesame seeds – or a mix – instead of buckwheat.

Lunchtime rooty Bircher

Serves 2

100g chunk of celeriac

1 medium eating apple

100g jumbo oats

50g raisins or sultanas

50g whole, skin-on almonds

50g mixed seeds, such as sunflower, pumpkin and sesame (or just one type if you prefer)

3 tbsp extra virgin olive or rapeseed oil

Juice of ½ lemon

200ml cloudy apple juice

Sea salt and black pepper

Bircher muesli, traditionally, means oats soaked with fruit juice and grated apple so they soften into a sort of raw porridge. It's one of my favourite breakfasts and I see no reason to confine it to the morning. This lunchtime version includes raw celeriac, lemon juice and olive oil to give it a more savoury slant, but retains a delicious sweetness from the apple. You can make it in the morning and leave it soaking until lunchtime.

Slice the knobbly, grubby outer layer off the celeriac, revealing the creamy-white interior. Grate this coarsely into a large bowl.

Grate the apple into the bowl too. There's no need to peel or cut the apple, just grate it on one side down to the core then turn it and grate the other side, and so on. Mix with the celeriac.

Add all the remaining ingredients, including a pinch of salt and a grinding of pepper. Mix together well, making sure the grated fruit and veg is well distributed.

If you're going to be eating the Bircher at home, cover the bowl and leave in the fridge for at least 1 hour, up to 6 or 7. Stir once or twice during that time if you can and let it come up to room temperature before eating. If you're taking the muesli to work, divide it between a couple of plastic tubs, snap the lids on and it's good to go – keep it cool until you're ready to eat.

Swaps

Roots Try grated carrot or parsnip in place of celeriac – or beetroot, for a splendidly colourful Bircher!

Dried fruit Choose your favourite dried fruit here: chopped apricots, dried cherries, sliced dates and prunes are all good.

Nuts Replace the almonds with whole or roughly chopped hazelnuts, pecans or walnuts.

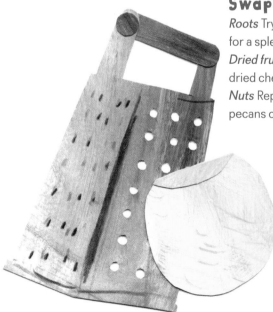

Summer slaw with peanut dressing

Serves 4

½ pointed summer cabbage such as hispi/sweetheart (about 200g)

1 medium red pepper

2 small-medium carrots (about 150g in total)

50g raisins

A small handful of coriander leaves

FOR THE PEANUT TOPPING

75g raw peanuts, coarsely chopped

1 tbsp sesame seeds

2 tbsp tamari

1 tsp sugar

FOR THE DRESSING

1½ tbsp no-sugar-added peanut butter (crunchy or smooth)

Juice of ½ large lime

2 tsp toasted sesame oil

2 tsp tamari

2 tsp rice vinegar (or you can use cider vinegar)

2 tsp sugar

A scrap of garlic (about ¼ clove), finely grated

1 tsp freshly grated ginger

This makes a big, colourful bowlful of sweet and tangy flavours.

First make the peanut topping. Put the chopped peanuts into a medium non-stick pan and toast them gently over a moderate heat, tossing often, until they start to turn golden. Add the sesame seeds and tamari and continue to cook for a couple of minutes. Use a spatula to stir the nutty, seedy mix with the tamari as it reduces and thickens. Stop cooking when the tamari is reduced to a sticky coating on the nuts. Take off the heat and stir in the sugar, then set aside to cool.

To make the dressing, put the peanut butter into a large bowl, add the lime juice and whisk to combine. Now whisk in the other ingredients, one by one, until you have a nicely amalgamated dressing.

Cut the cabbage half in half again, trim out the core from each section, then slice the cabbage thinly and add it to the dressing.

Quarter the red pepper and remove the stalk, seeds and membranes. Slice the flesh fairly thinly and add it to the bowl with the cabbage.

Peel or scrub and trim the carrots and grate them coarsely into the bowl with the other prepared veg. Add the raisins and mix everything together thoroughly.

Transfer the salad to a serving dish. Scatter with coriander, then the tamari-coated peanuts and seeds, and it's ready to serve.

Swaps

Leaves In winter, use red or white cabbage.
Veg Try replacing the red pepper with fennel, and/or the carrot with beetroot.
Dried fruit Substitute dried cherries, or chopped dried apricots or dates, for the raisins.

Tomato and black bean salad with cumin dressing

Serves 4

350g cherry tomatoes (or any flavourful tomatoes)

½ small onion (ideally red), halved again and finely sliced

400g tin black beans or carlin peas, drained or rinsed

1 little gem lettuce, quartered and sliced

Sea salt and black pepper

FOR THE DRESSING

2 tsp cumin seeds

A good pinch of flaky sea salt

½ garlic clove

1 tsp sugar

Juice of 1 small lemon

4 tbsp extra virgin olive oil

TO FINISH

Basil or mint leaves, ribboned or roughly shredded

With its rich colours and garlicky, spicy dressing, this is a treat to find in your lunchbox, or take on a picnic.

First make the dressing. Using a large pestle and mortar, pound the cumin seeds, sea salt, garlic clove and a grinding of black pepper to a paste. Add the sugar and lemon juice and mix, then add the extra virgin oil and stir well. Taste and add more salt and pepper if needed then transfer to a large bowl.

Halve the cherry tomatoes (or cut larger ones into small-ish pieces) and add to the dressing. Stir and then mix in the onion, breaking up the layers as you go.

If you have time, leave the dressed tomato mix to macerate for an hour or so, but if you need to serve the salad straight away it will be fine. (If you're taking this salad somewhere in a lunchbox, you will, of course, have maceration time built in.)

Add the drained and rinsed beans to the tomatoes and mix well.

Scatter the lettuce over a serving dish (or pack into plastic tubs). Spoon the dressed tomato mixture over the lettuce. Sprinkle with a pinch each more salt and pepper, then the basil or mint, and it's ready to eat, or to pack up for later.

Swaps

Leaves You can introduce any kind of lettuce here, or baby spinach leaves, or chicory.
Pulses Use another tinned pulse, such as white beans or chickpeas, in place of the black beans. Cooked Puy lentils are great too.

Kohlrabi, cucumber and sprouted beans

Serves 2–3

2 small or 1 large kohlrabi (about 400g in total)

½ cucumber (about 200g)

125g sprouted beans, lentils or seeds

2 tbsp finely shredded mint

FOR THE DRESSING

2 tbsp extra virgin olive or rapeseed oil

1 tbsp pomegranate molasses

A scrap of garlic (about ¼ clove), finely grated or crushed

Sea salt and black pepper

This vibrant, crunchy salad includes some intriguing ingredients. Kohlrabi comes in the form of a curious-looking pale-green sphere. It is delicious served raw in salads like this – and fantastic with sprouted beans, lentils or seeds, which you can now buy ready-sprouted in many health food shops and supermarkets. The simple dressing is based on pomegranate molasses: a syrup of cooked-down pomegranate juice with a unique tangy-sweet flavour.

For the dressing, whisk all the ingredients together in a small bowl, adding a good pinch of salt and a grinding of pepper, then set aside.

Peel the kohlrabi and trim the tops and bases. Cut into thin slices then cut each slice into slim batons (or simply grate the kohlrabi coarsely if you prefer). Put the kohlrabi into a large bowl.

Slice the cucumber in half lengthways, then cut into thin half-moons. Add these to the kohlrabi, along with the sprouted beans, lentils or seeds, and most of the mint.

Give the dressing another whisk then pour it over the raw veg and sprouts and mix well. Taste and add more salt or pepper if required. Transfer to a serving dish, scatter over the remaining mint, and serve.

Swaps

Veg If you can't get hold of kohlrabi, use one of its brassica cousins such as raw, shredded red cabbage or grated raw cauliflower.
Herbs Basil or coriander can stand in for the mint.
Dressing If you don't have pomegranate molasses, use 1 tbsp cider vinegar and a good pinch of sugar.

Cauliflower, apple, almond and date salad

Serves 2–3

50g whole, skin-on almonds

½ medium cauliflower (about 400g untrimmed)

1 eating apple

75g pitted dates, thickly sliced

50g rocket

FOR THE DRESSING

2 tbsp tahini

3 tbsp extra virgin olive or rapeseed oil

3 tbsp cloudy apple juice

1 tbsp lemon juice, plus an extra spritz if needed

1 tsp nigella (black onion/kalonji) seeds

A scrap of garlic (about ¼ clove), finely grated or crushed

Sea salt and black pepper

This lovely, crunchy, all-raw salad is a feast of tastes and textures – nuttiness from the cauliflower, sweetness from the apples and dates, a touch of bitterness from the tahini dressing, and the unique, oniony flavour of nigella seeds. It makes for a hearty bowlful.

If you have time, put the almonds to soak in cold water in the fridge for a few hours – even an hour makes a difference – so they become more plump and juicy.

To make the dressing, whisk the tahini, oil, apple and lemon juice together until smooth and creamy textured. Stir in the nigella seeds, garlic and some salt and pepper. Set aside.

Cut up the cauliflower: first slice off the florets and cut them into very small pieces (1–2cm); then cut the stalk into small, thin pieces. Discard any very thick-stemmed leaves, but keep the small, tender leaves, slicing them roughly. Put all the chopped cauliflower into a large bowl.

Quarter, core and roughly chop the apple, then add to the bowl with the dates. Drain the almonds if they've been soaking. Roughly chop the almonds and add to the salad. Pour over the dressing and stir well.

Finally, fold through the rocket. Taste and add more salt, pepper or lemon juice, as needed. Serve straight away or pack in a tub as a portable lunch.

Swaps

Fruit A nice, firm, slightly under-ripe pear makes a lovely alternative to the apple here.

Nuts Add hazelnuts, walnuts or pecans in place of the almonds.

Leaves Use watercress or any peppery leaf instead of the rocket.

Spices Replace nigella with sesame or poppy seeds.

Summer spelt salad with gremolata

Serves 4

150g pearled spelt or pearl barley

3 tbsp extra virgin olive, rapeseed or hempseed oil

Juice of 1 lemon

250g asparagus, tough ends snapped off

200g peas or petits pois (fresh or frozen)

200g radishes, quartered

Sea salt and black pepper

FOR THE GREMOLATA

A small bunch of flat-leaf parsley (25g), leaves picked from the stalks

1 small garlic clove

Finely grated zest of 1 lemon

I enjoy summer veg tossed with something earthy and substantial. Pearled spelt fits the bill, while fresh, zesty gremolata (a mix of garlic, parsley and lemon rind) keeps everything bright and zingy. The spelt is cooked, dressed and cooled ahead – so you only need to briefly cook the green veg and cut up the raw radishes before serving.

If time, soak the spelt or barley in cold water first, for 20–30 minutes. Either way, rinse well in a sieve. Tip into a saucepan, cover with plenty of cold water and add a pinch of salt. Bring to the boil, lower the heat and simmer for about 20 minutes for spelt, 40 minutes for barley.

Meanwhile, prepare the gremolata: roughly chop the parsley leaves and garlic separately, then combine the two, add the lemon zest and chop them finely together, mixing them as you go.

Drain the spelt or barley well, then tip back into the hot pan. Add the oil, lemon juice, gremolata and some salt and pepper. Mix well and leave to cool completely.

Just before serving, bring a pan of water to the boil. Add the asparagus and peas to the boiling water and return to a simmer. Cook for a couple of minutes, until the veg are just tender. Drain, run them under the cold tap to cool, then drain again.

Add the radishes to the seasoned spelt, then the asparagus and peas. Stir, check the seasoning and it's ready to eat – just as it is or heaped onto a pile of salad leaves.

Swaps
Aromatics In the spring and summer, replace the parsley and lemon zest in the gremolata with a couple of handfuls of ribboned sorrel.
Veg Use slivers of raw carrot in place of the radishes and/or green beans instead of asparagus.
Grains/pulses You can use pearl barley, wholegrain rice or Puy lentils instead of the spelt.

Quinoa, tomatoes and courgettes

Serves 2

125g quinoa

1–2 fat limes

1 tbsp olive or rapeseed oil

A pinch of sugar

1 medium-hot red chilli, deseeded (for less heat if preferred) and finely chopped

A good pinch of bashed cumin seeds (optional)

200g flavourful tomatoes, cut into small bite-sized pieces

6 very fresh baby courgettes, sliced about 1cm thick

3 tbsp roughly chopped coriander

A pinch of dried chilli flakes (optional)

50g pumpkin seeds

Sea salt and black pepper

This zingy, sustaining salad is built around quinoa, a nutritious, protein-rich little seed native to South America (but now grown in Britain too, see britishquinoa.co.uk). The salad travels well and makes a great lunchbox option.

Rinse the quinoa very thoroughly in a sieve, then tip it into a saucepan. Cover with plenty of cold water – about three times as much water as quinoa. Add a pinch of salt. Bring to the boil, reduce the heat, then simmer for about 10 minutes, until the quinoa is just tender but not mushy – it's a good idea to start checking after 6–7 minutes because it's quite easy to overcook this tiny grain. Drain thoroughly in a sieve.

While the quinoa is cooking, prepare the tomatoes. Squeeze the juice of 1 lime into a large bowl and add the oil, sugar, chopped chilli, cumin if using, and some salt and pepper. Now add the tomatoes and mix well.

Once drained, tip the hot quinoa into the bowl with the lime-dressed tomatoes. Stir well and leave to cool.

Stir in the courgettes and coriander, then taste the salad. You may well want more lime juice (I usually add the juice of another ½ lime at this point). You might also want more salt, pepper, cumin, possibly even more chilli (I sometimes add a pinch of dried chilli flakes to pep it up).

Stir through the pumpkin seeds, and your salad is ready to eat. Either serve it straight away or pack in a lunchbox.

Swaps

Tomatoes If you come across plump, green, tangy tomatillos, they make a great swap for the tomatoes (to which they are related).
Courgettes Use cubed avocado in place of the courgettes.
Herbs Swap mint or flat-leaf parsley for the coriander.
Seeds Use sunflower (or mixed) seeds instead of pumpkin seeds.

Fennel, white beans and lettuce

Serves

50g hazelnuts (skin on or off)
3 medium fennel bulbs (about 700g in total)
2 tsp fennel seeds
1 tbsp olive or rapeseed oil
2 garlic cloves, sliced
Finely grated zest and juice of 1 lemon
400g tin white beans, such as haricot or cannellini, drained and rinsed
2 tbsp extra virgin olive or rapeseed oil
1 large butterhead or a large cos/romaine lettuce, or a mix of both, leaves separated
Sea salt and black pepper

In this lovely, aromatic salad, wedges of fresh fennel are roasted with fennel seeds and garlic until caramelised and sweet, tossed with a tin of white beans then left to marinate with lemon and extra virgin oil. This can all be done an hour or two ahead of time. The fennel is then heaped onto a pile of lettuce leaves and finished with toasted hazelnuts before serving.

Preheat the oven to 180°C/Fan 160°C/Gas 4. Using a pestle and mortar, bash the hazelnuts roughly to break them up a bit. Put them into a large roasting tray (you'll be using it for the fennel later). Roast in the oven for 5–8 minutes until lightly browned, shaking the tray once or twice and watching the nuts carefully. Tip the hazelnuts onto a plate and set aside. Turn the oven setting up to 190°C/Fan 170°C/Gas 5.

Trim off the tops and bases of the fennel bulbs and remove the outer layer if it seems fibrous. Quarter the bulbs, then slice each quarter into 2 or 3 wedges. Place in the roasting tray with the fennel seeds. Trickle over the 1 tbsp oil, season with salt and pepper and stir well. Roast for about 35 minutes, stirring once, or until the fennel is tender to the tip of a knife and taking on some nice golden brown colour.

Add the garlic, lemon zest and beans to the roasting tray and stir well. Return to the oven for 10 minutes.

Sprinkle with the lemon juice and trickle over the extra virgin oil. Give everything a final stir then set aside to cool.

Arrange the lettuce leaves in a large salad bowl. Taste the fennel and bean mix and add more salt and/or pepper if needed, then spoon over the lettuce leaves, making sure you scrape in any juices from the tray. Scatter over the toasted hazelnuts and serve.

Swaps

Pulses Use tinned chickpeas, or cooked brown or green lentils, instead of white beans.
Nuts Replace the hazelnuts with walnuts or pecans.

Aubergine and spinach with cumin and rosemary

Serves 3–4

2 tbsp olive oil

3 medium aubergines (about 750g in total), trimmed and cut into roughly 2cm cubes

2 garlic cloves, sliced

1 medium-hot chilli, deseeded and sliced, or a pinch of dried chilli flakes

1 tbsp cumin seeds, roughly bashed

A sprig of rosemary, leaves picked from the stems and roughly chopped

About 100g baby spinach leaves

50g pine nuts, lightly toasted

Sea salt and black pepper

FOR THE DRESSING

Finely grated zest of ½ large (or 1 small) orange

2 tbsp extra virgin olive oil

2 tsp balsamic or sherry vinegar

1 tsp sugar

1 tsp chopped rosemary

Aubergine is great at soaking up other flavours. For this big salad I've roasted it with garlic, chilli, cumin and rosemary before dousing it in a tangy, fragrant, orangey dressing. The hot aubergine is added to raw baby spinach and left to stand, so that the spinach wilts a little before serving. Pine nuts add a lovely contrasting crunch.

Preheat the oven to 190°C/Fan 170°C/Gas 5. When it's hot, put the olive oil into a large roasting dish and place in the oven for 10 minutes.

Tip the cubed aubergines into the hot oil. Add the sliced garlic, chilli, bashed cumin and rosemary. Season with salt and pepper and stir well. Don't worry that the oil seems to completely disappear at this point! Roast the aubergine in the oven for 30 minutes, stirring well halfway through. The aubergine should be quite tender, and richly golden brown in places – give it a few minutes longer if necessary.

Meanwhile, for the dressing, whisk the ingredients together in a bowl, making sure the sugar dissolves, and season with salt and pepper.

When the aubergine is cooked, heap the raw spinach leaves onto a serving dish and trickle over about half of the dressing. Spoon the hot aubergine on top, which will start to make some of the leaves wilt. Scatter over the pine nuts, then trickle over the remaining dressing.

Leave the salad to cool to room temperature then gently toss the aubergine and semi-wilted leaves together before serving.

Swaps

Veg Use a combination of roasted courgettes and peppers in place of the aubergines.

Leaves Other tender leaves, such as baby kale or pak choi, or butterhead lettuce, can be used instead of the spinach.

Citrus Replace the grated orange zest with some finely chopped preserved lemon.

Griddled cauliflower with orange, pecans and tahini

Serves 2–3

1 medium cauliflower (about 800g), untrimmed

1 tbsp olive or rapeseed oil

A pinch of dried chilli flakes

2 medium-large oranges

1 tbsp extra virgin olive oil

1 tsp nigella (black onion/kalonji) seeds (optional)

A good squeeze of lemon juice, plus extra to finish

About 50g pecan nuts, ideally toasted, roughly broken

Sea salt and black pepper

FOR THE TAHINI DRESSING

¼–½ garlic clove, finely grated or crushed

2 tbsp tahini

Finely grated zest and juice of ½ lemon

½ tsp sugar

1 tbsp extra virgin olive, rapeseed or hempseed oil

One of my favourite ways to eat cauliflower is a little bit burnt. Griddled, grilled or barbecued, that sweet white flesh takes on some quite delicious, smoky-nutty flavours. Here, it's finished with oranges, olive oil and a trickle of my very tasty tahini dressing.

To make the dressing, put the garlic into a bowl with the tahini, lemon zest and juice, and the sugar. Stir together well; the mix will probably thicken and go grainy, which is fine. Thin it down by whisking in a little water until you get a creamy, trickling consistency. Stir in the oil, season with salt and pepper, then set aside.

Heat a large, ridged grill pan over a medium-high heat, or heat the grill or barbecue. Remove any damaged or dirty outer leaves from the cauliflower. Slice into quarters then cut each piece from top to stalk into 1cm thick slices. Put the sliced cauliflower into a large bowl, along with any tiny florets or loose leaves that have come away while slicing. Add the olive or rapeseed oil, some salt and pepper and the chilli flakes and toss well.

Now cook the cauliflower slices, in batches if necessary, turning a few times for about 10 minutes, until slightly softened and marked with char stripes. Any tiny florets can be left in the bowl – you can toss them, still raw, with the rest of the cauliflower later.

While the cauliflower is cooking, finely grate the zest of 1 orange into another bowl. Cut a slice from the top and base of both oranges. Stand one on a board and use a sharp knife to cut away the peel and pith, working around the orange in sections. Once you have a whole, peel-less orange, cup it in your hand and, working over the bowl, slice out the segments from between the membranes, dropping them onto the zest. Repeat to segment the other orange. Add the extra virgin olive oil, nigella seeds, if using, lemon juice and some salt and pepper.

Put the griddled cauliflower back in the bowl with any bits of raw cauliflower and toss to absorb any remaining oil and seasonings. Transfer to a serving dish. Add the orange segments, then trickle over the seedy oily juice from the bowl. Scatter over the pecans and give the dish a final squeeze of lemon and a sprinkle of salt. Trickle over some tahini dressing and serve, warm or at room temperature.

Roast squash and apple with raw sprouts

Serves 3–4

About 1kg squash, such as a medium butternut or acorn squash, or ½ Crown Prince

2 tbsp olive or rapeseed oil

4–5 bay leaves, roughly torn

2 sprigs of rosemary, roughly torn

A small handful of sage leaves, roughly torn (optional)

1 tsp fennel seeds

A pinch of dried chilli flakes

About 175g Brussels sprouts

2 medium eating apples

25g sunflower seeds (or other seeds of your choice)

Sea salt and black pepper

FOR THE DRESSING

2 tbsp extra virgin olive or rapeseed oil

2 tsp English mustard

1–2 tsp sugar

1 tbsp cider vinegar

This wonderful autumnal salad, from my ever-brilliant collaborator Gill Meller, is hot and tender, spicy and aromatic, crisp and raw – the range of textures and flavours is superbly satisfying. And it's so easy to throw together.

Preheat the oven to 200°C/Fan 180°C/Gas 6.

Halve the squash and scoop out the seeds, but don't remove the peel. Cut into slim wedges, about 2cm wide at the outside edge, and place in a large roasting tray. Trickle over the oil then scatter over the herbs, fennel seeds, chilli flakes and some salt and pepper. Turn the pieces of squash over in the oil and seasonings, then place in the oven and roast for about 30 minutes until tender and nicely browned in places.

Meanwhile, combine all the ingredients for the dressing in a large bowl, adding salt and pepper to taste.

Trim the sprouts and remove any damaged or dirty outer leaves then slice very thinly. Add them to the bowl of dressing and mix well, breaking up the layers of sprout a bit as you go.

Quarter the apples, remove the cores and cut each quarter into 2 or 3 wedges (again, no need to peel). Set aside.

When the squash is tender and starting to brown, add the apple wedges and stir them in with the squash and seasonings. Return to the oven for about 15 minutes or until the apples are tender but not broken down. Scatter the seeds over the veg and apple for the last few minutes of cooking, so they toast lightly.

Spoon the dressed sprouts over the hot squash and apple wedges, then serve.

Swaps

Squash Replace the squash with a combination of peeled and roughly chunked-up parsnips and carrots.
Greens Use finely shredded Savoy cabbage instead of the sprouts.

Tofu, mushrooms and seaweed

Serves 2–3

20g dried seaweed, such as sea spaghetti

About 200g pak choi or baby pak choi, roughly sliced (small leaves can be left whole)

400g tofu (not silken)

1 tbsp rapeseed oil

250g mushrooms, thickly sliced

75g cashew nuts

1 medium-hot red chilli, halved, deseeded and sliced

1 large garlic clove, finely chopped

2 tbsp tamari

Juice of ½ lime juice, or to taste

Sea salt

This is a hearty salad, with Asian overtones, that I like to eat warm. However, leftovers can do good service in a lunchbox. I use sea spaghetti for this (from cornishseaweed.co.uk) but you can use any kind of dried seaweed.

Soak the dried seaweed in cold water as instructed on the packet, probably between 5 and 30 minutes. Then rinse, drain and squeeze out excess water. Check over it for any tough stalks or roots, then chop it very roughly.

Put the raw pak choi into a serving dish.

Take the tofu out of its packet, pouring away any liquid. Wrap the tofu in a clean tea towel and press quite firmly to get rid of a little more excess liquid, then unwrap the tofu and cut it into 1.5–2cm chunks.

Heat the oil in a large wok over a high heat. Add the tofu (take care, it will spit) and a shake of salt. Cook for about 4 minutes, stirring once or twice, until each piece of tofu is golden on at least a couple of its surfaces. Add the mushrooms and cook for another 4 minutes, stirring once or twice.

Add the seaweed, cashews, chilli, garlic and tamari and stir-fry for another minute or so until everything is piping hot. Heap the hot contents of the wok over the pak choi leaves, spritz with the lime juice and serve.

Swaps

Leaves Replace the pak choi with baby spinach, baby kale or any tender salad leaf.

Seaweed Spring onions, trimmed and halved lengthways, are delicious stir-fried with the tofu instead of seaweed.

Kale, mushroom and quinoa salad

Serves 3–4

150g quinoa

150g curly kale or cavolo nero

1 tbsp red wine vinegar or cider vinegar

A pinch of sugar

200g very fresh mushrooms, thinly sliced

2–3 tbsp coarsely chopped dill

1 tsp celery seeds

2 tbsp extra virgin olive or rapeseed oil

Juice of ½ lemon

Sea salt and black pepper

In this raw-meets-cooked salad, raw kale leaves are massaged with a little salt and vinegar so that they wilt. It's a great way to tenderise kale without cooking it (see also page 266). The kale is combined with raw mushrooms and cooked quinoa – both of which have a nice, substantial texture – and all are boosted by the lovely aniseedy tones of dill and celery seeds.

Rinse the quinoa very thoroughly in a sieve, then tip it into a saucepan. Cover with plenty of cold water – about 3 times as much water as quinoa. Add a pinch of salt. Bring to the boil, reduce the heat, then simmer for about 10 minutes, until the quinoa is just tender but not mushy. Start checking after just 6–7 minutes' simmering because it's quite easy to overcook this tiny grain. Drain the cooked quinoa thoroughly in a sieve then transfer to a large bowl or dish to cool completely. Speed up the cooling by giving it a stir now and then.

While the quinoa is cooling, strip the kale leaves off their stalks, tearing them into rough pieces as you go; discard the stalks. Put the torn kale leaves into a bowl with the vinegar, sugar and some salt and pepper. Now massage the kale with your hands: crush, squeeze, pound or rub, whichever you find easiest, until the leaves darken, wilt and reduce in volume. Around 3 minutes of massaging should be sufficient. (An alternative method is to bash and pound the kale with the end of a rolling pin or a large pestle.) Set the kale aside until the quinoa is completely cool.

Add the sliced mushrooms to the kale along with the chopped dill, celery seeds, extra virgin oil and lemon juice. Add the quinoa and tumble everything together. Taste and add more salt, pepper or lemon if needed, then serve.

Swaps
Herbs Use chives or flat-leaf parsley instead of dill.
Spices Use coriander seeds rather than celery seeds.

Roast parsnip
and mushroom salad

Serves 4–5

600–700g parsnips, peeled and cut into bite-sized chunks

2 medium onions, cut into slim wedges

2 tbsp olive or rapeseed oil

250g chestnut mushrooms, quartered (or cut into 6–8 chunks if they are very large)

100g walnuts

2 fat garlic cloves, thickly sliced

100g salad leaves

75ml cloudy apple juice

2 tbsp balsamic vinegar

Sea salt and black pepper

Extra virgin olive oil, to finish

The dressing for this hearty, warm salad is an intense glaze, made from reduced apple juice mixed with balsamic vinegar. Get a really good balsamic if you can – something sweet, syrupy and rich that you can happily sip from a spoon without wincing! It will certainly cost more but the flavour will blow you away.

Preheat the oven to 190°C/Fan 170°C/Gas 5.

Put the parsnip chunks and onion wedges into a large roasting tray (suitable for use on the hob). Add the 2 tbsp oil and some salt and pepper and stir well. Roast for 30 minutes.

Add the mushrooms, walnuts and garlic, stir well and return to the oven for 15–20 minutes, or until all the veg are tender and nicely coloured, and the walnuts are well browned (but not burnt).

Heap the salad leaves onto a large serving plate. Spoon the hot, roasted vegetables over the leaves (they'll start to wilt a little with the heat, which is exactly the idea).

Put the roasting tray over a low heat on the hob and pour in the apple juice. Let it simmer for a few minutes, using a spatula to stir and scrape up any little bits of caramelised veg from the base of the tray. When it's reduced by about half, take it off the heat. Stir in the balsamic vinegar, then immediately trickle this intense balsamic glaze all over the salad.

Trickle over a little extra virgin olive oil, sprinkle with salt and pepper, and serve straight away.

Swaps
Roots Celeriac, carrots or potatoes, or any combination of these, are lovely alternatives to the roasted parsnips.

Spudzanella

Serves 4

750g new potatoes

500g cherry tomatoes or other well-flavoured tomatoes

75g pitted black olives, such as kalamata (about 100g stone-in), roughly chopped

1 tbsp roughly chopped tarragon

2–3 inner celery stems, chopped

A bunch of spring onions, sliced, or ½ small red onion, chopped

4 tbsp extra virgin olive oil

1 tbsp red wine vinegar

Sea salt and black pepper

This is a spin on *panzanella* – a lovely Italian bread-and-tomato salad – with new potatoes taking the place of the bread. You can serve it while the potatoes are still warm from the pan, or let it cool to room temperature, by which time the spuds will have soaked up lots of the savoury tomato juices. Either way, it's a satisfying summer lunch.

Cut the potatoes into even, large-bite-sized pieces (keep them whole if they are baby potatoes) and place in a large saucepan. Cover with cold water, add salt, bring to the boil and simmer for 12–15 minutes, until tender. Drain in a colander.

While the potatoes are cooking, prepare the other ingredients. Halve the cherry tomatoes (if using larger tomatoes, cut them into bite-sized chunks) and put them into a large bowl. Now give the tomatoes a really good squeeze with your hands to get the juices flowing and break up the flesh a little.

Add the chopped olives, tarragon, celery, onion, oil, vinegar and some salt and pepper to the squished tomatoes and mix well.

Add the hot potatoes straight to the tomatoey mixture and toss well. Serve straight away, or leave the spudzanella until it has cooled to room temperature. Either way, taste it just before serving and add more salt, pepper or vinegar if needed.

Swaps

Celery Replace this with diced cucumber or slivered fennel.
Herbs Swap roughly shredded basil or flat-leaf parsley for the tarragon.

Chickpea, fennel and olive salad

Serves 4

150g dried chickpeas, soaked overnight in cold water

100g rocket

1 medium fennel bulb (about 250g), trimmed and thinly sliced

A trickle of extra virgin olive oil

A squeeze of lemon juice, to taste

50g walnuts, broken or roughly chopped

Sea salt and black pepper

FOR THE DRESSING

1½ tbsp extra virgin olive oil

1½ tbsp walnut oil (or use more olive oil)

1½ tbsp cider vinegar

1 tsp English mustard

A scrap of garlic (about ¼ clove), finely grated or crushed

½ small onion (ideally red), very finely chopped

75g pitted olives (about 100g stone-in), roughly chopped

1 tsp thyme leaves

Sometimes it's really worth cooking chickpeas from scratch for their lovely, fresh, nutty flavour, but tinned ones work fine in this salad too. It's a dish you can make at any time of the year, varying the fresh veg element depending on the season.

Drain the soaked chickpeas, tip them into a saucepan and cover with plenty of cold water. Bring to the boil, turn the heat down to a gentle simmer and cook, covered, until tender. This can be anywhere from 1–2 hours.

Meanwhile, make the dressing by whisking all the ingredients together in a bowl and seasoning with salt and pepper.

Drain the chickpeas in a colander, then return them to the hot pan and add the dressing. Stir to combine and leave to cool completely.

To serve, arrange the rocket over a serving dish. Taste the chickpeas and add more salt and/or pepper if you think they need it. Spoon the chickpeas and their dressing over the leaves.

Toss the fennel with a little extra virgin oil and a spritz of lemon juice, then add to the salad. Scatter over the walnuts and serve.

Swaps

Pulses Substitute other dried or tinned pulses, such as haricot or cannellini beans, or use 150g Puy lentils, simmered for 15–20 minutes, then drained.

Veg The fennel can be swapped with sliced blanched asparagus, blanched broad beans, raw baby peas, sliced raw baby courgettes, sliced boiled new potatoes, cherry tomatoes or raw celeriac cut into matchsticks.

Leaves Use mild salad leaves or flat-leaf parsley leaves – or a combination of the two – instead of rocket.

Soups and broths

NO TWO SOUPS are ever quite the same in my house, but almost all are generous with vegetables. Sometimes they are only part veg but more often than not they are a riot of plant-based goodness. The soup pan is one of the best tools I know for both celebrating veg and ensuring that none of it ever goes to waste.

On the more extemporary side of things, I always enjoy 'compiling' a soup from seemingly random veg foraged from the fridge (or garden), chopped up and perhaps combined with a tin of beans and a jugful of stock. Well-built versions of these often end up so hearty and chunky that they become what I call a 'stoup' (a stew/soup).

Alternatively, veg leftovers can be blitzed into something smoothly delicious with the help of a flavourful stock (more on that below). I like to feel and taste my way along – sometimes tweaking for acidity with a dash of wine or fruit juice, or enriching with a blob of nut butter or coconut milk in the blender. I've yet to come across the leftover roast roots, wilted leaves or frozen oddments of veg that cannot worthily take their place in one of these concoctions.

Sometimes, however, I want to make a 'destination soup', a more premeditated mingling of flavours and textures. Perhaps a pared-back broth, bobbing with neatly chopped roots and greens, or a soup that showcases just one or two beautiful, in-season vegetables – as do many of the recipes in this chapter. Even then, I always let a spirit of inventiveness and flexibility take precedence, and so should you. Why not play fast and loose with combinations? Tinker with quantities? You need only stick to a few basic principles to ensure success.

A good soup often relies on a good stock. You can use a stock cube or granules, of course, and indeed, I often do. My 'go-to cube' is a yeast-free organic veg stock, and the outcome is reliably good. (If you're vegan or avoiding gluten, do check the ingredients on stock cubes and powders as some contain milk powder and wheat flour.) Of course, ready-made stock is never *quite* the same as the home-made version, simmered up from fresh vegetables and herbs. There is a certain cleanness of flavour that comes with DIY veg stock and the recipe on page 190 shows you how easy – and thrifty – it is to make. But stock is not always essential. You can make great soup using plain water, as several of these recipes show. The required bass note of flavour might then come from an ingredient like seaweed, which is rich in umami tones, or from big-hitting aromatics, such as the tamari, orange and spices in my sweet potato soup on page 217. In the case of the traditional veg soup on page 188, the main ingredients are the vegetables that would go into a stock anyway.

Another thing that makes all the difference to soup is the way you start the cooking process. If you're beginning with sautéed vegetables such as onions and celery, or any root veg, it pays to let them sweat for a bit, in a little oil. Sizzle them gently, taking them to the edge of goldenness, and they will grow sweeter and more flavoursome in a way that really informs the finished dish.

Not all soups involve cooking, however. At the end of this chapter there's a bevy of delicious raw soups. Essentially, these are savoury smoothies, blitzed up bowlfuls of boisterous raw goodness and tangy flavour. They generally take just minutes to put together, making them the easiest soups of all.

Raw or cooked, a final flourish of flavour and texture is often the making of a good soup. You are after something rich, salty, spicy, crunchy or aromatic — to pique the appetite and point up the flavours in the bowl. It's easy to get this right. A glossy thread of good virgin oil on its own will invariably do the trick, but you can have a lot of fun 'souping up' soups with thick dots of velvety-dark tamari or balsamic, little heaps of crunchy seeds or smashed nuts, dustings of sea-sweet flaky salt, bashed whole spices or generous drifts of fresh herbs (not mean little sprigs, you want to *taste* them!). Happily, perfecting a soup in this way is pretty much guaranteed to make it look irresistible too.

Soup is a movable feast. It can be a starter — even a petite little *amuse-bouche* — or a whole meal, depending on the quantity you dish it up in. For that reason, I have been deliberately fluid (ha!) regarding how many people each of these recipes serves, specifying 2–4, 3–6 etc. The smaller number is for when you are relying on the soup alone to fill you up, the larger number is for when you're serving it as a starter or part of a multi-layered meal.

Vegetable soup

Serves 4–6

2 medium onions, roughly chopped

1 head of celery (500–600g), trimmed, outer 3–4 stems removed, thinly sliced

2 medium carrots (250–300g in total), trimmed, peeled and chopped

3 small or 2 medium leeks (250–300g in total), topped, tailed and outer layer removed, cut into 1cm thick slices

1 large or 2 small parsnips (about 200g in total), or a 200g chunk of celeriac, trimmed, peeled and chopped

2 tbsp olive or rapeseed oil

2 garlic cloves, roughly chopped

1–2 bay leaves

½ bunch of flat-leaf parsley (about 15g)

Sea salt and black pepper

This is a classic veg soup, tasting not dominantly of one vegetable or another, but offering a soothing, mingled, earthy, vegetabley-ness. What's more, the trimmings from the veg are precisely the raw materials you need to make a fantastic fresh stock – as you prepare the veg, err on the side of generosity with the trimmings (peels, tops and tails) and put them aside for the stockpot.

Have two large saucepans or small stockpots ready: one for the soup and one for the trimmings.

The only trimmings you don't want to keep are the onion tops, tails and skins – these contain tannins that can sometimes make a stock bitter. As you prepare the other veg, set aside the tops, tails and peels, being reasonably generous with what you cut off so you end up with a good panful. Make sure the trimmings are clean, then chop them roughly and put them into one of the large pans. This will become your veg stock (see overleaf for the method).

Heat the oil in the second large pan over a medium heat. Add the chopped soup veg, garlic and bay leaves, along with a good pinch of salt and some pepper. Once the veg is sizzling nicely, turn down the heat, cover the pan and sweat the veg for about 15 minutes, stirring a few times.

Pour in 1 litre water. Cover the pan and bring to the boil, then lower the heat and let it simmer for around 20 minutes, or until all the vegetables are soft.

Meanwhile, chop the leaves from the bunch of parsley (put the stalks in the stock pan). Remove the bay leaf from the soup and add the chopped parsley. Using a jug blender, purée the soup in 2 or 3 batches until smooth. Return all the soup to the pan. Taste and season with more salt if necessary, and some pepper. Reheat if necessary.

Ladle the soup into warmed mugs or bowls and serve.

Swaps

Veg To the onion, celery and carrot base, you can add all kinds of alternative veg, including leftovers (which you should add at the end). Cauliflower, broccoli, spinach, peas and fennel would all be good swaps or additions.

Veg stock

Makes about 1 litre

1 large onion, roughly chopped

Stalks from a small bunch of flat-leaf parsley

2–3 bay leaves

6–8 black peppercorns

CLEAN TRIMMINGS FROM:

3 small or 2 medium leeks

2 medium carrots

1 head of celery (i.e. the 3–4 coarse outer stems)

1 large or 2 small parsnips, or a 200g chunk of celeriac

I love a home-made veg stock – more subtle, complex and, well, *vegetabley*, than a stock cube version. It's easy to make a simple veg stock from scratch using fresh, chopped onion, leek, carrot, celery and herbs but, in a quest for a minimal-wastage alternative, I've come up with this, made from the trimmings left after preparing the classic veg soup on the previous page.

Roughly chop all the veg trimmings and put them into a large saucepan with the chopped onion, parsley stalks, bay leaves and peppercorns. Add 1.5 litres cold water and bring to the boil.

Reduce the heat and allow to simmer fairly gently, uncovered, for 20–30 minutes, or until the veg stock tastes good. It should not be too concentrated, but tasty enough that you could use it as the base for a broth.

Strain out the veg trimmings and the stock is ready to use, or to chill and freeze.

Veg broth with summer cabbage and tomatoes

Serves 2–4

½ pointed summer cabbage, such as hispi/sweetheart (200–300g)

1 tbsp olive or rapeseed oil

500ml veg stock (see page 190 for home-made)

½ x 400g tin haricot or aduki beans, drained and rinsed

2–3 fat spring onions, trimmed and sliced

1 garlic clove, thinly sliced

1 small nugget of ginger, very thinly sliced

1 medium-hot chilli, deseeded and thinly sliced

1–2 tbsp tamari

A generous squeeze of lime juice

100g cherry tomatoes, quartered

Sea salt

TO FINISH

Coriander leaves

Toasted sesame oil, to trickle

This quick recipe is satisfying but light. The cabbage is only briefly cooked and the tomatoes are still raw: they release their savoury juices into the hot broth as it is poured over them. I like to use my home-made veg stock here.

Cut the cabbage half in half again, trim out the core from each half, then slice the cabbage thinly.

Heat the oil in a large saucepan over a medium heat. Add the cabbage and stir-fry briskly for about 3 minutes until it is wilted and perhaps starting to colour in a couple of places. Add the stock, beans, spring onions, garlic, ginger and chilli and bring to the boil, then remove from the heat.

Stir in 1 tbsp tamari and taste the broth. You will probably need more tamari, and perhaps a pinch of salt too, to give it a good, well-seasoned flavour. When you're happy with it, add a squeeze of lime juice.

Use tongs to lift most of the cabbage out of the broth and place in warmed soup bowls. Divide the cherry tomatoes between the bowls. Pour over the steaming broth and add any remaining cabbage and beans from the pan. Sprinkle each bowl generously with coriander leaves, give each a swirl of toasted sesame oil, and serve.

Swaps

Greens Use thinly sliced chard or kale in place of the summer cabbage.
Pulses You can use any cooked bean or pulse in the soup, including chickpeas and lentils.

Soupe au pistou

Serves 4–6

1 medium onion

1 small carrot, scrubbed or peeled

2 tender inner celery stems

1 small fennel bulb (150–200g), trimmed

200g potatoes (any kind), scrubbed

2 tbsp olive oil

1 garlic clove, chopped

1 litre veg stock (see page 190 for home-made)

200g courgettes, sliced if small, or cut into 1cm dice if medium-large

150g green beans, stalk ends trimmed, cut into 2cm lengths

400g tin white beans, such as haricot, drained and rinsed

Sea salt and black pepper

FOR THE PISTOU

50g walnuts

A bunch of basil (about 50g), leaves picked from the stems

A small bunch of flat-leaf parsley (about 25g), leaves picked from the stems

1 garlic clove, finely chopped

A pinch of flaky sea salt

About 100ml extra virgin olive oil

1 fat plum tomato (about 75g), chopped (or other flavourful tomato)

I'm all for innovation – throwing out the rule book is often the way to discover delicious new ways with veg. However, there are times when it pays to honour the time-tested classics. *Soupe au pistou*, a hearty but summery Provençal soup, is a case in point. Served with a generous spoonful of garlicky, herby *pistou*, it's hard to beat. I haven't been *entirely* true to tradition, but I think you'll like my veg-only version.

First, make the pistou. Put the walnuts, basil and parsley leaves, garlic and flaky salt in a food processor. Grind in some black pepper. Blitz, stopping once or twice to scrape down the sides of the processor, until the ingredients are very finely chopped. With the motor running, trickle in the olive oil. Stop when you have a thick, coarse purée – like a pesto – 100ml should do it but use a little more or less if you like. Add the chopped tomato and stir in (don't blitz it, just stir). Taste the pistou and add more salt or pepper if needed. Set aside.

For the soup, chop the onion, carrot, celery, fennel and potatoes into roughly 1cm dice. Heat the olive oil in a flameproof casserole or small stockpot over a medium heat. Add the chopped veg with the garlic and some salt and pepper. When the veg are sizzling nicely, cover the pan, lower the heat and sweat for about 15 minutes, stirring once or twice.

Add the stock to the pan and bring to a simmer. By this time, the carrot and potato should be tender. If they still seem very undercooked, simmer them for another couple of minutes.

Now add the courgettes, green beans and tinned beans to the pan. Return to a simmer and cook for 3 minutes or so, until the green beans are *al dente*. Take off the heat. Taste and add some more salt and pepper if needed.

Ladle the soup into warmed bowls and serve with the pistou, getting everyone to spoon a good dollop into their soup before tucking in.

Swaps

Veg Aside from the base of onion and carrot, you can swap out any of the veg for alternatives such as peas, broad beans, leeks, shredded summer cabbage or chopped tomatoes.

Nuts For the pistou, swap the walnuts with almonds, pine nuts or pumpkin seeds.

Roast fennel and tomato soup

Serves 3–5

3 medium fennel bulbs (about 700g in total)

1 medium onion, roughly chopped

500g large, ripe tomatoes, halved

3 garlic cloves, sliced

1 tsp fennel seeds

2 tbsp olive or rapeseed oil

500ml hot veg stock (see page 190 for home-made)

Sea salt and black pepper

TO FINISH

Extra virgin olive or rapeseed oil, to trickle

Dried chilli flakes or fresh chopped chilli (optional)

As you start roasting the veg for this soup, the aroma wafting from the oven will tell you good things are in store. Warming, delicately aromatic and surprisingly creamy in texture, it's really easy to make and very satisfying. A perfect late-summer lunch.

Preheat the oven to 190°C/Fan 170°C/Gas 5.

Trim the fennel bulbs and remove the outer layer if it seems fibrous. Reserve a few of the frondy green leaves if there are any. Roughly chop the fennel bulbs, core and all, and put into a large roasting tray.

Add the chopped onion and the halved tomatoes. Scatter over the garlic, fennel seeds and some salt and pepper. Trickle the 2 tbsp oil over the surface and stir well. Roast in the oven for about 50 minutes, stirring halfway through, until the fennel and onion are soft and starting to caramelise, and the tomatoes are pretty much collapsed.

Scoop about half the roasted veg into a blender, add half the hot veg stock and blitz thoroughly until smooth. Transfer to a saucepan. Repeat with the remaining veg (making sure you include any caramelised bits and tasty juices from the roasting tin) and the remaining stock.

Combine the two batches of soup in the pan. It will probably be quite thick at this stage, so stir in a few splashes of hot water from the kettle to thin it a little. Taste and add more salt or pepper if needed. Reheat gently if necessary.

Serve the soup finished with a few drops of virgin oil, any reserved fennel fronds (chopped), and some black pepper. A sprinkle of chilli flakes or fresh chilli is also very good if you like a bit of heat.

Swaps

Veg You can use a whole head of celery instead of the fennel. For a very different soup, you can replace the fennel with beetroot; the method is exactly the same.

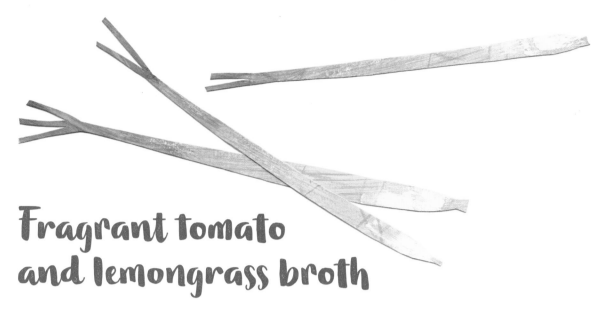

Fragrant tomato and lemongrass broth

Serves 3–5

2 lemongrass stems

1 tbsp virgin coconut or rapeseed oil

2 garlic cloves, grated

1 tbsp freshly grated ginger

1 hot green chilli, such as a bird's eye, deseeded and finely chopped

1 tsp ground turmeric or 1 tbsp freshly grated turmeric root

400ml tin coconut milk

400ml hot veg stock (see page 190 for home-made)

500g cherry tomatoes, quartered (or any flavourful tomatoes, in small pieces)

125g cashew nuts

1 tbsp tamari

A large bunch of coriander (about 50g), leaves picked from the stems and roughly chopped

1 large lime

Sea salt and black pepper

A riot of colour with a fusion of wonderful, savoury flavours, this is both comforting and uplifting.

Strip the tough outer layers off the lemongrass stems, but don't discard them; finely slice the tender inner shaft.

Heat the oil in a large saucepan over a medium-low heat. Add the sliced lemongrass, garlic, ginger and chilli. Fry gently, stirring often, for about 5 minutes.

Stir in the turmeric, then add the coconut milk, stock and the reserved lemongrass trimmings. Bring up to a simmer, stirring to ensure the coconut milk amalgamates smoothly. Let the broth simmer gently for a couple of minutes.

Add the tomatoes and cashews. Let the broth just return to a quivering bare simmer, then take off the heat. You don't want to cook the tomatoes, just heat them gently. Stir in the tamari and taste the broth. Add a pinch of salt and/or pepper if necessary.

Distribute the chopped coriander between 3–5 bowls. Ladle the soup over the coriander, removing the big bits of lemongrass stem as you go, and ensuring each bowl has a roughly equal portion of tomatoes and cashews.

Finely grate the zest of the lime over the bowls of soup, then halve the lime and give each bowl a good squeeze of juice too. Eat straight away.

Swaps

Herbs In place of the coriander, use basil, Thai basil or mint, or any combination of these.

Beetroot and rhubarb soup

Serves 3–6

2 tbsp olive or rapeseed oil

1 medium onion, roughly chopped

2 garlic cloves, chopped

250g beetroot

500ml veg stock (see page 190 for home-made)

100g rhubarb, chopped into roughly 5cm lengths

Sea salt and black pepper

TO FINISH

Extra virgin olive, rapeseed or hempseed oil, to trickle

Chopped herbs, such as chives, chervil, flat-leaf parsley or thyme (or a mixture)

Rhubarb, with its startling sourness, is the perfect foil to beetroot. Just a little added to this soup brings the sweetness of the root down a notch or two, allowing its lovely vegetal flavour to shine. This is delicious served chilled in small quantities as a starter, but you can also serve it hot.

Heat the oil in a saucepan over a medium heat. Add the onion and garlic and some salt and pepper. When the onion is sizzling, turn the heat down, cover the pan and let the onion sweat for 7–8 minutes, stirring a few times.

Meanwhile, peel the beetroot and roughly chop it. Add it to the softened onions and sweat, covered, for a few more minutes.

Add the stock and bring to a simmer then cover the pan again and simmer for 10 minutes, or until the beetroot is just tender.

Add the rhubarb and simmer gently for another 10 minutes or so until the beetroot is completely tender and the rhubarb is quite soft.

Transfer the mixture to a jug blender and blitz until smooth. Taste and add more salt and pepper as needed.

Serve the soup straight away, piping hot, or cool it and then chill it. Either way, finish it with a swirl of extra virgin oil and a few herbs.

Fennel, lentil and seaweed soup

Serves 4–6

2 tbsp olive or rapeseed oil

1 large or 2 small onions, chopped

1 garlic clove, chopped

2 large or 3–4 smaller fennel bulbs (about 700g in total)

100g red lentils

20g 'sea salad', or other ready-to-eat flaked, dried seaweed

Sea salt and black pepper

Extra virgin olive or rapeseed oil, to finish

This subtle, soothing soup is velvety in texture. A little dried seaweed deepens the savoury flavour and provides a beautiful finishing sprinkle too. I like a 'sea salad' mix (which is available from cornishseaweed.co.uk or clearspring.co.uk).

Heat the oil in a large saucepan over a medium heat. Add the onion and garlic with a pinch each of salt and pepper. When the onion is sizzling, turn down the heat, cover the pan and leave to sweat while you prepare the fennel.

Trim the tops and bases off the fennel bulbs and remove any tough or damaged outer layers, then cut the fennel bulbs into 5–8mm thick slices (including the core). Add the sliced fennel to the sweating onions, stir, cover and leave to cook gently for about 10 minutes, stirring once or twice.

When the onion is nice and soft, add the lentils, together with half of the sea salad. Pour in 750ml water and bring to a simmer, then put the lid on the pan and simmer gently for 15–20 minutes until the lentils are completely soft.

Transfer the contents of the pan to a jug blender (work in two batches if necessary), add some salt and pepper and blitz until velvety smooth, adding a little more hot water if it seems very thick. Re-combine the soup in the pan if you have blitzed it in two batches.

Taste to check the seasoning, then ladle into warmed bowls. Top each portion with a trickle of extra virgin oil, then sprinkle generously with the remaining sea salad before serving.

Celeriac, kale, barley and apple broth

Serves 4–6

50g pearl barley or pearled spelt

2 tbsp olive or rapeseed oil

1 onion, chopped

2 garlic cloves, chopped

½ small celeriac (about 250g), peeled and cut into roughly 1cm cubes

1 litre hot veg stock (see page 190 for home-made)

150g curly kale or cavolo nero, leaves stripped off the stalks and roughly shredded

5–6 sage leaves, sliced into fine ribbons

2 medium eating apples, quartered, cored and chopped into roughly 1cm cubes

Sea salt and black pepper

Extra virgin olive or rapeseed oil, to finish

A lovely autumn-into-winter soup, this is nice and chunky with a sweet, aromatic note from the apples.

Put the pearl barley or spelt to soak in cold water while you prepare the vegetables.

Heat the oil in a large saucepan or small stockpot over a medium heat. Add the onion and garlic with some salt and pepper. When everything is sizzling, turn the heat down low, cover the pan and let the veg sweat, stirring once or twice, for about 10 minutes.

Meanwhile, rinse the barley or spelt well.

Add the barley or spelt to the pan with the celeriac. Sauté, stirring, for 2–3 minutes, then pour in the hot stock. Bring to a simmer and cook, partially covered, until the grain is almost tender (about 15 minutes for spelt, 25 minutes for barley).

Stir in the shredded kale and sage and bring back to a simmer. Cook for 5 minutes, then add the cubed apple and cook for a further 2 minutes only. Remove from the heat, taste the soup and add more seasoning if needed.

Ladle the soup into warmed bowls and finish with a trickle of extra virgin oil and a grinding of black pepper, then serve.

Swaps
Roots Replace the celeriac with parsnips, turnips, beetroot or carrots.
Greens Swap shredded chard or spring greens for the kale.
Fruit Use firm, slightly under-ripe pears instead of apples.

Red pepper and chickpea soup

Serves 4–6

3 medium red peppers (400–450g in total)

2 tbsp olive or rapeseed oil

3 medium onions (ideally red), chopped

3 garlic cloves, finely chopped

1 medium-hot red chilli, deseeded and chopped, or a pinch of dried chilli flakes

2 tsp sweet smoked paprika

2 tsp ground turmeric

1 tbsp coriander seeds, bashed (or 2 tsp ground coriander)

2 x 400g tins chickpeas, drained

500ml hot veg stock (see page 190 for home-made)

Juice of 1 large lime or ½ lemon

Sea salt and black pepper

TO SERVE

Extra virgin olive or rapeseed oil

Lime or lemon wedges

A gently spiced, richly coloured, veg-packed soup, I like to finish this off with a good squeeze of lemon or lime juice.

Halve, core and deseed the red peppers, then chop the flesh into roughly 1cm pieces.

Heat the oil in a large saucepan or small stockpot over a medium heat. Add the onions, garlic, peppers, chilli and some salt and pepper. When the veg are sizzling nicely, turn down the heat and cover the pan. Let everything sweat gently, stirring from time to time, for 20–30 minutes until the peppers are nice and soft.

Stir in the spices, then add the chickpeas and pour in the hot stock. Bring to a simmer and cook gently for a few minutes, then take off the heat. Add the lime or lemon juice, then taste the soup and add more salt or pepper if needed.

Ladle into warmed bowls, trickle over a little extra virgin oil and finish with a little black pepper. Have lime or lemon wedges on the table so people can spritz on a little more juice as they eat.

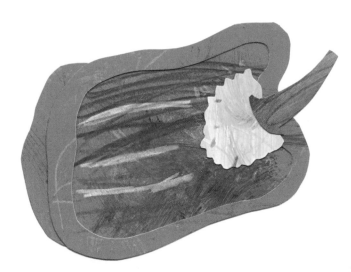

Squash and cauliflower soup with sage

Serves 6–8

1 small-medium cauliflower (about 700g)

About 600g squash, such as a small onion squash, or ½ large butternut or a chunk of Crown Prince

1 large onion, roughly chopped

4 garlic cloves, peeled but left whole

2 tbsp roughly chopped sage, plus a few finely ribboned leaves to finish

2 tbsp olive or rapeseed oil

1 litre hot veg stock (see page 190 for home-made)

Sea salt and black pepper

TO FINISH

Balsamic vinegar

Flaky sea salt, to sprinkle

This is so easy to make: the veg are simply roasted then blitzed. It's fantastic finished with a trickle of good, sweet balsamic vinegar.

Preheat the oven to 200°C/Fan 180°C/Gas 6.

Remove any very damaged or tough looking leaves from the outside of the cauliflower and trim the very end of the stalk. Then roughly chop the rest of the cauliflower – stem, leaves and all – and put into a large roasting tray.

Peel and deseed the squash then cut into bite-sized chunks. Add these to the roasting tray with the onion, whole garlic cloves and chopped sage. Trickle over the oil, season with salt and pepper and stir well.

Roast for about 45 minutes until the vegetables are soft and nicely caramelised, stirring halfway through. Make sure there's some good colour on the cauliflower especially – this adds to the flavour of the finished soup.

You now need to purée the soup with the hot veg stock. There's a lot of veg here, so do this in two batches: blitz half the veg with half the stock in a blender until smooth then pour into a large saucepan; repeat with the rest of the veg and stock.

Once the two batches are reunited, you may want to add a touch of hot water to thin the soup a little. Taste and add more salt and pepper if needed, and reheat if necessary.

Ladle the soup into warmed bowls, splash some balsamic onto each serving then add a little finely ribboned sage, ground pepper and a few grains of flaky sea salt.

Celeriac and parsley soup

Serves 4–6

2 tbsp olive or rapeseed oil

1 medium onion, chopped

2 garlic cloves, chopped

4 celery stems, thinly sliced

½–1 medium celeriac (about 500g), peeled and diced

1 tsp thyme leaves

A large bunch of flat-leaf parsley (about 50g)

750ml hot veg stock (see page 190 for home-made)

Sea salt and black pepper

Celeriac, parsley and celery are all members of the umbelliferae family and they partner each other beautifully in this recipe. It should really be called 'umbelliferous soup'...

Heat the oil in a large saucepan or small stockpot over a medium heat. Add the onion, garlic, celery, celeriac and thyme with a good pinch of salt and some pepper. When everything is sizzling, turn down the heat, cover the pan and let the veg sweat gently, stirring once or twice, for about 15 minutes.

Meanwhile, pick the parsley leaves off the stalks. (It's worth the time it takes to do this – it ensures your soup is silky smooth.)

Add the hot stock to the sweating vegetables, bring to a gentle simmer and partially cover the pan. Simmer for 15–20 minutes, until the celery and celeriac are soft.

Add the parsley leaves, reserving a small handful for finishing, and cook for just a minute or two more, then take off the heat. Transfer the contents of the pan to a blender and blitz thoroughly until velvety smooth; do this in batches if necessary. Thin with a splash of hot water if it's very thick.

Taste the soup and add more salt and pepper if needed. Reheat if necessary. Ladle into warmed bowls, scatter over the reserved parsley leaves and serve.

Swaps

Roots Parsnip, another umbellifera, is a good swap for celeriac – as is salsify, a more unusual root.

Leek and cauliflower soup with mustard and thyme

Serves 4–6

2 tbsp olive or rapeseed oil

3 medium leeks (about 500g in total), trimmed and cut into 5mm slices

2 garlic cloves, thickly sliced

1 celery stem, thinly sliced

2 tbsp thyme leaves

1 medium-large cauliflower (800g–1kg untrimmed)

850ml hot water or veg stock (see page 190 for home-made)

2 tsp English mustard

Sea salt and black pepper

Extra virgin olive or rapeseed oil, to finish

Both leeks and cauliflower have a naturally velvety texture when puréed, giving this simple veg soup a deliciously 'creamy' feel.

Heat the oil in a large saucepan over a medium heat. Add the sliced leeks, garlic, celery, half the thyme leaves and some salt and pepper. When the veg are sizzling nicely, cover the pan, reduce the heat and let them sweat for about 10 minutes, until the leeks are fairly soft, stirring from time to time.

Meanwhile, prepare the cauliflower: trim off any thick outer leaves (the little inner leaves are fine to keep) and the base of the stem if it looks coarse or grubby, then roughly chop the rest of the cauliflower – stalk and all.

Add the chopped cauliflower to the softened leeks and stir well then pour in the hot water or stock. Bring to a simmer, cover and cook for 5–10 minutes, until the cauliflower is tender but not too soft.

Remove the pan from the heat. Add the mustard, then purée the soup until smooth – either in two batches in a jug blender, or using a stick blender, in the pan. Re-combine the soup in the pan if you have blitzed it in two batches. Add a splash of hot water if it's very thick. Taste and add more salt and/or pepper if needed, then reheat if necessary.

Ladle the soup into warmed bowls, trickle some extra virgin oil over the surface and finish with the remaining thyme leaves and a grinding of black pepper.

Swaps
Alliums Replace the leeks with a couple of medium onions.
Herbs Swap rosemary for the thyme.

Celery soup with pear

Serves 4–6

1 head of celery

2 tbsp olive or rapeseed oil, plus a trickle for frying the pear

1 medium-large onion, chopped

3 garlic cloves, chopped

½ tsp celery salt

1 small, floury potato (about 125g), peeled and cut into 1cm cubes

40g cashew nuts

750ml hot veg stock (see page 190 for home-made)

1 large, slightly under-ripe pear

Black pepper

Extra virgin olive or rapeseed oil, to finish (optional)

It's hard to beat the velvety, savoury, earthy loveliness of a good celery soup. This one is made creamy with cashew nuts and a little potato, and finished off with slivers of fried pear, which provide a delicious contrast.

Trim the root end off the bunch of celery, to separate the stems. Remove the 3 or 4 coarse outer stems (use these for stock, or the pickle on page 354). This should leave you with 300–350g inner stems. Slice these stems thinly.

Heat the 2 tbsp oil in a large saucepan or small stockpot over a medium heat. Add the onion, garlic, celery salt and some pepper. When sizzling, cover the pan, turn down the heat and sweat the veg gently for about 5 minutes.

Add the sliced celery, cubed potato and cashews and continue to sweat, stirring from time to time, for another 10 minutes.

Pour in the hot stock and bring to the boil, then turn down the heat. Simmer, partially covered, for about 25 minutes, until the celery is soft.

Meanwhile, cut the pear lengthways into quarters and remove the core. Slice each quarter quite thinly. Heat a trickle of oil in a non-stick frying pan over a medium heat. Add the pear slices and fry for a few minutes, turning once or twice, until golden brown. Remove from the heat and set aside.

Transfer the contents of the soup pan to a blender and blitz thoroughly until the soup is velvety smooth; do this in batches if necessary. Add a splash of hot water if it's very thick. Taste it and add more celery salt and/or black pepper if needed.

Reheat the soup if necessary. Ladle into warmed bowls or soup plates. Top with a few slices of pear, a trickle of extra virgin oil if you like, and a dusting of black pepper.

Swaps
Fruit Finish the soup with fried apples rather than pears.

Spicy sweet potato soup with orange

Serves 3–4

500g sweet potatoes

Finely grated zest and juice of 2 medium-large oranges

1 tbsp sugar

2 tbsp tamari

2 garlic cloves, chopped

1 cinnamon stick

2 star anise

A pinch of dried chilli flakes

Sea salt and black pepper

TO FINISH

Coriander leaves

Finely chopped red onion, (optional)

A little extra tamari (optional)

This intensely flavoured soup is warming, fragrant and beautiful to look at. It's also an absolute breeze to make and happens to be fat-free!

Peel the sweet potatoes, then cut into 2–3cm chunks and place in a medium-large saucepan. Add the orange zest and juice, sugar, tamari, garlic and spices. Pour in 500ml water and add some salt and pepper.

Bring to the boil then reduce the heat and simmer, uncovered, for about 15 minutes, until the sweet potato is completely tender.

Fish out and discard the cinnamon stick and star anise. Now purée the soup until smooth – I do this in the saucepan, using a stick blender, but you can use a jug blender. Taste the soup and add more salt or pepper if needed.

Ladle the soup into warmed bowls. Top with coriander leaves and a little finely chopped red onion, if you like. Splash on a few more drops of tamari, if you wish, and serve.

Swaps

Veg Replace the sweet potato with 500g peeled, deseeded squash.

Fava bean soup with parsley

Serves 4–6

1 tbsp olive or rapeseed oil

1 medium onion, roughly chopped

1 medium carrot, peeled and cut into 2–3mm thick slices

1 celery stem, thinly sliced

2 garlic cloves, chopped

1 bay leaf

1 tbsp cumin seeds, bashed (or 2 tsp ground cumin)

250g dried, split fava beans (ready-skinned variety)

Sea salt and black pepper

TO FINISH

A large bunch of flat-leaf parsley (50g), leaves picked from the stems

1 small garlic clove, finely chopped

4–5 tbsp extra virgin olive oil

A squeeze of lemon juice

Fava beans are dried broad beans. They have a unique, bittersweet flavour that I find irresistible and, if you buy them in their skinned, split form, they cook quickly and can be easily puréed into a lovely, hearty soup like this one. Traditionally used to make *ful medames*, an Egyptian staple, you can now buy English-grown, dried split fava beans (see hodmedods.co.uk).

Heat the oil in a large saucepan over a medium heat. Add the onion, carrot, celery, garlic, bay and cumin and stir well. When the veg are sizzling nicely, reduce the heat, cover the pan and let everything sweat gently for 10–15 minutes, stirring once or twice.

Add the dried fava beans and pour in 1 litre water. Bring to the boil then reduce the heat and simmer, uncovered, until the beans are soft enough to crush – around 30–45 minutes. Don't worry if a little scum forms on the surface – this is just protein from the beans and will be amalgamated when the soup is puréed.

While the soup is cooking, finely chop the parsley leaves on a large board. Add the chopped garlic and chop it together with the leaves. Transfer this mixture to a bowl and add the extra virgin olive oil, some salt and pepper and a few drops of lemon juice. Stir to combine.

Remove the bay leaf from the soup. Add salt and pepper, then purée the soup – either using a stick blender in the pan, or in a jug blender. Add a little more hot water if it seems excessively thick. Taste and add more seasoning if needed.

Pour the soup into warmed bowls and spoon on the parsley/oil mixture. Sprinkle with a little extra black pepper, and serve.

Swaps

Pulses Use yellow split peas instead of fava beans.

Winter veg broth with quinoa

Serves 4–6

2 tender inner celery stems, leaves trimmed off

1 medium-large leek (about 200g), trimmed

2 tbsp olive or rapeseed oil

1 large onion, chopped

2 medium carrots (about 200g in total), peeled and chopped into roughly 1cm cubes

About 200g celeriac, peeled and chopped into roughly 1cm cubes

1 large garlic clove, chopped

1 tsp chopped rosemary

1 tsp thyme leaves

75g quinoa, rinsed

1 litre hot veg stock (see page 190 for home-made)

400g tin black beans, carlin peas or any other smallish bean, drained and rinsed

Sea salt and black pepper

Extra virgin olive, rapeseed or hempseed oil, to finish

Ideal as a warming winter lunch, this is a great way to use quinoa – especially British quinoa. It adds body, protein and a lovely texture to the soup, which is thickened by being partially puréed.

Halve the celery stems and leek lengthways, then slice finely. Heat the oil in a large saucepan or small stockpot over a medium heat. When the oil is hot, add the celery, leek, onion, carrots, celeriac, garlic, herbs and some salt and pepper. Get everything sizzling and stir well.

Cover the pan and turn the heat down. Let the veg sweat, stirring from time to time, for about 15 minutes, until nicely softened.

Add the quinoa to the pan, then pour in the hot veg stock. Bring to a simmer and cook, covered, for about 15 minutes until the quinoa and veg are tender.

Spoon 4 big ladlefuls of the soup into a blender (aiming for a good mix of veg and broth in each ladleful) and blitz until smooth. Pour this purée back into the pan of soup and stir well. Add the beans and return to the heat for a minute or two to warm the beans through.

Taste the soup and add more salt and pepper as needed. Serve in warmed bowls, with a good splash of extra virgin oil on each.

Swaps

Roots Replace the celeriac with parsnips.

Celeriac and seaweed miso broth

Serves 2

10g dried seaweed, such as wakame

75g peeled celeriac, cut into thin matchsticks

2–4 tsp white miso paste or shiro miso paste (see page 270)

1 tbsp tamari, plus extra to serve

2 tsp rice vinegar (or you can use cider vinegar), plus extra to serve

Sea salt

TO FINISH

Dried chilli flakes

Sesame seeds, ideally lightly toasted

Quick to make, this is hot, savoury and comforting, but delicate – the sort of thing you can knock together easily when you need to feel warmed up but not weighed down.

Put the dried seaweed to soak in a bowl of cold water for the time suggested on the packet, probably 20–30 minutes.

Drain the seaweed, squeeze out excess water and check for any tough stalks. Then chop or shred the seaweed roughly.

Bring 400ml water to the boil in a saucepan. Add the seaweed and celeriac matchsticks. Return to a simmer and cook for 3 minutes, then remove from the heat.

Make a little gap in the centre of the seaweed and celeriac and blob in 2 tsp miso. Use a whisk to work the miso into the broth.

Add the tamari and vinegar and whisk again, then taste the broth. You might want more miso, you'll probably want to add a little salt and you might want a drop more vinegar or tamari. Adjust to taste.

Ladle the hot soup into warmed bowls. Sprinkle a pinch of chilli flakes and some sesame seeds over each portion, then serve. Put the tamari and vinegar bottles on the table so you can add a little more as you eat if you like.

Rhubarb gazpacho

Serves 4 as a starter

400g rhubarb stalks

2 medium cucumbers (about 700g in total), chilled

4 tbsp extra virgin olive or rapeseed oil

About 1 tbsp sugar

Sea salt and black pepper

Pure refreshment in a bowl, this chilled soup is just the thing to cool and revive you on a hot day, with cucumber softening the rhubarb's sharp acidity. Start cooking the rhubarb well ahead of time so you can get it nicely chilled before you blitz the soup.

Trim the rhubarb and cut into roughly 5cm pieces; set a couple of these pieces aside. Put the rest into a saucepan with 200ml water and bring to a simmer. Cook gently for 7–10 minutes until soft, stirring every now and again so all the rhubarb cooks evenly. Transfer the rhubarb and its cooking liquid to a bowl, leave to cool completely, then chill.

Put the chilled rhubarb, with its liquor, into a jug blender.

Cut a 10cm length from one of the cucumbers and set aside. Peel the rest of the cucumbers then roughly chop them, seeds and all, and add to the blender. Add 100ml cold water, 2 tbsp oil, 1 tbsp sugar and some salt and pepper. Blitz to a smooth, velvety texture. Taste and add more seasoning or sugar if needed.

Finely chop the reserved raw rhubarb and cucumber and combine them with some salt, pepper and the remaining 2 tbsp oil.

Pour the soup into chilled bowls. Spoon the dressed raw rhubarb and cucumber mix on top of the soup. Give each bowl a scattering of pepper and serve.

Chilled cucumber and melon soup

Serves 2–3 as a starter

250g piece of Galia or Honeydew melon (¼ medium melon), chilled

1 cucumber (about 400g), chilled

½ garlic clove, chopped

Juice of ½–1 lemon

3 tbsp extra virgin olive oil, plus extra to serve

1 tsp balsamic vinegar, plus extra to serve

2 tbsp roughly chopped flat-leaf parsley, plus extra to serve

Sea salt and black pepper

Like the recipe on the previous page, this is a kind of gazpacho – one of my favourite genres of soup! Melons and cucumbers both come from the cucurbit family and their cool, mild flavours work beautifully together.

Cut the melon into 2 or 3 wedges. Use a small, sharp knife to slice out the seedy section from the centre of each wedge then cut the melon flesh away from the skin. Cut the flesh into chunks and drop these into a blender.

Peel the cucumber then cut it into chunks – seeds and all. Add to the blender, along with all the other ingredients, including a pinch of salt, a grinding of pepper and the juice of ½ lemon.

Blitz the soup until smooth – it might take a little while to get going, so stop the blender a few times and tamp down the ingredients inside to enable the blender blades to get to work on them. Taste and adjust the seasoning, adding more lemon juice too, if needed.

Pour into chilled bowls. Trickle a whisper more balsamic vinegar and a thread of extra virgin oil over the top of each portion. Scatter over some chopped parsley and grind over a little pepper, then serve.

Swaps
Herbs Replace the parsley with basil or mint.

Raw kale soup

Serves 2–3 as a starter

30g cashew nuts

¼ large avocado (ideally chilled), skinned and roughly chopped

2 large crisp, fresh kale leaves (about 50g in total), stripped off their stalks and roughly chopped

Juice of ½ lemon

50ml cloudy apple juice

1 tsp freshly grated ginger

A scrap of garlic (about ¼ clove), finely grated or crushed

1 tsp tamari

Sea salt and black pepper

FOR THE TOPPING

Choose from the following:

1 heaped tbsp sauerkraut or celeriac 'kimchi' (pages 274–6)

A sprinkle of dried seaweed

A few morsels of pickled veg (page 354)

A generous splash of Tabasco

A trickle of olive, rapeseed or hempseed oil and a sprinkle of whole toasted buckwheat 'groats' (kasha)

This easy raw soup is delicious and rammed with good things: kale, avocado, ginger, garlic and lemon juice. I love to eat it topped with a little sauerkraut or celeriac 'kimchi', but the choice is yours (see suggestions below).

Put all the ingredients, including a pinch of salt and a grinding of pepper, into a blender with 150ml very cold water (or use 100ml water and a few ice cubes, if your blender is the sort that can cope with ice!).

Blitz thoroughly until you have a velvety-smooth, green purée. Add a splash more water if it seems very thick.

Taste and add more salt if needed. If you have used cold ingredients, the soup should be lightly chilled already; if not, chill it for half an hour or so before serving.

Pour into small bowls and add your chosen topping to serve.

Curried raw mushroom soup

Serves 2–3 as a starter

250g very fresh chestnut mushrooms

300ml oat milk, chilled

1 rounded tsp medium-hot curry paste (the home-made curry paste on page 95 is ideal)

Sea salt (optional)

TO FINISH

½ mild red chilli, halved, deseeded and sliced

A pinch of garam masala

A trickle of rapeseed oil

This is made by simply throwing raw mushrooms, oat milk and curry paste into a blender. To quote Nikki, my key collaborator on this book, 'it's a bit wacky, but it tastes totally amazing'. That's good enough for me.

Wipe or brush the mushrooms to remove any debris, then cut into halves or quarters – stalks and all. Put the mushrooms into a blender or food processor, add the oat milk and curry paste and blitz until smooth and velvety.

Taste and add salt if necessary – but you may find that there is already enough (from the curry paste, and probably the oat milk, too).

The soup will start to discolour after a short while, so serve straight away, topped with a few slices of chilli, a sprinkling of garam masala and a trickle of rapeseed oil.

Raw

DESPITE ALL THE cooking you'll find in this book – the roasting, grilling, sautéeing and simmering that transform vegetables so successfully into dinner – I'm always aware that one of the best ways to enjoy good, fresh veg is unashamedly raw. It's certainly one of the ways *I* choose increasingly often. Raw is the state in which most veg does you most good – but that's only part of the appeal. Untouched by the heat of pan or oven, virgin veg is cool, crunchy, bursting with natural juices, and often manifests its inherent character in surprisingly subtle ways.

I want to expand your horizons regarding what raw veg can be – both in terms of ways of preparing it, and in terms of the sheer variety of veg that can be relished without the application of heat. There are very few veg that cannot be enjoyed raw, so when you're deciding how to cook a particular vegetable, I believe 'not cooking it at all' should be one of the options you consider. You'll find raw veg recipes throughout this book – salads, soups etc. – but this chapter is populated entirely by delicious recipes for uncooked veg and fruit.

It's true that, if mishandled, raw veg can be challenging – no one wants to munch through great mountains of it, or tackle huge, unwieldy chunks and slabs. But if you apply a few simple principles, you'll make the path of raw-veg eating a wide and welcoming one.

You have to begin, of course, with quality veg – the perkiest of leaves, the firmest and freshest of roots, the sweetest of brassicas. Then it all comes down to how you cut it – literally. Take time to reduce raw veg to slivers and matchsticks, wafers and shreds and it will meet the mouth in the most appealing way.

Even easier than setting to with a knife, grater or mandoline, is to use a food processor or blender. In fact, if you want to increase your intake of veg in general, and of raw veg in particular, these tools can be your greatest friends. Try one or two of my raw 'blitz' recipes (pages 281–7) or my carrot and apricot breakfast bars (page 298), and you'll see just how much lovely, lush, uncooked veg and fruit, nuts and seeds can be crammed into a bowl or a lunchbox when you call a food processor into play. Once sliced, grated, blitzed or shredded, simple seasoning and a good dressing are usually all that's required to make raw veg sing.

There are recipes in this chapter that demonstrate just how good a single raw vegetable can be with a well-chosen dressing. The remainder of the dishes are more multi-layered, but only a little. Sometimes I pair two raw vegetables together and, just as often, I find myself adding a raw fruit to a raw vegetable. I've used fruits throughout the book – really as additional, honorary vegetables – but perhaps most liberally in this raw chapter. Their juiciness, sweetness, acidity and colour are particularly welcome at the all-raw party.

Dried fruits have their place too. These are ingredients that, along with the rolled oats used in a few recipes, are not in themselves completely raw, since at least some degree of heat has been applied to them – but not by you! This is one chapter where you don't have to turn on the cooker.

You'll also find here recipes for home-fermented vegetables, including a simple sauerkraut. For me, these are a natural and delicious progression from eating fresh raw veg. The benign bugs that get to work during fermentation are effectively a tasty, living marinade that give shredded leaves and grated roots a delicious tang. There is also a growing consensus that fermented foods are good for us, helping to grow a spectrum of beneficial bacteria in our guts, improving not just digestion, but general well-being. I now eat fermented foods several times a week, often at the beginning of a meal. I find a nibble of homemade 'living pickle' is a great way to both stimulate the appetite and, literally, get the gastric juices flowing.

There are really no rules for how or when you eat the raw food in this chapter. You can enjoy them before or alongside a main dish, as a solo snack, or out of a plastic box when you're on the move. Personally, I like to eat a 'plate of raw' at least once a day. I think we all should.

Lettuce with gooseberries

Serves 4

1 large cos/romaine lettuce, leaves separated

1 head of elderflower (optional)

Sea salt and black pepper

FOR THE GOOSEBERRIES

100g gooseberries (fresh or frozen)

2 tbsp extra virgin olive or rapeseed oil

1 tsp sugar

A good squeeze of lemon juice, or more to taste

With their distinct sharpness and fragrant flavour, gooseberries are a fantastic fruit to use in savoury dishes. Seasoned with lemon juice and balanced with a little sweetness, they make a delicious addition to green leaves: both in a dressing and as a characterful ingredient in their own right. During their brief, early summer season, I like to scatter this pretty dish with fresh elderflowers too.

If you're using fresh gooseberries, halve them (or cut into quarters if large) and place in a small bowl. If using frozen gooseberries, leave to defrost in a small bowl – they'll soften and release quite a lot of juice. Crush the gooseberries in your hands to break them down further.

Add the oil, sugar, lemon juice and some salt and pepper to the berries, mix well and leave to macerate for 20–30 minutes. Mix again, taste, and add more lemon, salt or pepper as needed.

Arrange your lettuce leaves on a large platter or in a serving bowl with the paler bases of the leaves all pointing inwards. Give the dressed gooseberries a final mix and spoon it into the centre of the leaves. If you have a head of elderflower, use a fork to gently rake the little flowerheads from the stalks, allowing them to fall over the salad.

Serve straight away – I like to eat this with my hands, scooping up the juicy berries with the leaves.

Swaps

Leaves Instead of the cos/romaine, use 2 little gems or 1 large oak leaf or butterhead lettuce.

Berries Replace the gooseberries with whole redcurrants, very slightly squished in the dressing – or chopped strawberries or plums.

Radish with poppy seed dressing

Serves 3–4

200g radishes

Flaky sea salt

FOR THE DRESSING

2 tbsp extra virgin olive or rapeseed oil

1 tsp sugar

1 tbsp lemon juice, plus an extra spritz if needed

½ tsp English mustard

½ tbsp poppy seeds

Sea salt and black pepper

When they're really fresh, raw radishes are incredibly juicy and crunchy – and full of natural peppery flavour. Get yourself a good bunch and only the simplest treatment is needed: this nutty-tasting poppy seed dressing works a treat.

For the dressing, in a bowl, whisk all the ingredients thoroughly together, adding only a little salt (as you'll be adding more later).

Slice the radishes thinly and spread out on a plate. Spoon the dressing over them. Sprinkle with a little flaky sea salt. Taste one slice of radish and add a spritz more lemon juice to the whole plate if needed.

Eat straight away, to enjoy the radishes' fresh crunch, or let them soften for 15 minutes or so – either is delicious.

Swaps

Veg Use thinly sliced raw carrot, beetroot, kohlrabi or a mixture of roots, instead of radishes. Thin 'coins' of raw courgette are good too.
Seeds Replace the poppy seeds with sesame seeds, or ½ tsp nigella (black onion/kalonji) seeds.

Beetroot, rhubarb and orange

Serves 4

3 medium beetroot (300–350g in total)

2 tsp cider vinegar

1 rhubarb stalk (about 85g)

1 tsp sugar

2 medium oranges

Sea salt and black pepper

Sprigs of chervil or flat-leaf parsley, or carrot leaves, to finish

Full of bright, fruity flavours, this makes a palate-piquing appetiser before something hearty and spicy, such as one of the veg curries on pages 68 and 71.

Peel and trim the beetroot then coarsely grate into a bowl (or grate it in a food processor and transfer to a bowl). Sprinkle the cider vinegar over the beetroot, season with salt and pepper, and stir to distribute the seasonings.

Trim the rhubarb stalk and slice it across thinly – into 2–3mm slices. Toss the sliced rhubarb into the seasoned beetroot, add the sugar and mix well. Leave to macerate for about 10 minutes while you prepare the oranges.

Cut a slice from the top and base of each orange. Stand one orange on a board and use a sharp knife to cut away the peel and pith, working around the orange in sections. Once you have a whole, peel-less orange, cup it in your hand and, working over a bowl, use the knife to slice out the segments from between the inner membranes, dropping them into the bowl. Repeat with the other orange.

Add the orange segments to the beetroot and rhubarb (you can drink any orange juice left in the bowl). Toss lightly then transfer the salad to a large serving plate. Top with a few sprigs of chervil or parsley (or, if you happen to have some nice, fresh perky carrot tops to hand, use a few of those). Season with a little more salt and pepper, and serve.

Swaps

Roots Use grated raw carrot, celeriac or kohlrabi in place of the beetroot.

Herbs If the beetroot have some tender, perky leaves still attached, finish the dish with a few of these, instead of herbs. Or go for peppery rocket or watercress.

Cauliflower, walnuts and capers

Serves 4–6

1 medium very fresh cauliflower (about 800g untrimmed weight)

3 tbsp extra virgin olive oil, plus extra to finish

1–2 tsp sugar, to taste

Juice of 1 medium orange

Juice of ½ lemon

2 tbsp capers, rinsed, drained and roughly chopped if large

75g walnuts

Sea salt and black pepper

Coarsely grated raw cauliflower has a pleasingly uneven texture and a lovely ability to soak up dressings – like this tangy citrusy one. Salty little capers add piquancy to the dish and walnuts give colour, body and crunch.

Trim off the coarse outer leaves of the cauliflower and the base of the stalk. Now cut it vertically into quarters, going down through the stalk.

Using a box grater, grate the cauliflower into a large bowl. Start by grating the floret side of each quarter, until you get down to the stalk, then turn the piece round and grate the tender inner part of the main stem. You should be able to grate almost all of the cauliflower, barring a few fibrous, stalky bits. Any little florets that fall off as you go can be added to the bowl – just break them up if they are more than about 2cm across. The small, tender leaves from the base of the cauliflower can be included too. (Alternatively, you can cut the cauliflower into chunks and blitz it to a coarsely chopped texture in a food processor before transferring it to a bowl.)

Add the olive oil, sugar, orange and lemon juice, capers and some salt and pepper to the cauliflower and mix well. Then add the walnuts: you want them to be in chunky pieces, so either chop them roughly first or just break them up with your hands as you drop them into the bowl. Toss them into the cauliflower.

Taste and add more seasoning if necessary. Transfer to a serving bowl, add a final trickle of extra virgin olive oil and it's good to go.

Swaps

Capers Replace these with about 50g black or green olives, pitted and roughly chopped.

Nuts Try bashed-up almonds, hazelnuts or pumpkin seeds instead of the walnuts.

Beetroot and redcurrants

Serves 4

1 tsp fennel seeds

125g redcurrants

2 tbsp extra virgin olive oil

1–2 tsp sugar, to taste

Juice of ½ lemon

1 tbsp chopped fennel tops
or fennel herb (optional)

3 medium beetroot (about
350g in total)

A few fennel flowers (optional)

Sea salt and black pepper

Redcurrants are in season from June to August, and they make a fantastic pairing with young summer beetroot in this juicy, fresh and gloriously coloured dish.

Roughly crush the fennel seeds using a pestle and mortar.

Use a fork to strip the redcurrants off their stems. Put half of them into a bowl and crush them with a fork. Add the olive oil, sugar, crushed fennel seeds, lemon juice, chopped fennel (if you have it) and some salt and pepper. Stir well to combine with the redcurrants.

Peel the beetroot and either grate it coarsely or cut into very thin julienne matchsticks using a sharp knife or a mandoline. Put the beetroot into a bowl, spoon over half the crushed redcurrant mixture and stir together.

Scatter the dressed beetroot out over a large plate. Shake over the remaining redcurrants and spoon over the rest of the dressing. If you have any fennel flowers, scatter these over the salad before serving.

Swaps

Roots Instead of, or as well as, beetroot, use grated carrot – it works equally well with the redcurrant dressing.
Cabbage You can bulk up this dish by adding shredded red cabbage to the beetroot and/or carrot.
Fruit Swap chopped gooseberries or roughly crushed raspberries for the redcurrants.
Spices Use coriander seeds rather than fennel seeds.
Herbs Add roughly chopped parsley, dill or basil in place of the fresh fennel fronds.

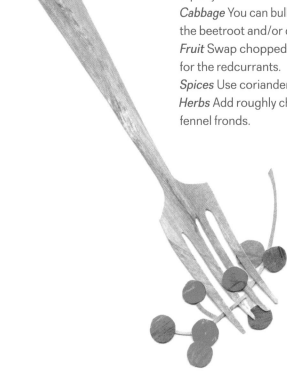

Courgettes with strawberries

Serves 4

4 very fresh small-medium courgettes (about 400g in total)

3 tbsp extra virgin olive oil

1 tbsp balsamic vinegar

4 tbsp shredded mint leaves

About 250g strawberries

Sea salt and black pepper

Fresh, raw courgette has a silky texture and mild, nutty flavour, while strawberries bring fragrance and rosy good looks to this lovely, summery mix. It's fine to use slightly under-ripe strawberries.

To prepare the courgettes, top and tail them, then either use a potato peeler to slice them into thin ribbons, or slice them thinly on the bias with a sharp knife or a mandoline. Put them into a bowl.

Add the olive oil, balsamic vinegar, some salt and pepper and 2 tbsp of the shredded mint. Use tongs or your hands to toss the courgette ribbons with the dressing and seasonings.

Hull the strawberries and then slice them about 3mm thick, working from the top to the bottom of the fruit. Drop these slices into the bowl of dressed courgette and toss again very gently, to distribute the strawberries without breaking them up.

Taste and add more salt or vinegar if needed, then divide the salad between serving plates, pouring over any juices left in the bowl. Scatter over the remaining shredded mint, add a final dusting of black pepper then serve.

Swaps

Veg Use thin slivers of fennel or cucumber instead of courgette.
Fruit Try whole blueberries or raspberries in place of the strawberries.
Herbs Swap mint with basil.

Fennel, melon and basil

Serves 4

1 large or 2 small fennel bulbs (about 350g in total)

3 tbsp extra virgin olive oil

Finely grated zest of ½ lemon, plus a squeeze of juice

½ medium-hot red chilli, deseeded and finely sliced

3–4 tbsp shredded basil leaves

½ medium Galia or Honeydew melon (about 500g)

Sea salt and black pepper

With its medley of wonderful, fragrant flavours, this is a lovely, refreshing summer dish. Make sure your melon is ripe and perfumed – it should give just a little when pressed at the base, and have a delicate melony aroma, even before you cut it open.

Trim off the top and base of the fennel bulbs, reserving any nice, fresh-looking green fronds if there are any. Remove the outer layer if the bulbs look a bit damaged or fibrous. Quarter the fennel bulbs and slice them as thinly as you can, using a sharp knife, or a mandoline if you prefer.

Put the sliced fennel into a large bowl and add the olive oil, lemon zest and juice, chilli, most of the basil and some salt and pepper. Toss together well and set aside for at least 10 minutes – up to an hour – to allow the flavours to mingle and the fennel to soften.

Scoop out and discard the seeds from the melon half and slice the fruit into thin wedges. Cut away the skin with a small sharp knife, then slice each wedge in two.

Add the melon pieces to the fennel and give it another gentle toss, then use tongs, or clean hands, to heap the salad onto a large serving plate. Trickle any juices from the bowl over the top and scatter over the rest of the basil and any fennel fronds you had in reserve. Give the dish a final grinding of black pepper, and serve.

Swaps

Veg Replace the fennel with deseeded, sliced cucumber. Thin slivers of carrot, cut with a veg peeler, also work well.
Herbs Mint is a lovely alternative to basil here.

Carrots with dukka and preserved lemon

Serves 3–4

2 tsp cumin seeds

2 tsp coriander seeds

2 tsp caraway seeds (optional)

A pinch of dried chilli flakes

100g whole, skin-on almonds

1 tbsp finely chopped preserved lemon (peel and flesh, but no pips)

3 tbsp extra virgin olive oil

Juice of ½ lemon

3 medium carrots (about 300g in total)

Sea salt and black pepper

Dukka is a tempting mix of bashed nuts and spices. In this simple dish, it's soaked with preserved lemon, olive oil and lemon juice, then tossed with grated raw carrot. Try serving it with pea hummus (page 304) or nutty, seedy, herby hummus (page 306), or alongside my pepper, potato and chard stew (page 18).

Using a pestle and mortar, pound the spice seeds with the dried chilli to grind them coarsely, then tip into a bowl. Put the almonds into the mortar and pound them to break them up into chunky bits (or chop them roughly if you prefer), then add to the bashed spices.

Add the preserved lemon, olive oil and lemon juice to the nutty, spicy mix and stir together. Leave to macerate while you prepare the carrots.

Peel and trim the carrots then grate them coarsely into a large bowl.

Pour the spicy, oily almond mixture over the grated carrots. Season with some salt and pepper and mix the whole lot together thoroughly. Taste and add more salt, pepper and/or lemon juice if needed, then it's ready to serve.

Swaps

Roots Use grated raw beetroot or celeriac in place of the carrots.
Nuts Try bashed hazelnuts or walnuts instead of almonds.
Spices Fennel seeds can replace the cumin, coriander or caraway seeds, and the dried chilli flakes can be swapped with 1 tsp sweet smoked paprika.
Citrus If you don't have preserved lemon, use the finely grated zest of 1 large orange or a couple of lemons.

Tomatoes, plums and basil

Serves 4

500g ripe tomatoes, any shape
or size (a mix is ideal)

350g ripe plums

3 tbsp extra virgin olive oil

4–5 tbsp shredded basil

Sea salt and black pepper

Marigold petals or other edible
flowers, to finish (optional)

I like to cut the fruit for this dish in a pleasingly haphazard way so
it feels generous and chunky. In late summer, when tomatoes and
plums are at their flavoursome best, it's a stunning raw centrepiece.

If you have small tomatoes, halve them. With larger ones, pick up the
tomato and use a small, sharp knife to slice chunks off it, until you've
chunked the whole tomato. Put the prepared tomatoes on a large
serving dish.

Halve or quarter and de-stone the plums and add to the tomatoes.

Trickle the olive oil over the tomatoes and plums. Sprinkle with some
salt and pepper, and then scatter over the shredded basil. If you have
any edible flowers, sprinkle these over too, then it's ready to serve.

Swaps

Fruit Thickly sliced strawberries work really well with tomatoes,
in place of the plums.
Herbs Try using mint instead of basil.

Cucumber with almond dressing

Serves 4

1 large cucumber (350–400g),
not fridge-cold

A pinch of sugar

50g whole, skin-on almonds,
soaked in cold water for at least
3 hours then drained

1 tbsp extra virgin olive, rapeseed
or hempseed oil

1 tbsp balsamic or sherry vinegar

¼–½ garlic clove, finely grated
or crushed

Sea salt and black pepper

This is a great, zero-waste way to use a cucumber: the juicy seedy section from the middle forms the base of a lovely, creamy-textured almond dressing. Make sure you allow time to pre-soak the nuts.

Cut the cucumber in half across the middle, then cut each half into quarters lengthways. Using a teaspoon, scoop out the seeds from the centre of each quarter and put them into a blender.

Cut each cucumber quarter into four fat 'fingers' (slice once lengthways and once widthways). Put these into a bowl, add a good pinch each of sugar, salt and pepper, stir gently to distribute the seasonings, then set aside while you make the dressing.

Put the drained, soaked almonds into the blender with the cucumber seeds. Add the oil, vinegar and a scrap of grated garlic – start with ¼ clove and add more later if you want to. Add salt and pepper and blitz to a creamy dressing, stopping periodically to scrape down the sides of the blender. It might take a little while for the almonds to start breaking down but keep going – they will eventually.

If the seasoned cucumber has released any juices, drain these off and add to the almond dressing. Arrange the cucumber pieces on a plate.

Taste the almond dressing and add more salt, pepper, garlic and/or vinegar if needed. Spoon the dressing into the middle of the cucumber pieces and serve straight away – the cucumber may release more juices if left to stand for too long.

Swaps

Veg If you have scooped-out cucumber seeds left over from another recipe, use them to make this dressing – you can serve it with almost any raw veg, from baby globe artichokes to tomatoes.
Nuts Replace the almonds with cashew nuts – again, it's best to soak them first.

Celeriac, rocket and cashews

Serves 4

½ large celeriac (350–400g)

1 tbsp extra virgin olive or rapeseed oil

A squeeze of lemon juice

Sea salt and black pepper

FOR THE DRESSING

75g cashew nuts

75g rocket

3 tbsp extra virgin olive or rapeseed oil

A squeeze of lemon juice

This fresh green dressing is a bit like a pesto, but much lighter, with no garlic and less oil. Use rocket with a good peppery flavour and you'll find it really brings out the nutty quality of the raw celeriac.

To make the dressing, put the cashews and rocket into a food processor and add the oil, lemon juice and 3 tbsp water. Add some salt and pepper and process to a coarse, loose paste, stopping once or twice to scrape down the sides of the processor. Taste and add more salt, pepper and lemon juice if needed, or a drop more water if it seems very thick.

Slice the rough outer layer from the celeriac, then slice the root thinly and cut each slice into thin matchsticks (you can grate it coarsely if you prefer). Put the prepared celeriac into a bowl, add the 1 tbsp oil, the lemon juice and a little salt and pepper and toss together well.

Transfer the celeriac to a serving bowl, spoon over the dressing and it's ready to serve.

Swaps

Veg This dressing tastes good with lots of other root veg – try carrot, beetroot or kohlrabi.
Leaves Peppery watercress is a good swap for rocket (remove the tougher stalks before blitzing).
Nuts Replace the cashews with whole, skin-on almonds, soaked in cold water for 2–3 hours.

Squash, blackberries and apple

Serves 4

250–300g young squash, such as ½ small butternut or a chunk of Crown Prince

1 tbsp extra virgin olive oil, plus an extra trickle

½ medium eating apple, cored and chopped

100g blackberries

Juice of ½ small lemon

1 tsp sugar

About 50g hazelnuts (skin on), roughly bashed

Sea salt and black pepper

Young, firm, fresh squashes have a nutty, almost melony flavour when eaten raw – and the beginning of the harvest coincides pleasingly with the blackberry season! This is a beautiful plateful, just the thing to start an autumn meal.

Use a vegetable peeler to peel the squash (or a knife if it's a tough, thick-skinned variety). Then use the peeler to pare the squash flesh into ribbons. It's easiest to cut it into manageable pieces, removing any seedy bits as you go, then pare each piece. The ribbons needn't be long – in fact, short curls are easier to eat.

Put the squash ribbons into a large bowl, add a trickle of olive oil, season with some salt and pepper and toss together.

Put the chopped apple and about half the blackberries into a mortar or robust bowl. Use the pestle, or the end of a rolling pin, to bash up the fruit a bit – just enough to crush some of the apple and get the blackberry juices flowing. Add the lemon juice, 1 tbsp olive oil, the sugar and some salt and pepper and mix well.

Arrange the raw squash over a large serving plate, or individual plates and spoon the juicy blackberry and apple mix on top. Scatter over the remaining whole blackberries and then the roughly bashed hazelnuts. Give the dish a final grinding of pepper, and serve.

Swaps

Veg Replace the squash with ribbons of raw carrot, beetroot or celeriac – they all work well.
Fruit Try using autumn raspberries in place of the blackberries. And pear can certainly be used instead of apple.

Celeriac, grapes and radicchio

Serves 4

½ large celeriac (about 350g)

100g grapes, halved

A couple of sprigs of thyme, leaves picked from the stalks

1 small or ½ large radicchio

FOR THE DRESSING

3 tbsp extra virgin olive or rapeseed oil

1 tbsp cider vinegar

1 tsp sugar, plus a little extra to finish

1 tsp English mustard

Sea salt and black pepper

This beautiful winter dish is crisp, colourful and vibrant. It makes a good precursor to the hearty dishes in the first two chapters.

First whisk all the dressing ingredients thoroughly together in a bowl, until well amalgamated.

Slice the rough outer layer from the celeriac then, working over a large bowl, use a veg peeler to cut the celeriac into thin ribbons, dropping them into the bowl. (Or grate it coarsely if you prefer.) Add the dressing and toss well, making sure all the celeriac ribbons get coated in dressing. Add the grapes and thyme and toss them with the celeriac.

Coarsely shred the radicchio and arrange over a large serving plate. Use your hands to distribute the dressed celeriac over the leaves, spreading out the ribbons of celeriac if they clump together. Drop the grapes and any remaining dressing from the bowl over the celeriac. Give the salad another dusting of salt and pepper, then serve.

Swaps

Veg Replace the raw celeriac with parsnip, carrot or Jerusalem artichoke.
Leaves As an alternative to radicchio, use chicory or crisp lettuce, such as cos or little gems.

Mushrooms with olives

Serves 4

300g very fresh chestnut mushrooms

About 3 tbsp extra virgin olive oil

A scrap of garlic (about ¼ clove), finely grated or crushed

A squeeze of lemon juice

50g pitted kalamata or other well-flavoured olives (about 70g stone-in), coarsely chopped

Sea salt and black pepper

Dried chilli flakes, to finish (optional)

The deep flavours and dense textures of these two ingredients combine to create something intensely savoury and satisfying. You can serve this dish soon after making it or happily leave it for 24 hours or longer – as it sits, the dressing softens the mushrooms so they seem 'cooked'. Either way, it's good alongside leafy salads, wilted greens or bashed potatoes and broad beans (page 28).

De-stalk the chestnut mushrooms, cut them into 4–5mm slices and place in a bowl.

In a small bowl, whisk together 3 tbsp olive oil, the garlic, lemon juice and some salt and pepper. Add this dressing to the sliced mushrooms, along with the chopped olives, and mix well. Don't worry if it seems there's not a huge amount of dressing – it will be enough!

Taste and add more salt, pepper and lemon juice if needed. You can add a trickle more oil if the mushrooms seem dry but they will release some liquid as they sit in the dressing, so don't overdo it.

Serve straight away or refrigerate for 1–2 days, returning the dish to room temperature and stirring well before serving. It's very good with a sprinkle of dried chilli flakes on top.

Swaps
Olives Replace these with 1–2 tbsp roughly chopped capers.

Cabbage and apple with rosewater

Serves 4

¼ red or white cabbage (about 200g)

1 medium eating apple

FOR THE DRESSING

3 tbsp extra virgin olive oil

1 tbsp lemon juice

1 tsp sugar

A few drops of rosewater

Sea salt and black pepper

Floral and delicately bitter, a touch of rosewater can be deliciously refreshing with raw veg. It also enhances the flavour of apple beautifully, making this very simple combination quite sophisticated.

For the dressing, whisk the olive oil, lemon juice, sugar and some salt and pepper together in a small bowl until well amalgamated. Add just a few drops of rosewater and taste the dressing. It should taste delicately fragrant and floral, not overpoweringly 'rosy'. Add a few more drops if necessary.

Cut away the thick white core of the cabbage, then slice thinly, using a sharp knife or a food processor. Place the shredded cabbage in a large bowl. Grate the apple coarsely (no need to peel it) directly into the bowl with the cabbage. Add the dressing and stir thoroughly.

Taste the salad and add a little more salt, pepper, lemon juice or rosewater if necessary, then heap onto a large plate and serve.

Swaps

Fruit Try using a crisp, firm pear in place of, or as well as, the apple.
Rosewater Swap with orange flower water.

Kale, celeriac and raisins

Serves 3–4

50g raisins

2 tbsp orange juice

About 300g kale or cavolo nero (or a mix of both)

2 tbsp cider vinegar

3 tbsp olive or rapeseed oil

½ tsp English mustard

¼ garlic clove, finely grated or crushed

¼ medium celeriac (about 150g), peeled

50g pecan nuts

1 mild red chilli, deseeded and sliced (optional)

Sea salt and black pepper

I'm a big fan of techniques that tenderise raw veg without the use of heat (see the mushroom dish on page 263) and 'massaging kale' is an exceptionally good one. The raw leaves are rubbed with a little salt and vinegar so that the cells start to break down and the kale wilts. Combined with grated celeriac, plump raisins and a tasty dressing, and left to mellow and mingle for a bit, the result is juicy, tender, sweet, crunchy and altogether very satisfying.

Put the raisins into a small bowl, add the orange juice and set aside.

Strip the kale leaves off their stalks, tearing them into rough pieces as you go; discard the stalks. Put the kale leaves into a large bowl with a couple of pinches of salt and the cider vinegar.

Now roll up your sleeves and get massaging: crush the kale leaves with your fingers, squeeze in your palms and rub the leaves against each other. As you do so, you'll see the leaves start to darken, wilt and reduce in volume and some of the kale's juices will probably be released. About 3 minutes of massaging should be enough – the kale should have reduced to about half its former volume by then. If you find this massaging rather hard work, an alternative method is to bash and pound the kale with the end of a rolling pin or a large pestle.

Whisk the oil, mustard, garlic and some pepper together in a small bowl. Add this dressing to the wilted kale and mix thoroughly.

Coarsely grate the celeriac into the bowl and mix with the kale. Add the raisins with their orange juice. Break up the pecans with your hands and add them too, along with the chilli if using. Mix the salad together then taste and add more salt and pepper if you like.

You can eat this straight away but it's even better left in a cool place for an hour or two to relax and develop in flavour. I can happily eat a big bowlful just as it comes but it's also good with something creamy-textured like hummus – try it with raw mushroom, walnut and parsley hummus (page 308).

Swaps

Fruit Replace the raisins with soaked dried cherries or chopped dates; or use fresh apple slices instead, and add the orange juice separately.
Nuts Use hazelnuts, walnuts or pumpkin seeds rather than pecans.
Roots Try grated carrot, parsnip or beetroot in place of the celeriac.

Lightly pickled beetroot, carrot and apple

Serves 4

1 small red onion (roughly egg-sized) or ¼ brown onion, finely chopped

1 tsp sugar

4 tsp cider vinegar

2 smallish carrots (about 150g in total)

1 small-medium beetroot (about 150g)

1 medium eating apple

Sea salt and black pepper

Dressed with a splash of cider vinegar, balanced by a little sugar and onion, this is fresh flavoured and nicely piquant. It's great to put on the table as a foil to richer, heartier veg – or as part of any big mezze-style spread.

Put the onion into a large bowl. Add the sugar, cider vinegar and some salt and pepper and mix well, breaking up the bits of onion as you go.

Peel and trim the carrots, then use the peeler to pare the carrots into wafer-thin slices. Drop these into the bowl of onion as you work. Peel and trim the beetroot then pare the raw flesh into the bowl – don't worry about being too consistent with the size and shape of your parings. Peel the apple and pare its flesh into the bowl (you can coarsely grate the carrots, beetroot and apple if you prefer).

Mix the veg thoroughly into the juicy onion – you might find it easiest to do this with your hands, or some tongs. Taste and add more salt or pepper if required, then serve.

Swaps

Veg Try adding slivers of fennel or celery in place of either the carrot or the beetroot.

Alliums Swap the onion with finely diced shallot or sliced spring onion.

Miso-dressed cabbage

Serves 4

½ small white or red cabbage (about 300g)

1 tsp black mustard seeds (optional)

Finely sliced red chilli, to serve (optional)

FOR THE MISO DRESSING

2 tbsp white miso paste or shiro miso paste

2 tbsp rapeseed oil

1 tbsp rice vinegar (or you can use cider vinegar)

1 tsp grated ginger

A scrap of garlic (about ¼ clove), finely grated or crushed

Miso, a Japanese ingredient, is a paste made from fermented soya beans. Intensely savoury, it's a great addition to any cook's box of tricks – with the added bonus that unpasteurised versions are also rich in live, friendly bacteria. Some of the darker varieties of miso can be really pungent but sweet white miso, made from soya beans and rice, is about the mildest you can buy and is great in dressings (see also pages 67 and 339). But you can, if you like, use the slightly stronger shiro miso in this recipe.

First put the ingredients for the miso dressing into a large bowl and whisk together until fully emulsified.

Slice the chunk of cabbage in half and cut out the thicker part of the stalk, then shred finely. Add it to the bowl with the dressing, along with the mustard seeds if using.

Mix the cabbage thoroughly with the miso dressing. You can serve it straight away, or leave it for up to 2 days in the fridge to soften a little. Either way, transfer it to a serving bowl and scatter with a little red chilli, if you like, before serving.

Swaps

Veg Replace the white cabbage with Savoy cabbage, or go for grated raw cauliflower or thinly sliced raw Brussels sprouts.

Home Fermenting

It is increasingly recognised that eating traditional fermented foods such as sauerkraut and kimchi, which are alive with friendly bacteria, can be beneficial to our health. This is just one reason why home-fermenting is an area I've been exploring. Fermenting vegetables is also extremely satisfying and, as the following three easy recipes demonstrate, the results are delicious, always pleasingly piquant and tangy. You can swap in different vegetables to spin dozens of exciting different ferments from these basic templates.

The process is very simple: raw veg is mixed with a brine and left at room temperature. Desirable lactic bacteria get to work under the surface, producing lactic acid, which preserves the veg and gives it a pleasantly sour flavour. Initially, these friendly bacteria also release carbon dioxide, which is why you'll see bubbles in the brine and why, in its early stages, the veg can taste slightly fizzy. The flavour will develop over time. As you'd expect, fermentation is quicker in warmer temperatures.

In our supermarket-dominated world, pasteurised, super-chilled foods and short use-by dates are the norm. So stepping into the realm of home fermentation, where bacteria are actively encouraged, can feel a little daunting. Don't worry: fermenting is a safe process because the lactic acid bacteria it relies on are very good at preserving food, and at keeping competing, unwanted micro-organisms at bay. The key thing is acidity. If you feel at all nervous, get a little book of pH strips. Use these to test the acidity of your ferments before eating. If they show a pH of 4 or below, they are safe to eat.

It is not unusual to find a white film of yeast growing on the surface of a ferment. This isn't harmful but it should be removed. Skim it off as best you can, wipe the inside of the jar and wash or replace any weight you're using. Repeat if the yeast grows again. If a ferment does go slimy or mouldy or has a bad, 'off' smell or taste, discard it.

For each of the following three recipes, you'll need a stout preserving jar, such as a Kilner jar, washed in hot, soapy water, rinsed and dried. If it has a rubber seal around the lid, remove it: you don't want it to be completely airtight or the carbon dioxide won't be able to escape during fermentation.

The chlorine in tap water can affect the fermentation process, so it's a good idea to use an inexpensive mineral water or filtered water for brining.

Simple sauerkraut

Traditional sauerkraut is dry-salted – the cabbage is sprinkled with salt and massaged or pounded so that it produces its own brine. This lightly tangy kraut is even easier – you just pour a ready-made brine straight on to the veg and let it do its thing.

Add the salt to the water in a jug and stir until fully dissolved to make a 4% brine.

Remove and reserve an outer cabbage leaf. Cut the cabbage half in two, cut out the thick white core then rinse the cabbage thoroughly. Cut the quarters into 5mm thick slices and put into a bowl.

If using carrots, coarsely grate them into the bowl with the cabbage. Add the bay leaves and juniper and roughly mix everything together.

Load the veg into a clean 2 litre preserving jar (see the previous page). About halfway through, tamp the veg down firmly in the jar with the end of a rolling pin. Do this again when all the veg is loaded in. Leave at least 5cm clear at the top of the jar.

Put the reserved cabbage leaf on top of the shredded veg. (This isn't essential but helps to stop bits of veg floating upwards in the brine.) Press down firmly on the cabbage with a very clean hand or the rolling pin and pour on enough brine to cover the veg by about 3cm when pressed. Tilt the jar to get rid of air bubbles.

You now need to weigh the cabbage down so that it stays submerged in the brine. (Cabbage exposed to the air may go mouldy.) The weight needs to fit inside the neck of the jar and still allow the jar to be closed. You can find designed-for-purpose pickling weights or 'pebbles' made of ceramic or glass. Alternatively, you can use a small, strong plastic bag, such as a freezer bag, part-filled with brine. Push the cabbage down, put the empty plastic bag inside the jar, open it and pour brine into the bag so that it fills the space in the jar, presses down on the veg and forces brine up above the veg (including the cabbage leaf 'lid'). Seal the bag. Use a teaspoon to scoop out any little bits of veg that float up above the bag. Then clip the jar closed.

Stand the jar on a cloth or a plate (sometimes brine can leak out) and leave undisturbed at cool room temperature for 7 days. You should be able to observe the mix releasing bubbles of carbon dioxide.

Transfer the weight/bag and cabbage leaf to a clean plate and taste the mix. If it is pleasantly sour and tangy, it's ready to eat. If not, re-weight the kraut and leave at cool room temperature for another 3–4 days to allow the flavour to continue to develop, making sure that the cabbage

remains submerged in the brine. When the kraut has reached a flavour that you like, discard the cabbage leaf lid, and transfer the jar to the fridge, which slows fermentation right down.

Each time you remove some kraut to eat, make sure the stuff still in the jar is all floating in brine. You don't have to keep the weight on it in the fridge, but you don't want the veg sitting above the brine, exposed to air. Top up with a little more brine if necessary.

Swaps

Brassicas Any cabbage can be used here – spring cabbage, Savoy etc. You could even throw some sliced Brussels sprouts into the mix.
Roots Try grated celeriac, beetroot, radish, turnip or kohlrabi in place of the carrot – or use a combination of roots.
Fruit Grated apple is another great addition to the mix.
Spices Instead of juniper, try adding 2 tsp bashed coriander, cumin or caraway seeds and/or some strips of citrus zest – or pep up your kraut with dried chilli flakes and sliced garlic.

Celeriac 'kimchi'

Makes at least 16 servings

2 large celeriac (1.5kg in total)

2–3 garlic cloves, finely grated or crushed

1 tbsp fennel or caraway seeds

2 tsp dried chilli flakes

500ml still mineral water or filtered water (if needed, see method)

Fine sea salt

True kimchi is a Korean dish of pungent, highly spiced fermented cabbage. This simple – though still strong and spicy – variation is inspired by a recipe from my River Cottage colleague, Naomi Devlin. It's delicious spooned next to salads, or dishes that major on earthy ingredients such as lentils or root veg. I also use it to top raw soups or just enjoy it as a healthy, probiotic, pre-dinner nibble.

Slice the rough outer layer from the celeriac, rinse well to get rid of any earth, then cut into chunks and coarsely grate (use a food processor for speed if you have one). Place a large, non-reactive bowl on your scales and weigh the grated celeriac into it. Add the garlic, fennel or caraway seeds, and the chilli flakes, and note the total weight. Calculate 2% of the weight of the celeriac mix – this is how much salt you'll need to add (e.g. for 1kg celeriac mix, you'd need 20g salt).

Add the salt to the celeriac mix and mix it in thoroughly, making sure the seasonings are evenly distributed. Set aside for 30 minutes, so that the salt starts to draw the juices from the celeriac.

Now pack the celeriac mixture into a clean 2 litre preserving jar (see page 273). Making sure your hands are very clean, put a couple of handfuls of celeriac into the jar. Then press the celeriac down into the jar, compressing it and forcing out some of its liquid.

Repeat with another couple of handfuls, pressing the celeriac again to pack it in and squeeze out juice. Keep going, filling and pressing, until you have used all the celeriac and/or the jar is filled to within 5–7cm of the top rim. If you happen to have a spare cabbage leaf to hand, you can use it to form a 'lid' (as for the sauerkraut on page 274), which will help to keep the celeriac submerged later.

Unless your celeriac is so juicy that it's already covered by around 3cm of its own salty liquid, you'll need to top up the jar with a small amount of home-made brine. Mix up a 4% brine by dissolving 20g fine sea salt in 500ml filtered or mineral water. Pour enough on to the celeriac to cover it, when pressed (and the cabbage leaf, if using), by about 3cm.

You now need to weigh the celeriac down so that it stays completely submerged in the brine. (Any exposed to the air may go mouldy.) The weight needs to fit inside the neck of the jar and still leave it possible to close the jar. You can find designed-for-purpose pickling weights or 'pebbles' made of ceramic or glass. A good alternative is to use a small, strong plastic bag, such as a freezer bag, part-filled with brine. Push the celeriac down hard, put the empty plastic bag inside the jar, open it and pour brine into the bag so that it fills the space in the jar, presses down on the veg and forces brine up above the veg – including the cabbage leaf 'lid'. Seal the bag. Use a teaspoon to scoop out any bits of celeriac or spice that float up above the bag. Then clip the jar closed.

Stand the jar on a cloth or a plate (sometimes brine can leak out) and leave undisturbed at cool room temperature for 7 days. You should be able to observe the mix gently releasing bubbles of carbon dioxide.

Transfer the weight/bag to a clean plate. Taste the mix. If it is pleasantly sour and nicely punchy, it's ready to use. If not, you can replace the weight and leave it at cool room temperature for 3–4 more days to allow the flavour to continue to develop, making sure that the celeriac remains submerged in the brine. When it has reached a flavour that you like, transfer it to the fridge, which slows fermentation right down.

Each time you remove some celeriac to eat, press the stuff still in the jar back down. You don't have to keep the weight on it in the fridge, but you do still want the celeriac to be covered with brine; top up with a little more if necessary.

Swaps

Roots Grated carrot, beetroot, radish or kohlrabi can all be fermented in this way (alone or in combination). Swede and turnip work too – try adding some grated apple to the mix to balance their peppery quality.
Spices Use coriander, cumin or Szechuan pepper instead of fennel seeds, or try a few smashed juniper or allspice berries, or 1 tsp smashed black peppercorns.

Brined fennel and red onion with orange and coriander

Makes 8–10 servings

40g fine sea salt

1 litre still mineral water or filtered water

1 very large or 2 medium fennel bulbs (about 500g in total)

1 medium red onion

Zest of 1 medium orange, pared in wide strips

1 tsp coriander seeds

This is an incredibly simple way to ferment raw veg, producing a crisp, delicately sour, light pickle in just a few days. The fennel has a lovely clean flavour, with a hint of orange. I like to nibble on it before a meal, or serve it next to something starchy, such as smashed new potatoes with coriander and bay (page 377).

Add the salt to the water and stir to dissolve fully to make a 4% brine.

Trim away any damaged or dirty outer layer from the fennel, then quarter the bulbs and slice thinly. Halve the onion and slice it thinly.

Pack the fennel, onion, orange zest and coriander seeds into a clean 1.5 litre preserving jar (see page 273), adding a little of each at a time so they are mixed. Leave at least 5cm clear at the top of the jar. Use the end of a rolling pin or your clean hand to hold the veg down in the jar while you pour in the brine – it should cover the pressed veg by 3cm.

You need to weigh the veg down so it stays completely submerged. The weight needs to fit inside the neck of the jar and allow the jar to be closed. You can buy ceramic or glass pickling weights or 'pebbles'. A good alternative is to use a small, strong plastic bag, such as a freezer bag, part-filled with brine. Push the fennel down, put the empty plastic bag inside the jar, open it and pour brine into the bag so that it fills the space in the jar, presses down on the veg and forces brine up above the veg. Seal the bag. Use a teaspoon to scoop out any little bits of veg or spice that float up above the bag. Then clip the jar closed.

Stand the jar on a cloth or a plate (sometimes brine can leak out) and leave undisturbed for a week. You should be able to observe the mix gently releasing bubbles of carbon dioxide.

Open the jar, lift up the weight and taste the veg. If it's pleasantly sour and aromatic, it's good to eat. Alternatively, replace the weight and give it another 2 or 3 days. When you're happy with the flavour, transfer the fennel to the fridge to slow fermentation. You can remove the brine bag or weight but the veg must stay submerged. It will keep for 3–4 weeks.

Swaps

Veg Try sliced radishes, carrots, kohlrabi, baby turnips or celery, or small cauliflower florets in place of the fennel.
Spices Add peppercorns, cumin or fennel seeds rather than coriander seeds. You can also add a pinch of dried chilli flakes to the brine.

Raw blitzes

I've had a lot of fun with the technique of blitzing raw veg (and often fruit, nuts and herbs) in a processor, taking it to the point where it's well-chopped but not pulverised or puréed. If you add some piquant or aromatic ingredients to the mix, you can make a fantastic salad-cum-relish in just a few minutes. Whizzing everything to a small size means these 'blitzes' are incredibly easy to eat — and every forkful has a little of everything in it. You'll find four of my favourite 'blitzes' on the following pages...

Celeriac Waldorf blitz

Serves 4

½ large celeriac (about 350g), peeled

1 medium eating apple

50g walnuts

A small bunch of flat-leaf parsley (about 25g), leaves picked from the stalks, plus extra to serve

30g raisins

2 tbsp extra virgin olive or rapeseed oil, plus extra to serve

Juice of ½ small lemon, or more to taste

Sea salt and black pepper

The classic Waldorf (celery, apples, walnuts) is one of the best conceived of all salads, I think, with a lovely balance of savoury, sweet, crunchy and tender. I also love a Waldorf that uses milder celeriac in place of celery — and this recipe is a pleasingly chunky, blitzed-up version of that combination. Try it as a starter before a hearty bake, such as nutty gratin of greens and leeks (page 24).

Roughly chop the peeled celeriac flesh into 2–3cm chunks and place in a food processor.

Don't peel the apple, but cut it into quarters, remove the core and roughly chop the flesh. Add to the processor.

Add the walnuts, parsley leaves, raisins and extra virgin oil. Add a good squeeze of lemon juice and plenty of salt and pepper.

Now pulse the salad in brief bursts, stopping several times to scrape down the sides of the processor. Stop when the salad is reasonably evenly chopped — you want it to be nicely chunky, not paste-like.

Taste a spoonful and add more lemon juice, salt or pepper as needed, then heap the mixture into a serving dish. Serve straight away, trickled with more extra virgin oil and scattered with more parsley.

Swaps
Roots Try carrot in place of celeriac.
Fruit For a really juicy blitz, add a handful of grapes instead of the apple.
Nuts Swap walnuts with pecans or hazelnuts.

Beetroot and peanut butter blitz

Serves 4

3 small-medium beetroot (about 300g in total), peeled and roughly chopped

5 tbsp crunchy, no-sugar-added peanut butter

1 tbsp tamari

Juice of 1 lime

¼–½ garlic clove, to taste, finely grated or crushed

A bunch of coriander (about 25g), roughly chopped, including tender stalks

A pinch of dried chilli flakes

A little more intense than some of my other 'blitzes' or hummus, I like to treat this delicious, sweet-savoury mix as a sort of hummus or relish, dishing it up with veg patties (such as the squash and chickpea patties on page 74), or a green salad – or both.

Put all the ingredients into a food processor and blitz to a fairly finely chopped, evenly mixed consistency, stopping to scrape down the sides of the processor once or twice. Don't reduce everything to a purée – the blitz should still have some texture.

Taste the mixture. You should find that the tamari, lime, garlic and chilli give it just the right balance of salty, sharp and piquant – but add a little more of any of those ingredients if you need to.

Serve the blitz straight away or store it in a plastic tub in the fridge for up to 3 days.

Swaps

Roots Replace the beetroot with carrot.
Herbs Use mint or Thai basil rather than coriander.
Nuts Instead of peanut butter, try a crunchy almond butter.

Moroccan carrot blitz

Serves 4

3 medium carrots (about 300g in total)

½ medium red onion, roughly chopped

50g pitted green olives (about 70g stone-in)

2 small or ½ large preserved lemon(s)

1 medium-hot red chilli, deseeded (for less heat, if preferred) and roughly chopped

A small bunch of coriander (about 25g), roughly chopped, including tender stalks

2 tbsp extra virgin olive oil

Sea salt and black pepper

This North-African-influenced carrot blitz is one of my favourites — great in a lunchbox and delicious alongside hearty veg dishes, such as roast fennel, new potato and tomato stew (page 16).

Peel the carrots and slice into 3–4mm thick slices. Put them into a food processor with the red onion and green olives.

Remove any pips from the preserved lemon, then roughly chop the rest (including the flesh) and add to the processor. Add the chilli, coriander, olive oil and a twist of black pepper.

Blitz to a well-chopped evenly mixed consistency, stopping to scrape down the sides of the processor once or twice. The idea is not to blitz it *too* much — you don't want a paste but a nicely chunky mix in which you can still distinguish the individual ingredients.

Taste the mixture and add salt if you like — but you will almost certainly find the olives and preserved lemon make it salty enough.

Serve the blitz straight away or keep it in a plastic tub in the fridge and use within 3 days.

Swaps

Veg Replace the carrot with beetroot.
Herbs Use mint or basil instead of the coriander.

Brussels, rhubarb and apple blitz

Serves 4

150g trimmed Brussels sprouts, halved

75g rhubarb, very roughly chopped

1 medium eating apple, quartered, cored and roughly chopped (no need to peel)

A squeeze of lemon juice, or more to taste

Sea salt and black pepper

Extra virgin olive, rapeseed or hempseed oil, to finish

It might sound a bit 'out there', but this is a tasty and easy winter blitz – perfect in January when Brussels, forced rhubarb and stored apples are all in season. Refreshing, light and vibrant, with the raw rhubarb contributing an almost citrusy tartness, it's delicious as a starter before the hearty and spicy dishes in the first two chapters. Go for small, sweet Brussels and trim off damaged outer leaves and any tough stalk before you begin.

Put the raw sprouts, rhubarb and apple into a food processor. Add some salt and pepper and a squeeze of lemon juice, and blitz. Keep going, stopping and scraping the sides down a few times, until the ingredients are well chopped and nicely mixed. Taste and add more seasoning or lemon juice if necessary.

Tip the mixture into a serving bowl, trickle generously with extra virgin oil and eat straight away (the apple will start to discolour after a while).

Swaps
Veg Try replacing the Brussels sprouts with roughly chopped Savoy cabbage, kale or cauliflower.

Overnight orange, almond and cardamom smoothie

Serves 1

40g whole, skin-on almonds

2 cardamom pods, seeds extracted

1 large orange

1–2 tsp sugar

This smoothie uses a whole (peeled) orange, which is cut up and left to soak overnight with a handful of almonds and a hint of cardamom. In the morning, the ingredients are blitzed together, to create a lovely, fragrant, breakfast-in-a-glass. The smoothie works best in a high-powered blender. A standard blender may not be able to render a completely smooth result – but your nubbly smoothie will still be delicious.

Measure 100ml water into a jug then add the whole almonds and cardamom seeds.

Cut a slice from the top and base of the orange. Stand it on a board and use a sharp knife to cut away the peel and pith, working around the orange in sections. Once you have a whole, peel-less orange, cut it into quarters, removing the thick piece of white pith running down the middle of the fruit as you go. Cut each quarter in half again.

Put the orange pieces in the jug with the water and almonds, and tip in any orange juice that may have puddled on your chopping board. Refrigerate the mixture overnight.

When you want to drink your smoothie, tip the chilled contents of the jug into a blender, add the sugar and give it a good blitz until smooth. Add a splash more cold water if necessary. Drink straight away.

Swaps

Nuts Use cashew nuts instead of the almonds.

Spices Omit the cardamom and add a pinch of ground cinnamon before blitzing.

Overnight banana, almond and cacao thickie

Serves 1

1 ripe medium banana (about 175g)

3 tbsp whole, skin-on almonds

3 tbsp porridge oats

2 tsp cacao or cocoa powder

A few drops of vanilla extract or paste (optional)

Rich, sweet and sustaining, this oat-thickened variation on a smoothie makes a fantastic quick breakfast. Put the banana in the freezer and the almonds, oats and water in the fridge the night before and all you have to do in the morning is whiz them together. For a really fruity thickie (or, as I like to call it, a frickie), leave out the cacao and add frozen raspberries or blueberries and a squeeze of lime juice.

The night before, peel the banana, slice it thickly and put it on a plate. Pop it in the freezer to freeze overnight.

Also the night before, put the almonds and oats into a jug or bowl and cover with 150ml cold water. Make sure the nuts and oats are fully submerged. Place in the fridge to chill and soak overnight.

In the morning, tip the swollen almonds and oats, and their soaking water, into a blender or food processor. Dislodge the frozen banana pieces from the plate and add those to the blender/processor too.

Now add the cacao or cocoa, and the vanilla, if using, and blitz. It might take a little while for everything to break down but within a few minutes, you will have a thick purée, flecked with tiny specks of almond skin. Keep blitzing, adding a little more cold water to get the thickie to a drinkable consistency – you'll probably need another 30–50ml water.

Pour it into a large glass and enjoy while it's still nice and cold.

Swaps
Nuts Use cashew nuts instead of the almonds.
Grains Try buckwheat flakes in place of the porridge oats.

Blackberry and beetroot shooters

Serves 3–6

2 small beetroot (about 175g in total), chilled

150g blackberries (chilled or frozen)

Juice of 1 lemon

1 tsp finely chopped rosemary

A pinch of sugar (optional)

Sea salt and black pepper

This intensely fruity, rooty purée is perfect served in little cups or small bowls as an *amuse-bouche* or starter. I like to make it with frozen blackberries and beetroot straight from the fridge so that it is ready to serve as soon as it's made.

Peel the beetroot and grate it coarsely, straight into a blender or food processor. Add the blackberries, lemon juice, chopped rosemary and 50ml cold water. Season with a little salt and/or pepper. Now blitz to a thick purée.

Push through a sieve into a bowl to produce a smooth purée, then taste and add more salt or pepper if needed. If your blackberries were particularly sharp, you might want a tiny pinch of sugar too, but generally this isn't necessary. If it's a bit too thick, add a trickle of water.

Serve lightly chilled in shot glasses or small tumblers.

Raw granola with banana and lime

Serves 6

75g whole raw buckwheat (buckwheat 'groats')

75g porridge oats

50g mixed seeds

50g hazelnuts (skin on or off)

75g pitted dates

75g pitted prunes

2 tbsp maple syrup

TO SERVE

2–3 medium bananas

1–2 limes

A fruity-sweet, blitzed-up mix of oats, buckwheat groats, seeds, maple syrup and dried fruit makes a filling, energising breakfast (or lunch!). I like to spritz it generously with lime juice to balance the sweetness and add a shot of vitamin C.

Put the buckwheat, oats, seeds and hazelnuts into a food processor.

Very roughly chop the dates and prunes (I do this by snipping each into 2–3 pieces with scissors). Add these to the processor and blitz until everything is well chopped. Add the maple syrup and blitz until the ingredients come together in a well-combined chunky, slightly sticky, clustery mix.

Spoon the granola into bowls. Slice half a banana over each portion then spritz generously with lime juice. Have more lime halves to hand so you can squeeze on more juice as you eat. Any unused granola mix can go into a plastic tub and be stored in the fridge for a few days.

Swaps

Nuts Add pecans, walnuts or pistachios instead of the hazelnuts.
Dried fruit Use raisins or chopped dried apricots in place of either the dates or prunes.

Pinhead 'overnight' muesli

Serves 2

50g unsulphured dried apricots, roughly chopped

50g whole, skin-on almonds, coarsely chopped

100g pinhead oatmeal

150ml hot black tea

150ml cloudy apple juice

TO SERVE

A squeeze of lemon juice

A pinch of sugar (optional)

Here, I've added a handful of roughly chopped fruit and nuts to chunky pinhead oatmeal and soaked the mix overnight in a blend of tea and apple juice. This gives a tender but nicely textured Bircher-style muesli that needs only a squeeze of lemon before you tuck in.

Put the chopped dried apricots and almonds into a heatproof bowl and add the pinhead oatmeal. Pour on the hot tea and mix well, then add the apple juice and mix again. Once cool, cover and leave in the fridge overnight.

The muesli is nicest when not absolutely fridge cold, so try and get it out of the fridge the next morning about 20 minutes before you want to eat it.

Give the mixture a good stir then divide between two bowls. Add a squeeze of lemon juice and a sprinkle of sugar if you like, and serve.

Swaps

Dried fruit Try raisins or chopped prunes in place of the dried apricots.
Nuts Use roughly bashed hazelnuts instead of the almonds.
Fruit juice Replace the apple juice with orange juice, or use a mixture of the two.

Carrot and apricot breakfast bars

Makes 12–16

400g carrots, peeled and roughly chopped

200g unsulphured dried apricots, roughly chopped

3 tbsp virgin coconut oil

Finely grated zest of 1 lemon

Finely grated zest of 1 orange

6 cardamom pods, seeds extracted and roughly crushed

150g porridge oats (not jumbo, chunky or traditional oats)

100g mixed seeds, such as sunflower, sesame and pumpkin

These can be kept in the fridge for a few days, ready to provide an instant healthy breakfast or snack. They're packed with raw carrot, oats, dried apricots and seeds, and given plenty of fragrant flavour with orange and lemon zest and a little cardamom.

Put the carrots and apricots into a food processor and blitz until finely chopped and well mixed, stopping several times to scrape down the sides and ensure that everything is evenly chopped.

Add the coconut oil, citrus zests and cardamom. Process again until thoroughly combined.

Scrape the mixture into a large bowl and add the oats and seeds. Mix thoroughly together.

Line a small baking tray, about 18 x 20cm, with baking parchment. Tip the mixture into the tray and spread it out evenly so that it fills the tray. Tamp it down, smooth the top and fold the parchment over to cover it, or cover with a second piece. Refrigerate for at least 4 hours, until firm.

Cut into fingers – 12 or 16, depending on how greedy you're feeling! Keep in a plastic box in the fridge and eat within a week. As well as making a great breakfast, the bars can be packed in a lunchbox – just keep them fairly cool so they don't soften up too much.

Swaps
Veg Parsnip is a good alternative to the carrot.
Dried fruit Replace the apricots with pitted dates.
Spices Swap 1 tsp ground cinnamon for the cardamom.

Mezze, tapas and sides

VEGETABLES – VIBRANT, COLOURFUL and juicy, fresh from the greengrocer or the garden – are very inspiring ingredients and I frequently allow them to 'lead' my cooking. So, sometimes, rather than having a specific dish or complete meal in mind, I just ask myself, 'How can I make something extra-tempting from this carrot/cabbage/spud/courgette/bean/mushroom? How do I really want to eat it today?' By cooking and seasoning that vegetable in a way – often very simple – that promises to give pleasure, I more often than not come up with something fun and delicious without much trouble or effort. And this approach has given me the repertoire of tasty vegetable treats represented in this chapter. You might call them – to adapt a buzz-phrase of the moment – 'small plates of plants'.

These small plates are, however, designed to make a big impact. Some are simple combinations of contrasting, complementary veg – like asparagus and carrots with lemon and parsley (page 326), or baked mushrooms with kale and walnuts (page 348). Others take a decent quantity of a single vegetable, and give it a tempting twist: burnt beans with sesame seeds and miso dressing (page 339), for instance, or purple sprouting broccoli with a salsa made from its own leaves (page 320). Those simple twists and clever seasonings make it very easy indeed to eat a generous pile of something you know is going to do you good. The 'dress-it-up-a-little-bit' approach is especially well deployed with veg, such as greens and beans, that are not universally adored in their plain form – and you'll find examples of how deliciously it can work throughout this chapter.

The dishes in this chapter might not quite make a meal on their own, but they don't need much alongside – a grainy side dish, perhaps, from the final chapter, or a raw salad – to be satisfying. You can also enjoy any of them alone as a starter.

However, I more often eat intensely tasty dishes like these as part of an eclectic mix. They are tailor-made for my favourite kind of eating: the tapas/mezze/antipasti-style spread, where the table is laid with several bowls or platters, all holding enticing things that you can help yourself to, mixing and mingling them on your plate just as you please.

This is a way of sharing food that is vernacular in the Middle East, Asia and the Mediterranean. Not surprisingly, some of my recipes borrow spicing and techniques from these delicious and intoxicating food cultures. But many do not. I have been indulging all kinds of whims to create these dishes – the ones here are simply the whims that worked…

The passing-and-sharing approach is perhaps a little unconventional in our traditionally each-to-his-own-plate culinary culture. But it's gaining traction, thanks to the wonderful multi-culturalism of the British food scene. It's such a friendly, inviting, communal way to eat. It makes mouths water and conversation flow. And, actually, it's a really brilliant way to learn to relish the distinctive characters of a whole range of lovely veg.

You'll very quickly develop an instinctive sense of how to put together a gathering of these dishes that will stimulate and satisfy your family and guests. You just need to balance a couple of cleaner, lighter or greener choices, such as greens with sesame and seaweed (page 332) and raw pea hummus (page 304), with one or two more substantial, protein-rich or starchy ones – roasted tofu (page 369) or Puy lentils with veg and herbs (page 370), for example. You can easily add effortless extras too, such as marinated olives – or leftovers from a previous veg-based feast.

With this sort of mixing and matching in mind, I've included both lighter and heftier dishes, so that you can put together a substantial meal (adding something from the Spuds and grains chapter that follows if you like). The 'serves' line on each recipe tells you how many people it will feed if you're combining it with a couple of other tapas/mezze-type dishes – in whichever permutation of vegetal loveliness appeals to you!

Pea hummus

Serves 4

300g frozen peas, defrosted, or freshly podded peas (about 750g in the pod)

A bunch of coriander (about 50g), roughly chopped, including tender stems

3 tbsp tahini

¼–½ garlic clove, finely grated or crushed

A good squeeze of lemon juice, or more to taste

Sea salt and black pepper

TO FINISH

Extra virgin olive, rapeseed or hempseed oil

Sumac, to sprinkle (optional)

Chives or chive flowers (optional)

This works well – and is very quick – if made with defrosted frozen peas, but it's also very good with fresh peas straight from the pod.

Defrosted frozen peas can be used just as they are, without cooking. If you are using home-grown peas, and they are really young, silky and sweet, you can use them raw. Larger or older fresh peas should be lightly blanched first: bring a pan of water to the boil, add the peas, bring back to a rolling boil, then drain the peas in a colander and run under the cold tap to cool them. Drain well.

Put the peas into a food processor with the coriander, tahini, garlic, lemon juice and some salt and pepper. Process to a coarse, bright green purée, stopping to scrape down the sides a couple of times. Taste the hummus and add more lemon, salt and/or pepper if needed. You could add a scrap more garlic too, if you like.

Transfer the hummus to a serving dish, trickle with extra virgin oil and sprinkle with sumac if you have some. A few pinched-out chive flowers or some snipped chive stems make a lovely finishing touch. Serve with more raw veg for dipping, or spoon alongside squash and chickpea patties (page 74) or curried potato rösti (page 378).

Swaps

Veg Use blanched, skinned broad beans in place of the peas – or try a mixture of the two.

Herbs Use the leaves from a bunch of mint instead of the coriander leaves – or try flat-leaf parsley. If you have them, you can throw in a few lovage too, for an extra layer of slightly spicy flavour.

Nutty, seedy, herby hummus

Serves 4

100g whole, skin-on almonds

100g mixed seeds, such as sunflower, pumpkin, sesame and linseed, plus extra to finish

100ml extra virgin olive, rapeseed or hempseed oil, plus extra to finish

Juice of ½ lemon

1 tsp English mustard (optional)

¼–½ garlic clove, finely grated or crushed (optional)

Sea salt and black pepper

2–3 tbsp mixed herbs, such as flat-leaf parsley, thyme, basil, chives, chervil (or a mixture), to finish

This is a big bowlful of goodness – a heap of soaked raw nuts and seeds, blitzed to a purée with plenty of lovely, cold-pressed oil and a little seasoning. Rich and filling, it has a nicely creamy texture – just the sort of thing to serve with veg dishes, cooked or raw, when you want to bring some proteinaceous presence to a meal. I also love it as a dip. Put the nuts and seeds to soak at least 3 hours before you want to make it.

Put the almonds and mixed seeds into a bowl and cover with plenty of cold water (they will swell and expand a little). Leave to soak in the fridge for at least 3 hours, up to 24.

Drain the nuts and seeds and tip them into a food processor. Add some salt and pepper then blitz until the nuts and seeds are well chopped. Now, with the motor running, gradually trickle in the extra virgin oil. Stop and scrape down the sides of the processor a few times to help everything amalgamate.

Add the lemon juice to the processor. Measure out 100ml cold water into a jug. Start the motor again and trickle in enough of the water to create a creamy but slightly textured purée; you probably won't need all of it.

You can eat the hummus just like this, but I like to season it a little further with the mustard and a scrap of grated garlic. Add these and blitz until thoroughly combined.

Scoop the hummus out into a serving bowl. Top it generously with herbs, another handful of seeds and a final swirl of oil, and tuck in.

Raw mushroom, walnut and parsley hummus

Serves 4–6

75g walnuts

200g very fresh chestnut mushrooms

A small bunch of flat-leaf parsley (about 25g), leaves picked from the stems

A scrap of garlic (about ¼ clove), finely grated or crushed, to taste

Juice of ½ lemon, or more to taste

Up to 100ml extra virgin olive oil

Sea salt and black pepper

This has a lovely, mild earthiness from the raw mushrooms. Serve it with raw carrots or celery, cucumber and slivers of apple for dipping, or dollop it next to a leafy salad or a pile of slivered, dressed fennel.

Put the walnuts into a food processor and blitz until coarsely chopped.

Add the raw mushrooms to the processor: if they are large, break them up with your hands as you put them in; small mushrooms can go in whole. Add the stalks as well, as long as they are clean. Blitz the mixture again to coarsely chop the mushrooms.

Scrape down the sides of the processor then add the parsley leaves, garlic, lemon juice and some salt and pepper. Blitz again, gradually trickling in the olive oil as you do so. Stop adding the oil when you have a thick, coarse purée, flecked with green from the parsley – you may not need the full 100ml oil.

Taste the hummus and add more lemon juice, salt and pepper if you think it needs it. You can add more garlic too but I like this best when it doesn't taste too strongly garlicky.

Swaps

Nuts For a slightly sweeter flavour, use whole, skin-on almonds, soaked for a couple of hours in cold water and drained, instead of the walnuts.
Herbs Replace some or all of the parsley with basil.

Raw carrot hummus

Serves 4

300g carrots, peeled, trimmed and cut into 5mm thick slices

2 tbsp tahini

2 tbsp extra virgin olive or rapeseed oil

1 tsp cumin seeds

A scrap of garlic (about ¼ clove), finely grated or crushed, to taste

A good squeeze of lemon juice, or more to taste

Sea salt and black pepper

This super-simple, blitzed-up mix has all the fresh, sweet flavour of raw carrot, with a touch of creaminess from the tahini and oil. Ramp up the raw factor by eating it with cucumber or celery sticks, or stuffed inside lettuce leaves – or alongside a dressed salad of lettuce and sugar snap peas.

Put the carrots into a food processor and blitz until finely chopped. You may need to stop and scrape down the sides of the processor a few times.

Add the tahini, oil, cumin seeds, garlic, a good squeeze of lemon juice and some salt and pepper. Blitz again until you have a coarse orange paste. Again, you'll have to stop and scrape down the sides of the processor several times, to ensure all the ingredients combine evenly.

Taste the hummus and add more salt, pepper and/or lemon juice as needed. Serve straight away or keep in a plastic tub in the fridge for a day or two.

Swaps

Roots Raw young beetroot make a lovely alternative to the carrot, and gives you a glorious purple hummus.

Spices Replace the cumin with coriander or fennel seeds for a subtly different character.

Roasted red pepper salsa

4–6 servings

4 medium red peppers (about 500g in total)

1 garlic bulb

2 tbsp olive or rapeseed oil

2 tsp harissa

Juice of ½ small lemon, or more to taste

Sea salt and black pepper

This is so easy and delicious. I use it in the same sort of way I would use an olive tapenade. It's the perfect, piquant counterpoint to a dish of starchy grains and roasted veg – including the smashed new potatoes on page 377. It's also delicious rippled into a hearty soup or a tomato sauce before serving, and lovely heated gently with a tin of butter beans and some chopped parsley.

Preheat the oven to 200°C/Fan 180°C/Gas 6.

Quarter the peppers and remove their stalks, seeds and white membranes. Put the pepper quarters on a large, non-stick baking tray (one with a lip to catch any juices).

Slice the top 1cm or so off the whole head of garlic (save this top bit to add to a stew or stock). Put the head of garlic, cut side up, on the tray with the peppers. Trickle the oil over the pepper quarters and garlic, making sure some of the oil gets right into the garlic. Use your hands to rub the oil all over the pepper quarters, then make sure they're all positioned skin side up.

Roast the peppers and garlic for about 35 minutes until the peppers are blistered and browned, but not completely blackened. Remove from the oven and leave to cool completely.

Remove the skin from the peppers (it should pull away easily), then put the soft peppers into a food processor. Squeeze the garlic bulb in your hand so the softened cloves pop out. Add these to the processor.

Use a rubber spatula to scrape any caramelised, oily, peppery juice from the roasting tray into the processor. Add the harissa, lemon juice and some salt and pepper. Blitz everything to a smooth, velvety red purée, stopping to scrape down the sides of the processor a few times.

Taste and add more salt or lemon juice if needed. Use straight away or refrigerate in a plastic tub for up to 5 days.

Seaweed tapenade

About 6 servings

20g dried seaweed, such as dulse

75g pitted kalamata olives (about 100g stone-in)

½–1 garlic clove, to taste, finely chopped

Finely grated zest of ½ lemon, plus a squeeze of lemon juice to taste

3 tbsp extra virgin olive or rapeseed oil

Sea salt and black pepper

With its combination of seaweed and olives, this intense condiment packs a real umami punch. It's fantastic with raw vegetables such as thinly sliced cauliflower, or a simple cucumber or tomato salad. I also like it dotted onto soups or stirred into hot roasted potatoes and served on peppery greens. Dulse is my favourite seaweed for this, but you can use other varieties – just soak and/or cook them as instructed on the packet, until tender and easily chopped.

Put the dried seaweed to soak in cold water for the time instructed on the packet (probably between 5 and 30 minutes), then drain and rinse it. (Some types of seaweed also need to be cooked before use – check the packet instructions.) Squeeze out all excess water with your hands. Check through the seaweed and remove any tough stalks or stems, then chop it roughly.

Put the seaweed into a food processor with the olives, garlic, lemon zest, oil, some black pepper and a good squeeze of lemon juice. Process the mixture, stopping several times to scrape down the sides, until you have a thick, coarse purée.

Taste the tapenade – you might want to add more lemon juice and black pepper, possibly even a little salt, though the olives and seaweed are already salty. Use straight away or refrigerate in a plastic tub for up to 5 days. Serve trickled with a little more oil if you like.

Asparagus with spring onion dressing

Serves 4

About 250g asparagus

FOR THE DRESSING

2 tbsp chopped flat-leaf parsley

1 tsp sumac

2 tsp capers, rinsed, drained and roughly chopped

Finely grated zest of ½ lemon, plus a squeeze of juice to taste

1 tsp English mustard

4 spring onions, trimmed and thinly sliced

2 tbsp extra virgin olive oil

Sea salt and black pepper

The punchy dressing is spiked with sumac, a Middle Eastern spice with a deliciously lemony flavour. It's great for dressing all kinds of crunchy summer veg – either raw or lightly blanched (see the swaps below).

Bring a large pan of water to the boil. Snap the woody ends off the asparagus stems (they should naturally break at the point where they become woody). Drop the asparagus into the boiling water and simmer for about 3 minutes, until just tender. If you have very slender, fresh asparagus, it will only need 1–2 minutes.

Meanwhile, for the dressing, combine the parsley, sumac, capers, lemon zest, mustard, spring onions and olive oil. Season with a squeeze of lemon juice, some pepper and a little salt (the capers will add salt). Stir well.

When the asparagus is cooked, and before you drain it, take 3–4 tsp of the cooking water and add to the dressing to loosen it a little.

Drain the asparagus and place it in a warmed dish. Spoon over the dressing and serve.

Swaps

Veg Instead of asparagus, serve the dressing with steamed purple sprouting broccoli, lightly cooked green beans, roasted baby carrots, raw radishes etc…

Spices If you don't have any sumac to hand, replace with 1 tsp sweet smoked paprika.

Globe artichokes with orange and paprika dressing

Serves 4

2 large globe artichokes

FOR THE ORANGE AND PAPRIKA DRESSING

Finely grated zest and juice of 1 large orange

3 tbsp extra virgin olive oil

½ garlic clove, finely grated or crushed

1 tsp sweet smoked paprika

2 tbsp finely chopped flat-leaf parsley

A pinch of sugar

Sea salt and black pepper

At their best in early summer, globe artichokes are delectable, but notoriously time-consuming to prepare. However, this way of cooking them bypasses most of the faff! The artichokes are simply boiled whole, then halved, and the furry 'choke' removed. Each diner then dismantles their own artichoke while they eat.

Trim the artichoke stalks to a 2–3cm length. Put the artichokes into a very large pan and cover with cold water. Bring to the boil then simmer until you can easily press the tip of a sharp knife into the base of the artichoke, between the top of the stem and the base of the leaves – this can be anything between 20 and 45 minutes.

When the artichokes are done, use tongs to lift them out of the pan, holding them upside down for a moment so water can drain out from between the leaves. Set aside until they're just cool enough to handle.

Meanwhile, put all the dressing ingredients into a small saucepan, season with salt and pepper and heat very gently, stirring for a couple of minutes, just to get the flavours mingling nicely. Set aside.

When the artichokes have cooled a little but are still warm, use a very sharp knife to halve each one down through the centre. Now use the tip of a small, sharp knife or a teaspoon to remove the fibrous 'choke' at the centre of each artichoke half. Make sure you remove all the little fibrous bits, leaving you with a hollow at the centre of each artichoke.

Place the artichoke halves on a serving dish and spoon some of the orangey dressing into each hollow.

To eat, pull the leaves from the artichokes, one at a time, dunking their fleshy bases into the orangey dressing, then use your teeth to nibble and scrape that delicious fleshy morsel away from the tough upper leaf (discard these). When you've pulled away all the leaves and nibbled their bases, you'll be left with the tender heart of the artichoke – the very best bit. Pick it up with your fingers and devour.

Swaps

Veg Instead of artichokes, serve the aromatic dressing with boiled new potatoes, blanched broccoli or cauliflower, or wilted spring greens.
Citrus Replace the orange with lemon, using the grated zest of the whole lemon and half of its juice.

PSB with leafy PSB salsa verde

Serves 4

500g very fresh purple sprouting broccoli

¼–½ garlic clove, chopped, to taste

1 tbsp capers

A squeeze of lemon juice, or more to taste

¼ tsp English mustard, or more to taste

A pinch of sugar

4 tbsp extra virgin olive oil

Sea salt and black pepper

Salsa verde – a piquant, herby sauce typically made with parsley – is fantastic with purple sprouting broccoli. In this recipe, I have used the raw leaves from the PSB itself to form the herb element of the salsa.

Pick a generous handful of leaves off the purple sprouting broccoli stalks and chop them finely. (Leafiness varies a lot, but unless your PSB is light on leaves you won't need to pick off all of them.)

Add the garlic and the capers to the pile of chopped broccoli leaf and continue to chop, scraping and mixing the ingredients together as you go until they are all finely chopped and combined. Transfer to a bowl.

Add the lemon juice, mustard, sugar and some salt and pepper to the leafy mix and stir thoroughly together, then add the olive oil and mix well. Taste the salsa verde and add a little more salt, pepper, sugar, mustard and/or lemon juice, to taste. Set aside.

Bring a large pan of salted water to the boil. Snap or cut off the ends of the PSB stalks where they become fibrous. Drop the PSB into the pan of salted water and cook briefly, until just tender. Just 2 minutes will probably do – you don't want it to be soft or soggy. Drain it well.

Tip the PSB into a warmed serving bowl, spoon over the salsa verde and serve straight away.

Swaps

Leaves If you prefer to leave your PSB fully leafed, use parsley, or a mixture of parsley and baby spinach leaves, to create a more conventional salsa verde.

Green new potatoes

Serves 4–6

750g new potatoes

About 100g baby spinach leaves

A bunch of flat-leaf parsley (about 50g), leaves picked from the stems

50g pumpkin seeds, ideally lightly toasted

½ garlic clove, finely chopped

Juice of ½ lemon, or to taste

Up to 100ml extra virgin olive oil

Sea salt and black pepper

Hot little new potatoes are fantastic tossed with this lovely raw sauce – essentially a kind of spinach pesto.

If the potatoes are bigger than walnut-sized, cut them up into even-sized pieces. Place in a saucepan, cover with cold water and add salt. Bring to the boil then simmer for 12–15 minutes, until tender. Drain, return the potatoes to the pan and keep warm.

Put the spinach into a food processor and add the parsley, pumpkin seeds, garlic and some salt and pepper. Blitz until everything is well chopped. Add the lemon juice then, with the motor running, start trickling in the olive oil. Keep going until everything is thoroughly combined into a thick, coarse green purée. You may not need the full 100ml oil. Taste the sauce and add more salt, pepper or lemon juice if needed.

Spoon the green sauce over the hot, boiled new potatoes and toss gently together. Transfer to a serving dish and serve straight away, with a final trickle of oil if you like.

Swaps

Leaves If you don't have really fresh baby spinach, use about 250g larger leaf spinach. Blanch it in boiling water, drain and then squeeze out excess water with your hands before putting it into the processor. In late spring, you can replace the spinach with nettles, picking the top few leaves only of each plant, and blanching them to get rid of their sting. For an even wilder sauce, add a few wild garlic leaves too (leaving out the chopped garlic).

Herbs For a more conventional pesto, lose the spinach and double up the quantity of parsley – or use half and half basil and parsley.

Seeds Replace the pumpkin seeds with walnuts or pine nuts.

Starch If you don't fancy potatoes, the green sauce is also very good stirred through freshly cooked pearled spelt (or barley).

New potatoes, peas and spring onions

Serves 4

200g freshly podded small peas (about 500g in the pod), or frozen petits pois

500g new potatoes

3 tbsp olive oil

200g spring onions, trimmed and sliced

1 small garlic clove, finely chopped

Lemon juice, to taste

Sea salt and black pepper

Chives (and/or chive flowers), to finish

In this simple but lovely dish, the cooking juices from gently sweated spring onions and peas form a light sauce with which to bathe some lovely summer spuds.

If you're using frozen petits pois, put them into a sieve and pour about half a kettle of boiling water over them so they start to defrost. Set aside while you prepare the potatoes.

If the potatoes are bigger than walnut-sized, cut them up into even-sized pieces. Place in a saucepan, cover with cold water and add salt. Bring to the boil, then simmer for 12–15 minutes until tender.

Meanwhile, heat the olive oil in a small-medium frying pan or wide saucepan over a medium heat. Add the spring onions, garlic and a pinch each of salt and pepper. When the onions are sizzling, cover the pan, reduce the heat and let them sweat for about 5 minutes.

Add the fresh or frozen peas to the pan, cover again and sweat for another 7 minutes or so, until the spring onions and peas are tender.

Scoop about 3 tbsp water from the simmering pan of potatoes and add it to the pan of peas and onions. Stir well and cook gently for a minute or two, then take off the heat. Add a good squeeze of lemon juice. Taste the onion and pea mixture and add more salt if needed.

When the new potatoes are tender, drain them and transfer to a warmed serving dish. Spoon the spring onions, peas and all their cooking juices over the potatoes. Snip some chives (or chive flowers) over the top and serve straight away.

Swaps

Spuds Enjoy this simple combination later in the year with waxy salad potatoes, such as Pink Fir Apple or Charlotte.

Peas Replace the peas with baby broad beans or, later in the year, use finely shredded greens or cabbage.

Alliums Use leeks, finely sliced, in place of the spring onions.

Asparagus and carrots with lemon and parsley

Serves 3–4

10–12 slender spears of asparagus (about 250g)

10–12 slender baby carrots (about 150g)

1 tbsp olive or rapeseed oil

1 garlic clove, finely chopped

A trickle of extra virgin olive or rapeseed oil

A large sprig of thyme, leaves picked from the stems and finely chopped

A handful of flat-leaf parsley leaves, finely chopped

Finely grated zest of 1 lemon

Flaky sea salt and black pepper

The first baby carrots of the year come good in late May or June. They're delicious with beautiful British asparagus in this very easy, lightly cooked dish.

Wash the asparagus to get rid of any grit caught in the tips, then snap off the ends of the stalks (they will naturally break at the point where they become woody). If the baby carrots are more than 1cm diameter, slice them in half lengthways.

Heat the 1 tbsp olive or rapeseed oil in a large frying pan over a medium-high heat. When hot, add the asparagus spears and baby carrots with a sprinkling of salt and pepper. Cook fairly briskly for about 8 minutes, tossing the veg in the pan now and then, until the asparagus is tender but not soft, the carrots are just tender, and both have some patches of golden brown colour.

Add the chopped garlic and cook it with the veg for another minute to take the raw edge off it, then remove the pan from the heat.

Trickle over a little extra virgin oil, scatter over the chopped herbs, lemon zest and a pinch of flaky salt and give the pan a shake to distribute the seasonings over the veg. Transfer to serving dishes or just take the pan to the table and tuck in as soon as the veg is cool enough to pick up.

Stir-fried shredded Szechuan greens

Serves 2–3

1 large head or 2 smaller heads of spring greens (about 250g in total)

A good pinch of flaky sea salt

1 tsp Szechuan peppercorns

1 tsp sugar

2 tbsp rapeseed oil

2 garlic cloves, finely chopped

Szechuan pepper, which is a spicy berry unrelated to familiar black peppercorns, has a unique, tingling, fragrant heat. Combined with a pinch of sugar and salt, it turns wilted greens into a little dish so tempting that I usually find myself eating it straight out of the wok.

Trim off the very end of the spring greens stalk, then lay the head of spring greens on its side and shred the entire thing, stalks and all, cutting it 5–10mm thick.

Using a pestle and mortar, pound the salt, Szechuan peppercorns and sugar until finely ground.

Heat the oil in a large wok over a high heat. When hot, add the greens (take care because they will spit, unless they are completely dry). Stir-fry for about 4 minutes, keeping the heat high, until the greens are wilted and look dark and glossy.

Add the Szechuan pepper mix and the garlic and stir-fry for another minute or so, then serve.

Swaps

Leaves Use shredded Savoy cabbage or spring cabbage in place of the spring greens.

Spices If you don't have Szechuan pepper, try a pinch of dried chilli flakes and/or ½ tsp Chinese five-spice powder instead.

Lemony samphire and peas

Serves 4

About 200g marsh samphire

3 tbsp extra virgin olive or rapeseed oil

1–2 tbsp lemon juice

200g freshly podded small peas (about 500g in the pod), or frozen petits pois

1–2 tbsp coarsely chopped flat-leaf parsley

Sea salt and black pepper

Salty, succulent marsh samphire is at its best during June and July, which is just when fresh peas are at their peak. The two ingredients pair beautifully, as this simple dish demonstrates. When you are shopping, ask for British samphire, as it's often imported, even in season. Alternatively, you may be able to forage for it yourself if you're at the coast, near muddy tidal estuaries.

Prepare the samphire by washing it thoroughly and trimming away any coarse stems. Chop or break it into short lengths.

Combine the extra virgin oil and 1 tbsp lemon juice in a medium bowl. Add a small pinch of salt (the samphire is naturally salty) and some black pepper. Whisk together and set aside.

Bring a large saucepan of water to the boil (don't add salt), then tip in the samphire and peas. Begin timing as soon as you add the veg to the water, before it's returned to the boil. After 2 minutes, check a piece of samphire. If it is tender, drain the whole panful of veg into a colander. If not, cook for a minute more, then test again, erring on the side of caution. You don't want the samphire to overcook.

Leave the samphire and peas to drain and cool just for a minute or two, then tip the hot veg into the bowl with the dressing and toss together. Taste and add more salt, pepper and/or lemon juice if needed.

Transfer to a serving bowl and scatter over the parsley. If you come across any fibrous bits of samphire, just tease the tender flesh off the central fibre with your teeth.

Swaps

Peas Baby broad beans are excellent in place of the peas.
Herbs Snipped chives – and a few tiny chive flowers if you happen to have them – are a lovely alternative to parsley.

Greens with sesame and seaweed

Serves 4

2 tbsp sesame seeds

3 tbsp 'sea salad' (ready-to-eat mixed, flaked, dried seaweed)

About 400g spring greens

Sea salt

FOR THE DRESSING

2 tbsp tamari

2 tbsp cider vinegar

1 tsp freshly grated ginger

1 tbsp toasted sesame oil

1 tsp sugar

This is packed with flavour: barely-cooked greens in a rich, tangy tamari-and-ginger dressing, finished with a generous sprinkling of savoury sesame and seaweed. A prepared 'sea salad' mix (available from cornishseaweed.co.uk or clearspring.co.uk) works well here.

Put the sesame seeds and sea salad into a large, dry frying pan and toast them over a medium heat for 2–3 minutes, tossing often, until the sesame seeds are golden. Tip into a bowl.

For the dressing, put all the ingredients into a jug and whisk well to combine, making sure the sugar is dissolved.

Bring a large pan of water to the boil and add some salt. Discard the very thick base of the spring greens, then slice the leaves across into roughly 1cm strips, including the stalks. Drop the sliced greens into the boiling water. Let it come back to a full, rolling boil, which should only take a minute or two, then take the pan off the heat.

Drain the greens in a colander then run them immediately under the cold tap to cool them down and stop any further cooking. Leave to drain for a few minutes, then take handfuls of the greens and squeeze out excess water with your hands, before scattering them over a large serving plate.

Give the dressing another whisk then trickle it over the spring greens, distributing it as evenly as possible. Scatter the toasted sesame and seaweed over the greens and serve.

Swaps

Leaves Use Savoy cabbage, kale or a pointed spring cabbage (hispi) instead of spring greens. Calabrese and purple sprouting broccoli are also great with this dressing.
Seeds Try sunflower seeds in place of sesame seeds.

Courgettes with fresh tomato sauce

Serves 3–4

500g large, ripe, juicy tomatoes

400g small-medium courgettes

1 tbsp olive or rapeseed oil

1 garlic clove, thinly sliced

1 tbsp ribboned basil leaves

Sea salt and black pepper

Extra virgin olive oil, to serve

This is like a very simple version of ratatouille and I like it best served just warm or at room temperature. It's delicious with smashed new potatoes with coriander seeds and bay (page 377).

Cut the tomatoes in half around the 'equator'. Using a box grater placed in a large bowl, grate the flesh side of the tomatoes, so that the juice and pulp goes into the bowl and you end up with only the skin of the tomato still in your hand. Set the tomato pulp aside.

Top and tail the courgettes, then cut into chunky slices, 8–10mm thick.

Heat the 1 tbsp olive or rapeseed oil in a large frying pan over a medium heat. When hot, add the courgettes and a sprinkling of salt and pepper. Cook briskly, tossing or stirring the courgettes often, for 8–10 minutes, or until they are well browned and just tender but not soft. Add the garlic for the last minute or so of cooking.

Add the tomato pulp to the pan and stir well. Simmer for 5–10 minutes until the tomato juice is reduced to a loose sauce consistency – you don't want to cook the tomatoes too long, but neither should the courgettes be swimming in liquid.

Remove from the heat and leave to cool a little – or down to room temperature; either is good. Just before serving, stir in the basil. Taste and add more salt and/or pepper if needed, then trickle with extra virgin olive oil and serve.

Swaps

Veg Replace the courgettes with aubergine – cut into roughly 2cm cubes and fry until golden brown before adding the juicy tomato pulp. Mushrooms also work well. And, to any of these veg, you can add a handful of spinach – wilt in the pan towards the end of cooking.

Aubergine and courgettes with rosemary and fennel seeds

Serves 4

1 medium-large aubergine (about 300g)

2 medium courgettes (about 300g in total)

2 tbsp olive or rapeseed oil

1 tbsp chopped rosemary

A pinch of dried chilli flakes

1 tsp fennel seeds

A squeeze of lemon juice, to taste

2 tbsp extra virgin olive oil

Sea salt and black pepper

These aromatic fried vine veg are delicious as part of a summer tapas spread. You can prepare this dish well in advance and keep it in the fridge, but bring it to room temperature before serving.

Trim the ends off the aubergine and courgettes then cut into roughly 2cm cubes.

Heat the olive or rapeseed oil in a large, non-stick frying pan (ideally about 30cm in diameter) over a medium-high heat. When it is hot, add the cubed aubergine and courgettes with some salt and pepper and fry hard for 8–10 minutes. You need to drive off any water released by the veg, so keep the heat quite high. You also want them to take on some good, golden brown colour so don't move them around too often – give them a chance to brown.

Meanwhile, using a pestle and mortar, pound the rosemary, chilli flakes and fennel seeds, to help release the flavour of the rosemary and break up the spices a bit.

When the veg are cooked, take the pan off the heat. Add the fennel and rosemary mix and stir well, then leave to cool completely.

When cold, stir in a good squeeze of lemon juice and the extra virgin olive oil. Taste and add more salt, pepper and/or lemon juice if needed, and it's ready to serve.

Swaps

Veg Replace either the courgette or aubergine with chopped red pepper or chopped fennel.
Herbs A handful of shredded basil is delicious in place of the rosemary – don't pound this in the mortar, but add it once the veg are cool.
Spices Try using coriander seeds instead of fennel.

Burnt beans with sesame seeds and miso dressing

Serves 4

1 tbsp sesame seeds

400g fine green beans, stalk ends trimmed

½ tbsp rapeseed oil

Sea salt and black pepper

FOR THE DRESSING

2 tbsp white miso paste or shiro miso paste (see page 270)

2 tbsp rapeseed oil

1 tbsp rice vinegar (or you can use cider vinegar)

1 tsp freshly grated ginger

Green beans, like so many vegetables, reveal new charms when charred. Throw them on a barbie, under a hot grill or in a pan and they become tender, browned and smoky-sweet, ready to take on a great dressing like this one, which is based on savoury miso paste.

Put the sesame seeds in a frying pan and toast them over a medium heat for a few minutes until golden, tossing often to prevent burning. Tip onto a plate and set aside.

If you are barbecuing the beans, make sure the barbecue is hot and ready for cooking. Otherwise, preheat your grill to high or heat a frying pan. Put the beans into a large bowl, add the ½ tbsp oil and some salt and pepper and toss well to coat.

Transfer the beans to the barbecue, a foil-lined grill tray under the grill or the hot pan. Cook for 5–10 minutes, moving and turning the beans from time to time, until tender and coloured dark brown in places – even a little blackened here and there. In the frying pan, they may take a little longer.

Meanwhile, to make the dressing, whisk all the ingredients together thoroughly in a bowl.

Tip the beans into a serving dish or individual bowls, spoon on the miso dressing and scatter over the toasted sesame seeds. Eat hot or at room temperature. The beans are very good with roasted tofu (page 369) and plain rice if you want to turn them into a meal.

Swaps

Veg This miso dressing is also very good on steamed mangetout or purple sprouting broccoli, seared cauliflower or cabbage (as in the recipes on pages 170 and 34 respectively) or roasted carrots.
Seeds Use sunflower seeds rather than sesame seeds.

Baked green beans with olives

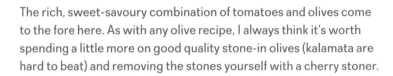

Serves 4

2 x 400g tins tomatoes

2 garlic cloves, sliced

1 tbsp olive oil

500g green beans, stalk ends trimmed

75g pitted black olives, such as kalamata (about 100g stone-in), very roughly chopped

Sea salt and black pepper

The rich, sweet-savoury combination of tomatoes and olives come to the fore here. As with any olive recipe, I always think it's worth spending a little more on good quality stone-in olives (kalamata are hard to beat) and removing the stones yourself with a cherry stoner.

Preheat the oven to 190°C/Fan 170°C/Gas 5.

Open the tins of tomatoes and tip them into a smallish roasting tray. Roughly crush the tomatoes with your hands, removing any white stalky ends as you go. Add the sliced garlic and stir in the olive oil with some salt and pepper. Cook in the oven for 20 minutes until reduced down to a thick sauce.

Take the tomatoes from the oven, stir them around well, then add the beans. Fold them over in the tomato sauce then return to the oven and roast for another 20–30 minutes or until the beans are tender.

Stir in the olives and serve, hot or at room temperature.

Swaps

Veg Instead of green beans, use purple sprouting broccoli. If the stalks are thicker than 1cm, split them lengthways to speed cooking. You can also use cauliflower, broken into small (walnut-sized) florets.

Cucumber with caramelised cashews

Serves 4

1 tbsp coconut oil

1 tsp tamari

2 medium cucumbers (about 400g each)

2 tbsp rice vinegar (or you can use cider vinegar)

½ tsp sugar

A large handful of coriander, mint or Thai basil leaves (or a mixture), roughly torn

A squeeze of lime juice, to taste

Sea salt and black pepper

FOR THE SPICY CASHEW MIX

100g cashew nuts

6 spring onions, or 1 echalion (banana) shallot, trimmed and roughly sliced or chopped

2 lemongrass stems, tough outer layers removed, finely sliced

2 garlic cloves, roughly chopped

1 heaped tsp freshly grated ginger

1 hot green chilli, such as bird's eye (deseeded for less heat, if preferred), chopped

Finely grated zest of 1 lime

1 tsp sugar

This is full of intense, Thai-inspired flavours. The fragrant cashew mix, once fried and seasoned, takes on a very satisfying, savoury quality. As well as making a great tapas dish, this is very good as a prelude to, or alongside, other dishes with a Southeast Asian feel, such as the summer veg coconut curry on page 68.

To prepare the spicy cashew mix, put all the ingredients into a food processor with a pinch of salt. Process to a coarse paste – it should be quite sticky and thick but with some bits of nut still visible.

Heat the coconut oil in a large non-stick frying pan over a medium-high heat. When hot, add the cashew mix and fry for about 5 minutes, turning almost constantly. The underside browns quickly in the hot pan, so keep turning and tossing until most of the mixture has some nice brown colour but nothing is burnt. Take the pan off the heat, stir in the 1 tsp tamari and set aside while you prepare the cucumber.

Trim the ends off each cucumber, then quarter lengthways and scoop out the seeds (see page 255 for a use for these). Cut each length of cucumber into 5–10mm slices and put into a large bowl. Add the vinegar, sugar and a pinch each of salt and pepper. Mix gently.

When the cashew mix is cool, stir most of the herb leaves into it. Spoon the dressed cucumber onto a serving plate and scatter the cashew mix on top. Squeeze over some lime juice, sprinkle on the remaining herbs and serve.

Swaps

Veg As an alternative to cucumber, the cashew mix is delicious heaped on to small lettuce leaves – with a little chopped avocado too if you like.

Seared lettuce and plums

Serves 3–4

1 garlic clove, finely chopped

1 tsp freshly grated ginger

1 medium-hot green or red chilli, deseeded and sliced

1–2 tsp sugar, to taste

1 tbsp tamari

1 tbsp rapeseed oil

2 little gem lettuces, quartered

4 ripe, sweet plums, such as Victorias (about 225g in total), quartered, stones removed

A squeeze of lime juice, to taste

Sea salt and black pepper

This is a lovely quick dish. The sweet-tart plum juices form a sticky, fruity sauce with the tamari and sugar. Use ripe, sweet plums – Victorias in late August are ideal. If your plums are under-ripe and/or very tart, add a little more sugar and go easy on the lime.

In a small bowl, whisk together the garlic, ginger, chilli, sugar, tamari and 1 tbsp water. Set aside.

Heat the oil in a large non-stick pan, or a wok, over a medium-high heat. Add the lettuce quarters with some salt and pepper and cook, turning often, for 8–10 minutes until softened and well coloured on all surfaces.

Add the quartered plums and cook for a further 3–4 minutes, tossing the fruit and lettuce together now and then, until the plums start to soften and release their juices. Add the tamari mixture and toss it with the plums and lettuce. Cook for a minute or two longer, to lose the rawness from the garlic.

Take the pan off the heat and squeeze over a little lime juice – not too much, as the plums already have a natural tartness. Serve straight away with a bowlful of rice and perhaps some roasted tofu (page 369).

Swaps

Leaves Use a large head of romaine or butterhead lettuce instead of the little gems.

Fruit Gooseberries, halved apricots and stoned cherries are all good alternatives to the plums.

Sautéed Waldorf salad

Serves 2

4–5 tender inner stems of celery, plus a few celery leaves

1 tbsp olive or rapeseed oil

1 medium-large eating apple

1 garlic clove, finely chopped

50g walnuts, roughly broken up

Finely grated zest of ½ lemon, plus a squeeze of juice

Sea salt and black pepper

This is the second dish in the book inspired by the ingredients of a classic Waldorf salad (though cooked here, rather than raw). This tasty autumnal sauté makes a nice little starter, or, alongside one of the spud or grain dishes in the next chapter, a good supper.

Cut the celery stems into 5mm–1cm thick slices.

Heat the oil in large frying pan over a medium-high heat. Add the celery with some salt and pepper and fry 'hard', tossing now and again, for about 10 minutes, until the celery is starting to colour. Meanwhile, quarter, core and chop the apple into 1–2cm cubes.

Add the apple, garlic and walnuts to the pan and cook for a further 5 minutes or so, keeping the heat high and tossing the ingredients often – you want everything to colour a little. Add the lemon zest and cook for a couple of minutes more.

Take the pan off the heat and stir in a good squeeze of lemon juice. Taste and add more salt and pepper if needed. Roughly chop a few celery leaves and scatter over the sauté before serving.

Swaps

Veg Replace the celery with a small fennel bulb.
Fruit Try using a firm, slightly under-ripe pear in place of the apple.
Nuts Swap bashed hazelnuts or pecans for the walnuts.

Baked mushrooms with kale and walnuts

Serves 4

3 tbsp olive oil

2 garlic cloves, chopped

1 medium-hot red chilli, deseeded and chopped, or a pinch of dried chilli flakes

4 large, open cap mushrooms (at least 8cm across)

100g kale or cavolo nero

About 1 tsp thyme leaves

50g walnuts, broken up or very roughly chopped

Sea salt and black pepper

It's hard to resist a big, baked mushroom, seasoned with lots of garlic and bubbling with its own juices. In this dish, those savoury juices soak into wilted kale, spiked with chilli and thyme. The earthy bite of a few walnuts finishes it off perfectly.

Preheat the oven to 190°C/Fan 170°C/Gas 5.

Put the olive oil, garlic and chilli into a small saucepan and heat briefly for a couple of minutes, just until the garlic is 'fizzing' in the oil. Take it off the heat before the garlic colours.

Place the mushrooms (no need to remove the stalks), gill-side up, in a small roasting tin. Brush about half of the garlic- and chilli-infused oil over the mushrooms, making sure each gets some of the garlic and chilli too. Season the mushrooms with salt and pepper and bake in the oven for 15 minutes.

Meanwhile, bring a pan of water to the boil. Tear the kale leaves off their central stalks. When the water is boiling, add the kale leaves and cook until just tender but not soft; 3 or 4 minutes should do it but some varieties of kale may take a little longer. When it is done, drain the kale in a colander for a few minutes, then use a pair of tongs to squeeze out excess water before transferring it to a board. Roughly chop the kale then put it into a bowl with the remaining garlic and chilli oil, the thyme and some salt and pepper. Mix well.

Take the mushrooms from the oven. Heap some of the kale mixture on top of each one (don't worry if a few bits of kale fall off into the roasting tin). Dot the broken bits of walnut over the kale. Return to the oven for 10–15 minutes, until everything is bubbling and the kale is dark and crisp on top.

Give the baked mushrooms a sprinkle more salt and pepper and serve straight away, with rice, or with mashed or fried potatoes – allow two each for a good meal, one for a lighter snack. Make sure you include any juices from the roasting dish too.

Swaps

Greens Replace the kale with other greens, such as spring greens, chard or spinach. Remove the stalks from greens or chard before cooking (see page 354 for a tasty way to use chard stalks).

Trio of alliums with roasted roots

In this simple dish, the three great alliums – onions, leeks and garlic – are sweated down gently with aromatic herbs until sweet and soft. The mix is delicious on roasted potatoes and celeriac, as it is served here, but also very good with herby spelt and lentils (page 394).

Preheat the oven to 190°C/Fan 170°C/Gas 5.

Cut the potatoes and celeriac into large bite-sized pieces and place in a roasting tray. Season with salt and pepper and trickle over 1 tbsp oil. Stir well. Roast for about an hour, until tender and nicely coloured, giving them a good stir halfway through.

Heat 2 tbsp oil in a large saucepan or a flameproof casserole, over a medium heat. Add the onions and a good pinch each of salt and pepper. Once the onions are sizzling gently, reduce the heat and cover the pan. Cook for about 10 minutes, stirring once or twice.

Add the leeks to the sweating onions, along with the garlic and thyme or rosemary sprigs. Cook the mixture gently for about 20 minutes. It's important to keep the heat quite low, so nothing browns or colours, and to keep the lid on – the steamy atmosphere keeps the veg tender, pale and sweet. Just take off the lid to stir the veg every few minutes or so. The veg are ready when they are silky soft and no longer crunchy or 'squeaky' between the teeth. Remove from the heat.

Add the roasted veg to the three-allium mix and toss together gently. Taste and add a little more salt and/or pepper if needed, then serve.

Serves 4

350–400g potatoes (any kind), scrubbed but not peeled

350–400g celeriac, peeled

3 tbsp olive or rapeseed oil

3 medium onions (about 250g in total), chopped

4 medium leeks (about 600g in total), trimmed, well washed and cut into 1cm thick slices

2 garlic cloves, sliced

A couple of sprigs of thyme or rosemary

Sea salt and black pepper

Baked celery agrodolce

Serves 4

2 heads of celery (about 600g each)

1 tbsp olive oil

1 garlic clove, sliced

1 medium-hot green chilli, deseeded and chopped

3 tbsp dry white wine or water

Sea salt and black pepper

2 tbsp chopped flat-leaf parsley, to finish

FOR THE AGRODOLCE DRESSING

1 large (or 2 small) shallot(s), finely chopped

1 tbsp capers, rinsed, drained and roughly chopped if large

2 tbsp raisins

2 tbsp balsamic vinegar

1 tbsp olive oil

1 tbsp sugar

Celery, baked until it is really tender and developing delicious, browned edges, then dressed in a sweet-sour 'agrodolce' mix, is rich, intense, sweet and tangy – almost like a relish.

Preheat the oven to 180°C/Fan 160°C/Gas 4.

Remove the coarse outer 3 or 4 stems from the heads of celery (you can use these for stock or the pickle recipe on page 354). Trim the very end of the celery root, then rinse the celery stems well under the cold tap to get rid of any earth or grit. Chop the stems, including all the leafy bits, into roughly 5–6cm lengths.

Put the chopped celery into a large roasting tin and add the olive oil, garlic, chilli and some salt and pepper. Toss together, then trickle the wine or water over the celery. Cover the dish tightly with foil (or a lid, if the dish has one). Bake in the oven for 45 minutes–1 hour, until the celery is completely tender and yielding to the tip of a knife, and browning a little in places.

In the meantime, for the agrodolce dressing, mix all the ingredients together in a small bowl and season with salt and pepper.

Spoon the agrodolce dressing all over the hot celery and stir well. Return the roasting tin to the oven, uncovered, for 10 minutes, then take it out and leave to cool to room temperature.

Taste and add a little more salt, pepper or balsamic vinegar if you like. Sprinkle over the chopped parsley before serving. This is very good with things that soak up its tasty juices: a green salad, crushed potatoes or herby spelt and lentils (page 394), for instance.

Swaps
Veg In place of the celery, use 3–4 fennel bulbs, cut into slim wedges.

Quick-pickled celery, chard and carrots

Makes a 500ml jar

400g mixed, prepared celery, chard stalks and carrot (see right)

1 tbsp fine salt

250ml cider vinegar (5% acidity)

2 tbsp sugar

1 bay leaf

A couple of sprigs of thyme or rosemary

1 tsp coriander seeds

A few black peppercorns

This is a very tasty way to ensure the more fibrous outer stems from a bunch of celery don't go to waste; likewise, the stems from a bunch of chard. I also add some carrot to the mix for sweetness and colour – but you can use just one or two of these veg, as long as it makes up the 400g raw weight.

Make sure the chard stems and celery are trimmed of any green leaves and dirty or damaged bits, then cut into roughly 1cm dice. Carrots should be peeled, trimmed then cut into thin half-moons or quarter-moons, depending on the girth of the carrot. Check that you have 400g prepared weight of raw veg.

Put the prepared veg into a bowl, add the salt and mix well, then transfer to a sieve or fine colander placed over a bowl. Leave for about half an hour. You'll see that the salt draws quite a lot of liquid out of the veg; it seasons it too, of course.

Meanwhile, thoroughly wash and dry a 500ml capacity Kilner or Le Parfait-type jar, or a robust jam jar with a vinegar-proof lid.

Pack the salted veg into the jar (don't rinse the veg first, but do discard the salty liquid in the bowl).

Put the cider vinegar, sugar, herbs, coriander seeds and peppercorns into a small saucepan. Bring to the boil and let bubble for 2 minutes. Immediately pour the pickling liquor over the veg in the jar, keeping the herbs out, but making sure the coriander seeds and peppercorns go into the jar. The veg must be completely submerged in the vinegar.

Seal the jar straight away and leave to cool completely.

Store in the fridge for at least a week before opening, then use within 10 weeks (keeping the jar in the fridge). It is delicious served with celeriac and seaweed bubble and squeak (page 387), tartare hash (page 388) or Berber barley (page 396).

Swaps

Veg You can happily include a small rhubarb stalk in this mix.

Wine-baked mushrooms

Serves 3–4

1kg mushrooms, cut into 5–10mm thick slices

3 garlic cloves, thickly sliced

A couple of bay leaves, torn

A few sprigs of thyme

3 tbsp olive oil

250ml red wine

1 tsp sugar

50g pitted kalamata olives (about 70g stone-in), roughly chopped (optional)

Sea salt and black pepper

You can use almost any kind of mushroom here, but large chestnut mushrooms or open cap varieties work best. The mushrooms absorb all the red wine and herby flavours as they cook, becoming tender and deliciously rich.

Preheat the oven to 190°C/Fan 170°C/Gas 5.

Put the mushrooms into a fairly large roasting dish. Add the garlic, herbs, olive oil, red wine and sugar, season with salt and pepper and stir well.

Bake in the oven for about 50 minutes, stirring a couple of times during cooking, until the winey liquor has almost completely disappeared and the mushrooms are tender and rich. Stir in the olives if using, check the seasoning and it's ready to serve.

This is delicious with brown rice with onions (page 400), or a dollop of split pea purée (see page 80), or both.

Swaps

Wine Use white wine instead of red for a slightly lighter finish.
Herbs Leave out the bay and thyme. Instead, add a cinnamon stick, snapped in half, and a pinch of dried chilli flakes with the wine.

Squash mash

Serves 4

1kg squash, such as a butternut or Crown Prince

1 tbsp olive or rapeseed oil

2 garlic cloves, chopped

3 tbsp crunchy, no-sugar-added peanut butter

Sea salt and black pepper

This lovely mash is enriched with peanut butter. If I'm serving it with something simple, such as roasted veg or steamed greens, I like to trickle it with chilli oil (made by infusing 2 tbsp olive or rapeseed oil in a small pan with 2 sliced hot chillies and some salt and pepper).

Halve the squash, peel it and scoop out the seeds. Cut the squash flesh into slices, about 2cm thick, then cut each slice into large chunks. Put the chopped squash into a large saucepan or small stockpot. Cover with water, add salt and bring to the boil. Reduce the heat and simmer for about 15 minutes, until the squash is completely tender. Tip the squash into a colander and leave it to steam for a few minutes.

While the squash is steaming off, heat the oil in the same pan you used to cook the squash, over a medium-low heat. Add the garlic and let it sizzle gently for a few minutes until it is just starting to colour. Add the peanut butter and, as it 'melts', stir it into the garlicky oil. Brands of peanut butter vary a lot in their consistency: most should blend nicely into the oil, but if you have a thick, stiff peanut butter, you can add a little more oil to help it loosen up in the pan.

When everything is well mixed, take the pan off the heat and add some salt and pepper (taking it easy if your peanut butter contains salt). Tip the squash back into the pan and use a potato masher to mash it into the peanut buttery mix. Finish off the mixing with a wooden spoon. If you've used a butternut squash, you'll get a relatively soft, wet mash. Other forms of squash will give a drier, fluffier result.

Taste the mash and add more salt and/or pepper if needed, then heap into a serving bowl and bring to the table.

Leek and parsnip mash with rosemary

Serves 4

600–700g parsnips, peeled, trimmed and cut into 3–4cm chunks

3 tbsp olive or rapeseed oil, plus extra to serve

3 medium leeks (about 500g), trimmed and thinly sliced

1 fat (or 2 small) garlic clove(s), chopped

2 tsp chopped rosemary

1 tsp English mustard

Sea salt and black pepper

I get so excited about roasted parsnips that I sometimes forget how good they can be just boiled – the flavour is a little less concentrated and therefore milder. Tender, sweated leeks and fragrant rosemary are perfect partners. This is particularly good alongside baked mushrooms (see pages 348 and 357).

Put the parsnips into a saucepan, cover with water, add salt and bring to the boil. Simmer for about 10 minutes until tender enough to mash.

Meanwhile, heat the oil in a large saucepan over a medium heat. Add the leeks, garlic and rosemary with some salt and pepper. When the leeks are sizzling, cover the pan, turn down the heat and let them sweat gently for 12–15 minutes, stirring occasionally, until completely tender. The leeks won't be getting any further cooking, so make sure they are done, with no 'squeak' left, at this point. Take the pan off the heat and add the mustard. Stir it thoroughly into the softened leeks.

Drain the parsnips and let them steam in their colander for a few minutes, then tip them into the pan with the leeks. Use a fork to mash the parsnips into the leek mixture and stir the whole thing together – the finished consistency should be quite textured and chunky, not super-smooth.

Taste and add more salt and/or pepper if necessary, then give the mash a final trickle of oil and it's ready to serve.

Swaps

Roots This also works well with a combination of roots – carrots, celeriac and spuds can all go in the mix.
Alliums You can swap the leeks with onions if you like.

Blitzed kale with lemon and garlic

Serves 4

3 large garlic cloves, peeled

400g curly kale, Red Russian or cavolo nero

Up to 75ml extra virgin olive oil, plus a little extra to serve

Sea salt and black pepper

TO FINISH

Finely grated lemon zest

A little flaky sea salt

Based on a recipe from my friend April Bloomfield, a British chef based in New York, this is a wonderful way to eat kale. In fact, you can eat a lot of kale, with a lot of pleasure, when it's prepared this way! I love it alongside spud-based dishes such as roast potatoes and grapes with bay and star anise (page 130).

Put the whole garlic cloves and a good pinch of salt in a large saucepan or small stockpot (big enough to hold all the kale). Add plenty of cold water and bring to the boil.

Meanwhile, prepare the kale by tearing the leaves away from the tough stalks (discard these) and tearing the leaves into large pieces.

When the water is boiling briskly, add the kale, pressing it down into the boiling water with a spatula. Let it simmer for 5–10 minutes until nice and tender but not too soft. (Cavolo nero will probably cook more quickly than the slightly more robust curly and Red Russian kales.)

Tip the kale and now soft garlic cloves into a large colander. Leave to drain for a couple of minutes, then use tongs to squeeze out a little more water from the leaves (there's no need to be too rigorous about this – a little moisture in the kale is ok).

Transfer the kale and garlic to a food processor. Add salt and pepper and start processing, stopping to push down the leaves as necessary. When the kale is roughly chopped, start pouring in the olive oil, stopping when you have a dark, dense, coarse purée (you may not need all the oil).

Heap the kale mixture into a warmed serving dish or individual bowls, trickle with a little more extra virgin oil, sprinkle with some lemon zest, a few flakes of sea salt and a grinding of black pepper, and serve.

Spiced cabbage with sunflower seeds

Serves 4

75g sunflower seeds

½ medium cabbage, such as pointed spring cabbage or Savoy (about 300g untrimmed)

1 tbsp rapeseed oil

1 medium onion, quartered and sliced

1 medium-hot red or green chilli, deseeded (for less heat, if preferred) and finely chopped

2 garlic cloves, chopped

1 tsp freshly grated ginger

1 tsp ground turmeric

2 tsp coriander seeds, bashed (or 1 tsp ground coriander)

Juice of ½ large lime, or more to taste

Sea salt and black pepper

When wilted in a hot pan, cabbage becomes tender and sweet, and tastes wonderful with aromatic spices and the nutty crunch of sunflower seeds.

Put the sunflower seeds into a large, dry frying pan over a medium heat and toast for a few minutes until the seeds start to colour a little and give off a nice, nutty aroma. Set aside.

Cut the cabbage half in half again and remove the thick core, then shred each quarter into roughly 5mm slices.

Heat the oil in the frying pan over a medium heat. Add the onion, chilli and a pinch of salt and, when sizzling, cover and turn down the heat. Sweat gently for 10–12 minutes, until the onion is soft and translucent.

Add the garlic, ginger, turmeric and coriander and cook for a couple of minutes longer. Toss in the sunflower seeds and stir well so they are coated in the spicy mixture.

Add the shredded cabbage to the frying pan, with a little more salt and some pepper. Cook gently, stirring frequently, for about 10 minutes, until wilted but still with a bit of body, covering the pan at least some of the time to help the leaves wilt.

Taste and add more salt if required, then transfer to a serving dish and spritz with the lime juice. Serve warm or at room temperature. I like to eat this with a dhal, such as the one on page 102.

Swaps

Brassicas Instead of cabbage, use shredded spring greens or chard.
Seeds Swap pumpkin or sesame seeds for the sunflower seeds.

Cavolo nero with oats

Serves 4

200g cavolo nero or curly kale

2 tbsp olive or rapeseed oil

1 medium onion, chopped

1 garlic clove, chopped

25g oats (porridge or jumbo)

Sea salt and black pepper

A pinch of dried chilli flakes (optional)

FOR THE OATY, NUTTY TOPPING

50g hazelnuts (skin on or off)

1 tbsp olive or rapeseed oil

50g oats (porridge or jumbo)

A large sprig of thyme, leaves picked from the stems (optional)

Oats are used two ways here: some are toasted to make a crisp topping, while a handful are mixed into the cooking cavolo nero or kale, adding a tender texture that contrasts with the leaves.

Strip the cavolo nero or kale leaves off their stalks, then roll up the leaves and slice them across into thin ribbons. Wash in a colander and set aside.

To make the topping, roughly bash the nuts using a pestle and mortar. Heat the 1 tbsp oil in a large frying pan over a medium heat. Add the nuts with a pinch each of salt and pepper and stir well, making sure the nuts are well coated in the oil. Toast them in the pan for 1–2 minutes.

When the nuts are sizzling nicely, add the 50g oats, with the thyme if using. Stir, then toast for 5 minutes more, stirring often but not continuously, so the oats get a chance to brown but don't burn. When the nuts and oats are golden brown, tip them out onto a plate; set aside.

Wipe out the frying pan, add the 2 tbsp oil and put it back over a medium heat. Add the onion with a pinch of salt and, when it's sizzling nicely, turn the heat down and cover the pan. Sweat gently, stirring a few times, until the onion is soft and translucent – at least 10 minutes. Add the garlic, cover the pan again and sweat for a few more minutes.

Now add the shredded cavolo nero or kale with the water still clinging from washing. Stir into the onion, then cover the pan and let the leaves wilt for about 5 minutes.

Scatter the 25g oats over the greens and trickle in 100ml water. Stir well. Cover the pan again and cook for 5–10 minutes, stirring once or twice, until the oats have absorbed the water and softened, and the greens are tender but not soft. Taste and add more salt and pepper if needed.

Spoon the greens into a warmed dish and sprinkle with a little dried chilli if you like. Finish with a good scattering of the oaty, nutty topping (you'll probably have more than you need). Serve straight away.

Swaps

Brassicas Try shredded spring greens or Savoy cabbage in place of the cavolo nero.

Nuts Replace the hazelnuts with walnuts or pecans.

Roasted tofu

Serves 2–3

1 tbsp olive or rapeseed oil

400g tofu (not silken)

3–4 garlic cloves, halved or quartered lengthways

About 1 tbsp chopped rosemary

A pinch of dried chilli flakes

Sea salt and black pepper

This simple way of cooking tofu drives off much of its moisture and leaves it with a lovely colour and tempting, slightly chewy texture. It works as a nibble on its own, or alongside green veg.

Preheat the oven to 200°C/Fan 180°C/Gas 6.

Trickle the oil into a small roasting tray and put it in the oven to heat up while you prepare the tofu.

Take the tofu from its pack, pouring away any liquid. Wrap the block(s) in a clean tea towel and press quite firmly to get rid of a little more excess liquid. Then unwrap the tofu and cut it into 3–4cm chunks.

When the tray of oil is hot, take it from the oven. Tip in the tofu (take care because it will spit). Add the garlic, rosemary, a small pinch of chilli flakes and a little salt and pepper. Use a spatula to turn the tofu over in the oil and seasonings.

Sprinkle on a little more salt, pepper and chilli and return the tray to the oven. Roast for 15 minutes, then stir the tofu with a spatula and give it another 10 minutes, until lightly coloured.

Serve straight away, piping hot, or let it cool to room temperature.

Swaps

Herbs Give the tofu a slightly different slant by replacing the rosemary with a good pinch of Chinese five-spice powder. This makes a great accompaniment to stir-fries and rice-based dishes.

Puy lentils with veg and herbs

Serves 6

2 tbsp olive or rapeseed oil, plus extra to finish

2 medium-large onions, chopped into large pea-sized dice

300g carrots, peeled and chopped into large pea-sized dice

200g celery, chopped into large pea-sized dice

2 garlic cloves, sliced

1–2 bay leaves

250g Puy lentils

Sea salt and black pepper

A handful of flat-leaf parsley, roughly chopped, to finish

Tiny, slate-green Puy lentils are a staple in my kitchen, dished up as an accompaniment to all kinds of savoury fare, from bubbling gratins to crisp salads. Often I just simmer, drain and season them. But in this recipe they are cooked with onion, carrot and celery, which imbue the lentils with extra flavour (and generally ups your veg intake, of course).

Heat the oil in a large, wide pan over a medium-high heat. Add the onions, carrots, celery, garlic, bay and a pinch of salt. Cook the veg, uncovered, stirring often and keeping the heat moderately high, for about 10 minutes until they are softened and very lightly coloured, but not browned.

Meanwhile, tip the lentils into a saucepan and cover with cold water. Bring to a full boil, then immediately take the pan off the heat and drain the lentils in a colander.

When the veg has had its 10 minutes, add the part-cooked lentils and 300ml fresh water (this won't cover the lentils – don't worry). Bring to a simmer then cover the pan. Cook gently for about 10 minutes until the lentils are tender but still with a little bit of nutty bite, stirring often to help them cook evenly.

Take the saucepan off the heat and leave to stand, covered, for about 5 minutes. You may have a little flavoursome cooking liquor left at the base of the pan at this stage. You can drain it off if you want your lentils to be completely 'dry' but there's no need to – it's very tasty! Season with salt and pepper to taste and add a little more oil. Serve warm or at room temperature, finished with a scattering of chopped parsley.

Swaps

Veg Replace the onion with sliced leek, the carrot with diced parsnip or celeriac, or the celery with chopped fennel.

Spuds and grains

WHEN THERE'S A CROWD of hungry people to feed, a dish of something starchy on the side can make all the difference. Every veg-centric cook needs a handy repertoire of such satisfying extras – the kind of things that turn a light and herby salad, a saucy curry, veggie hotpot, or cluster of well-flavoured tapas, into a varied and pleasing meal. And I think those side dishes should contribute more than mere bulk – they need to be tasty. Giving such dishes a little extra something to pique the appetite means they will always be more than basic ballast. It also means, I find, that you don't need quite so much of them. Add more to your rice, your grains or spuds in terms of texture and flavour and you can eat a little less in sheer volume.

For many these days, pasta is the easy and obvious choice for filling up the family. But I'm somewhat wary of it becoming a go-to 'starch on the side'. It just doesn't have the inherent goodness or, frankly, the culinary interest, of some of the less processed starchy options. The same goes for couscous. In fact, nutritional science is increasingly revealing that large quantities of refined carbohydrates like these, and the blood-sugar spikes they can cause, are just not good for us.

I think we should be paying more attention to the grains, seeds and root veg that represent starch in its more natural, unprocessed, fibre-rich form. They can partner other foods so well – and with greater nutritional benefits than the industrially made products of refined wheat. So it's recipes for these robust and tasty starches that you'll find in the pages that follow.

I still have, and always will have, a lot of time for potatoes. Spuds are rightly one of this nation's favourite vegetables – inexpensive, home-grown, all-year-round dependables that thoroughly deserve their staple status. And I never tire of finding new ways to explore their charms. They are versatile partners to all manner of more complex dishes, and this is just as true in veg-led cooking as in meat-based cuisine. So you'll find plenty of potato dishes here – including some nifty variations on the much-loved themes of mashing and roasting.

I have also included recipes for some of my favourite grains and seeds. Buckwheat, for instance, is a seed with an amazing nutty flavour. It can be eaten raw or toasted, but also cooks to a pleasing, tender, nubbly texture. It's great with something saucy, such as a mole or chilli. The same can be said of delicate quinoa, a protein-rich little seed that soaks up dressings and sauces beautifully. Delicious pearled spelt and barley, earthy lentils and good old brown rice have a place here too.

Such side dishes should be simple, but not plain or unseasoned. So while these recipes centre on foods that are, in their unadorned state, relatively bland, they are also shot through with herbs and spices, garlic and chilli, lemon, and even seaweed. These are all storecupboard stalwarts – things you can keep to hand in order to turn spuds or grains into partner dishes worthy of any supper table.

Thus seasoned and spiced or otherwise enhanced, these dishes fall very easily into the wonderful flow of mix-and-match eating that I've been proposing throughout this book. In fact they are great companions to almost all the other recipes. Many of them work as meals in themselves if you add a few extras – nuts, seeds, dried fruit etc. And even if you serve them in their simplest form. But I don't always need to have a plan for their final deployment to feel they are worth knocking out. I know they will always prove useful. And any leftovers can become the basis of a whole new dish – best augmented by a fresh helping of veg!

Smashed new potatoes with coriander seeds and bay

Serves 4

1kg large-ish new potatoes, or waxy salad potatoes, scrubbed or scraped but left whole

6 bay leaves, torn

6 garlic cloves, peeled but left whole

2 tbsp olive or rapeseed oil

2 tsp coriander seeds, roughly crushed

Sea salt and black pepper

This is a steal from Tom Hunt, a former River Cottage colleague of mine, now cooking at the excellent Poco in Bristol. Waxy spuds are simmered with garlic and bay leaves to perfume them, then 'smashed' to form nicely crisp-able pieces, before being roasted hard with more aromatics.

Put the potatoes, bay leaves and whole garlic cloves into a large saucepan. Cover with cold water, bring to the boil and simmer for about 15 minutes until tender.

In the meantime, preheat the oven to 200°C/Fan 180°C/Gas 6.

Drain the potatoes, garlic and bay in a colander and leave them there for 5 minutes or so, to steam-dry.

Meanwhile, put the oil into a large, shallow roasting tray – large enough to hold the potatoes in one layer, ideally with a little space between them here and there – and put it in the oven to heat up.

You now need to 'smash' the potatoes. Tip them back into their hot pan (bay leaves and garlic too) and use a heavy pestle, the end of a rolling pin or a potato masher to hit them gently, breaking them up but not crushing them completely. You want large, rough chunks of potato, with a few smaller bits of spud shrapnel here and there (not mash).

When the oil in the roasting tray is hot, take it from the oven and tip the smashed potatoes, bay and garlic into it. Add the crushed coriander seeds, season with salt and pepper and toss the potatoes in the hot oil. Roast in the oven for 30 minutes or until crisp and golden. Serve hot.

Swaps

Roots A mix of half spuds and half parsnips is a great variation.
Spices Replace the coriander with cumin seeds and/or a pinch of dried chilli flakes for a slightly warmer flavour.

Curried potato rösti

Makes 8

500g maincrop potatoes, such as Maris Piper

2 tbsp curry paste, ready-made or home-made (see page 95)

Rapeseed oil, for frying

Sea salt

These tasty potato cakes are an excellent way to use up a batch of home-made curry paste (see page 95). Serve them with a tomato and herb salad, or with dhal or a curry – with almost anything, in fact!

Peel the potatoes, then grate them coarsely on the largest holes of a box grater or, to make it extremely quick and easy, in a food processor.

Take handfuls of the grated potato and, holding them over a bowl, squeeze out as much starchy liquid from them as you can. Put the squeezed-out potato into a large bowl. Repeat with all the grated potato. If any has fallen into the bowl with the squeezed-out liquid, fish it out, squeeze it and add to the rest of the potato.

Add the curry paste to the grated potato and mix thoroughly, so it is evenly distributed.

Heat a large, non-stick frying pan over a medium-high heat and add enough oil to cover the base in a thin film.

When the oil is hot, take an eighth of the curried potato, squeeze it in your hand again to expel a little more liquid, then put it into the pan, squashing it down with a spatula into a thin cake. Repeat until there are another three cakes in the pan.

Fry the potato rösti over a brisk but not fierce heat for about 8 minutes, pressing them down periodically with your spatula, but trying not to move them too much, so they get the chance to form a good, golden, brown crust.

Take a peek at the base of one of the rösti and if you can see that a lovely crust has formed, carefully turn them all over and cook for a further 7–8 minutes until they are golden brown on the other side too, and crisp at the edges.

Transfer the cooked rösti to a plate lined with a double layer of kitchen paper; use more kitchen paper to blot the tops. Keep warm in a low oven while you cook the other half of the mixture. Serve the rösti as soon as they are all ready.

Swaps

Roots Grated celeriac, carrot or parsnip can all be mixed in with the potato to make mixed root rösti.
Spices Replace the curry paste with a couple of teaspoonfuls of harissa for a more Middle Eastern flavour.

Seaweed oven chips

Serves 4

1kg maincrop potatoes, ideally a floury variety such as King Edward

2 tbsp rapeseed oil

4 tbsp finely flaked dried seaweed, such as kombu

Sea salt and black pepper

The great thing about shaking a little dried seaweed over your chips is that you can add less salt. The taste of the seaweed itself is subtle, but the seasoning effect is significant; depending on the type of seaweed you use, you may not need any salt at all. I like to use flaked dried kombu for this (from maraseaweed.com) but any finely flaked dried seaweed will work.

Preheat the oven to 190°C/Fan 170°C/Gas 5.

Scrub the potatoes but don't peel them. Cut into chunky wedges and put them in a large saucepan. Cover with water, bring to the boil and boil for 5 minutes. Drain the potatoes and leave them to steam in the colander for a couple of minutes.

Meanwhile, pour the oil into a large roasting tray and place it in the oven to heat up.

Tip the potatoes back into their hot saucepan, put on the lid and shake the pan vigorously to roughen the potatoes' surfaces. If they are a very floury variety they will roughen up quite readily. If they're quite smooth, you can use a fork to break up their surfaces a little more. Add the flaked seaweed and a little pepper and toss well with the potatoes so each chip gets some seaweed.

Tip the potatoes into the hot oil and toss them in it, distributing the oil as well as you can. Return to the oven for about 50 minutes, stirring well halfway through, or until crisp and golden. Taste a tester chip and add salt to the rest of the chips if needed.

Eat the chips hot or at room temperature. They're great with a garlicky dip such as roasted red pepper salsa (page 312).

Swaps
Roots Use other root veg in combination with, or instead of, the spuds. Celeriac, Jerusalem artichokes and parsnips are all good with seaweed.

Bay mash

Serves 4

1kg floury potatoes, such as Maris Piper or King Edward

6 bay leaves

200ml oat milk or almond milk

50ml rapeseed oil

Sea salt and black pepper

Extra virgin olive, rapeseed or hempseed oil, to finish (optional)

Fragrant, almost-spicy bay is one of my very favourite herbs. It works deliciously with so many vegetables – roots in particular – and elevates plain mashed potato into something really special. I love this alongside big, baked mushrooms, like those on page 348.

Peel the potatoes and cut them into large chunks, no smaller than a large egg. Put them into a large saucepan. Add 3 bay leaves, giving each one a twist first, to tear it and help release its aromatic oils. Cover the spuds with cold water, add salt and bring to the boil. Reduce the heat and simmer the potatoes, partially covered, for 15–20 minutes until completely tender.

Meanwhile, put the oat or almond milk into another pan, large enough to mash the potatoes in. Add the oil and the remaining 3 bay leaves (twisted again). Bring the milk just to the boil, then remove from the heat and leave to infuse.

When the potatoes are cooked, tip them into a colander and leave to steam for 5 minutes or so. Meanwhile, gently reheat the bay-infused milk until steaming hot, then take off the heat, remove the bay leaves and add a good seasoning of salt and pepper.

Either tip the hot potatoes (minus the bay leaves) directly into the pan of hot milk and mash them with a potato masher or use a potato ricer to rice the potatoes into the milk. Either way, finish by stirring with a wooden spoon until the mash is smooth and creamy. Taste it and add more salt or pepper if needed.

Serve the mash straight away. You can finish it with a trickle of extra virgin oil if you like, which is very nice if serving it with something relatively 'dry' such as baked mushrooms, but not necessary if you're serving it with something saucy.

Swaps

Roots Replace half the potatoes with celeriac for a delicious spin on this simple mash.

Herbs Instead of the bay, use the leaves from a few good sprigs of rosemary or thyme, finely chopping them before adding to the almond or oat milk (no need to remove before adding to the spuds).

Potato and spring onion boulangère

Serves 4–6

4 bunches of spring onions (about 500g in total)

2 tbsp olive or rapeseed oil

1 garlic clove, chopped

1kg fairly large new or waxy potatoes, scrubbed and cut into 2–3mm thick slices

400ml hot veg stock (see page 190 for home-made)

Sea salt and black pepper

This summery spin on a classic boulangère is totally delicious. I can eat it on its own but it makes a lovely partner to courgette dishes, such as the one on page 334. Use larger new potatoes, or waxy salad potatoes (baby new potatoes are a bit too fiddly to slice).

Preheat the oven to 190°C/Fan 170°C/Gas 5.

Trim the roots from the spring onions, then cut off the dark green tops, but don't be too drastic here: leave some of the pale green section at the top of each spring onion shaft. Remove the outer layer of onion if it looks dry. Slice each onion in half lengthways.

Heat 1 tbsp oil in a large frying pan over a medium heat. Add the halved spring onions, season with some salt and pepper and sauté briskly for 5–7 minutes, stirring or tossing often, until they are slightly wilted and patched with golden brown. Add the garlic and cook for another minute, then take the pan off the heat.

Choose an oven dish around 28 x 20cm. Arrange a layer of sliced new potatoes over the base, overlapping them just slightly. Arrange a few sautéed spring onions over the potatoes and season with salt and pepper. Continue layering in this way, until you've used all the potatoes and onions, finishing with a layer of potato.

Pour the hot stock over the veg (it won't completely cover it). Trickle 1 tbsp oil over the top layer of potatoes and add a final seasoning of salt and pepper. Bake for 50–60 minutes, until a knife passes easily through the potato layers and the top is golden and crisp.

Leave the boulangère to stand for at least 10 minutes before serving.

Swaps
Alliums Instead of the spring onions, use a couple of large onions, sliced and sautéed until golden, before the garlic is added.

Celeriac and seaweed bubble and squeak

Serves 2–4

20g whole dried dulse or other seaweed

2 tbsp olive or rapeseed oil

1 medium onion (red or brown), sliced

400–500g cold, cooked celeriac and/or potatoes

Sea salt and black pepper

Celeriac, with its delicate, nutty flavour is delicious with seaweed in this great take on bubble and squeak. I usually make it with leftover cooked celeriac and spuds, but it's definitely worth cooking from scratch – in which case you may want to double the quantities to feed a few more people. Any dried seaweed is good here but I favour mildly spicy, red dulse.

Put the dried seaweed to soak in cold water for the time instructed on the packet – probably between 5 and 30 minutes. Drain the seaweed and squeeze out excess water with your hands, then roughly chop it, removing tough stalks if there are any.

Meanwhile, heat 1 tbsp oil in a large non-stick frying pan over a medium-low heat. Add the onion and fry gently for about 5 minutes, until it starts to soften. Increase the heat a little and add the celeriac/potato to the pan – you can slice the root veg thickly before adding, or just crush them with your hands, so they fall into the pan in nice, rough chunks. Season with a touch of salt and pepper.

Fry the onion and roots until nicely golden brown; this can take longer than you think, so be patient. Cook, without stirring them too much – so they get a chance to form a crust on the base of the pan, for at least 10 minutes, more likely 15 or 20 minutes. You'll probably need to add another 1 tbsp oil to help the veg brown.

When the bubble and squeak is starting to look temptingly coloured, add the chopped seaweed and cook for a few more minutes. Taste and add more salt and pepper if necessary, then it's ready to serve.

Swaps
Veg Use a couple of handfuls of leftover cooked cabbage, roughly shredded, in place of the celeriac.

Tartare hash

800g potatoes (any kind)

2 tbsp olive or rapeseed oil

1 medium onion, halved and sliced

1 fat gherkin or 6 cornichons (about 30g in total), roughly chopped

2 tbsp capers, rinsed, drained and roughly chopped if large

Finely grated zest of 1 lemon

3 tbsp coarsely chopped flat-leaf parsley, plus a handful of sprigs to finish

Sea salt and black pepper

Extra virgin olive or rapeseed oil, to finish

The flavourings for a classic tartare sauce – capers, parsley, onion and gherkins – turn plain potatoes into an incredibly moreish dish. Serve with a big salad, such as chickpea, fennel and olives (page 182) to make a fantastic, filling meal.

If you are using maincrop potatoes, peel them; new potatoes can just be scrubbed or scraped. Cut the potatoes into large chunks, no smaller than a large egg (for new potatoes that may mean not cutting them at all).

Put the potatoes into a saucepan, cover with cold water, add salt and bring to the boil. Reduce the heat and simmer the potatoes, partially covered, until tender: allow 15–20 minutes for maincrop potatoes, 12–15 minutes for newbies. Drain and leave to steam in the colander.

Heat the oil in a large non-stick frying pan over a medium heat. Add the sliced onion and season with salt and pepper. Stir well and get the onion sizzling, then let it cook for about 10 minutes, stirring once or twice, until soft and lightly coloured.

Add the gherkin or cornichons, capers, lemon zest and parsley to the pan. Give them a good stir, then add the potatoes. Use a fork to roughly crush the potatoes in the pan, breaking them up into lumps and crumbs, but not reducing them to a mash. Stir them with the oniony mix in the pan.

Cook for about 10 minutes, stirring every now and again, until the potatoes are piping hot again. Taste and season with black pepper, and more salt if necessary (the gherkins and capers may provide enough).

Serve the hash hot or at room temperature, trickled with a little extra virgin oil and finished with parsley.

Swaps

Roots You can use leftover cooked potatoes for this, and other leftover roots, such as sweet potatoes, parsnips or celeriac, can also go in the mix. Scale the other ingredients up or down, depending on how much veg you have.

Lightly spicy buckwheat

Serves 4

2 tbsp olive or rapeseed oil

2 garlic cloves, chopped

1 tbsp cumin seeds, bashed
(or 2 tsp ground cumin)

1 tbsp coriander seeds, bashed
(or 2 tsp ground coriander)

300g whole buckwheat
(buckwheat 'groats'), raw or
roasted

Juice of ½ large lemon

Sea salt and black pepper

Buckwheat is a seed (not a form of wheat at all), and makes a great alternative to pasta or rice. Naturally gluten-free, it's a good source of fibre, minerals and antioxidants. The flavour is distinctly earthy and it can be bland if served plain, but it takes beautifully to this spicy treatment. Try serving this with roasted vegetables such as roast spiced beetroot, radicchio and orange (page 128).

Heat the oil in a medium-large saucepan over a low heat. Add the garlic and spices and cook gently, stirring often, for a couple of minutes. Add the buckwheat groats and mix them into the spicy oil. Toast them gently, stirring a few times, for a couple more minutes.

Add 600ml water, a grinding of pepper and ¼ tsp salt. Stir well, bring to a simmer then turn the heat down low so the buckwheat is just simmering. Let it cook, uncovered, for about 15 minutes until all the water has been absorbed and there are steam holes forming in the grains (if you tip the pan, you shouldn't see liquid slopping to the side). Take the pan off the heat, cover and leave to stand for 5 minutes.

Add the lemon juice and fork through the buckwheat. Taste and add more salt, pepper and/or lemon juice if needed. Serve straight away, or let it cool to room temperature. The buckwheat will tend to clump together as it cools, but leftovers can easily be loosened with a spoon and fork and fried gently to reheat.

Swaps
Spices For curried buckwheat, replace the cumin and coriander with 1 tbsp ready-made curry paste (this will include salt so don't add salt to the water – just check the seasoning once the buckwheat is cooked); or use home-made curry paste (see page 95) if you have some to hand.

Nutty quinoa

Serves 4–6

1 tsp cumin seeds

1 tsp coriander seeds

1 tsp fennel seeds

A pinch of dried chilli flakes (optional)

A pinch of flaky sea salt

100g hazelnuts (skin on or off)

2 tbsp olive or rapeseed oil

100g mixed seeds of your choice, such as sunflower, sesame and pumpkin

200g quinoa

Juice of ½ lemon, or more to taste

Sea salt and black pepper

Quinoa provides both starch and protein, and makes a nutritious partner to roast veg or stews, particularly when tossed with a dukka-style mix of spiced nuts and seeds.

Start with the nutty mix: using a large pestle and mortar, pound the cumin, coriander and fennel seeds with the chilli flakes, flaky salt and a grinding of black pepper until coarsely ground. Add the hazelnuts and bash them up, mixing them with the spices as you go. You don't want the nuts to be completely pulverised, just bashed into chunks and shards. (Alternatively, blitz the spices and nuts in a food processor.)

Heat the oil in a large frying pan over a medium heat. Add the nutty, spicy mix, along with the mixed seeds. Fry for about 5 minutes until the nuts and seeds are golden and the whole mix smells beautifully toasty and aromatic – stir often to ensure nothing burns. Tip the nutty mix out on to a plate so it doesn't cook any further.

Rinse the quinoa very thoroughly in a sieve, then tip it into a saucepan. Add plenty of cold water – about three times as much water as quinoa. Bring to the boil, reduce the heat and simmer for about 10 minutes, until the quinoa is just tender but not mushy. It's a good idea to start checking after just 6–7 minutes' simmering because it's quite easy to overcook this tiny grain.

Drain thoroughly in a sieve and tip the quinoa back into the hot pan. Add the seedy, spicy, nutty mix and the juice of ½ lemon and fork through. Taste and adjust the seasoning with more salt, pepper and/or lemon if needed. Serve hot or at room temperature.

Swaps

Grains Instead of the quinoa, toss this delicious nutty, seedy mix into cooked wholegrain rice, spelt or buckwheat.

Herby spelt and lentils

Serves 4–6

200g pearled spelt

150g Puy lentils

½ garlic clove, finely grated or crushed

About 4 tbsp chopped mixed herbs (see right)

3–4 tbsp extra virgin olive, rapeseed or hempseed oil

Juice of ½ lemon, or more to taste

Sea salt and black pepper

A hearty, wholesome mix of grains and pulses, flavoured with herbs, lemon and garlic, this is a worthy side to anything from a saucy stew to a big salad. You can serve it hot or at room temperature, pack it in a lunchbox or fry up the leftovers. I like to add plenty of chopped herbs to the hot grains. Parsley, thyme and chives make a great blend; you could also include chervil, summer savory, marjoram or, in smaller quantities, pungent tarragon or lovage.

If you have time, soak the spelt in cold water for half an hour or so. Put the spelt into a sieve and rinse it well under a cold running tap then tip it into a large saucepan or small stockpot. Cover with plenty of cold water – the water should cover the spelt by at least 5cm. Bring to a rolling boil and boil steadily for 5 minutes.

Add the lentils to the pan, stir and reduce the heat a little. Simmer the spelt and lentils together for 12–15 minutes, stirring once or twice and skimming off any scum from the surface. Test the spelt and lentils – both should be tender but not soft, retaining a nice, nubbly texture.

Drain well then return the spelt and lentils to the hot pan. Immediately stir in the garlic (the heat of the grains will very lightly cook it), the herbs, oil, lemon juice and some salt and pepper. Stir well, then taste and add more salt, pepper and/or lemon if needed.

Serve hot or at room temperature.

Berber barley

Serves 4

250g pearl barley

2 tbsp olive or rapeseed oil

1 medium onion, chopped

2 garlic cloves, chopped

2 tsp ground turmeric

2 tsp sweet smoked paprika

1 litre hot veg stock (see page 190 for home-made)

1 bay leaf, torn

½ cinnamon stick

2 tbsp harissa paste, or to taste (brands vary in heat)

100g unsulphured dried apricots, roughly chopped

100g raisins or sultanas

Finely grated zest of 1 large orange

Sea salt and black pepper

Rich and warming, this is full of the flavours I associate with North Africa: garlic, paprika, cinnamon, dried fruit and the multi-layered, spicy loveliness of harissa paste. It's such a satisfying dish that I could eat it on its own, but it makes a great partner to a Moroccan carrot blitz (page 284), hummus (see pages 304–311), or a tray of roasted squash, or roast fennel, peas and parsley (page 116).

Put the pearl barley into a bowl and cover with cold water. Leave it to soak for 20 minutes then tip into a sieve or colander, rinse well and allow to drain.

Heat the oil in a large saucepan or small stockpot over a medium heat. Add the onion and fry for about 5 minutes, then add the garlic, turmeric and smoked paprika and stir well so they form a paste with the oil. Cook for another couple of minutes, stirring often to ensure the spices don't stick and burn.

Add the rinsed pearl barley, stir it into the spice mix and cook for a couple of minutes, stirring often. Now pour in the hot stock and add the bay leaf, cinnamon and some salt and pepper. Stir well and bring to a gentle simmer.

Cook the barley, uncovered, at this low simmer until it is tender and all the liquid has been absorbed; this will take around 50 minutes. Avoid stirring. If it looks like becoming dry before 50 minutes is up, trickle in a splash of boiling water.

When the barley is tender and the liquid has been absorbed, take the pan off the heat. Stir in the harissa, dried apricots, raisins or sultanas and the orange zest. Let the barley sit for 5 minutes, then stir again and taste. Add more salt or pepper if needed, and it's ready to serve.

Swaps

Spices Replace the turmeric with a big pinch of saffron strands.
Grains You can swap pearled spelt for the barley – use 800ml stock and simmer for about 35 minutes. Or you can use wholegrain basmati rice, which will take around 45 minutes.

Seedy black rice

Serves 4

200g wholegrain black rice

1 tbsp virgin coconut oil

100g mixed seeds, such as sunflower and pumpkin

Fine sea salt

Chopped flat-leaf parsley, to finish

Black rice is a form of wholegrain rice with a lovely, inky-coloured outer layer. It tastes – and looks – fantastic with dishes that feature a tomato sauce, such as charred radicchio and shallots (page 56) or baked green beans with olives (page 340).

Put the rice into a bowl, cover with cold water and leave it to soak for about 30 minutes (if you don't have that much time, just soak the rice while you're frying the seeds). Drain the rice in a sieve and rinse it under the cold tap.

Heat the coconut oil in a large saucepan (that has a tight-fitting lid) over a medium heat. When it's hot, add the seeds and fry them for about 4 minutes – keep them moving in the pan so that they develop a nice toasty brown colour but don't burn.

Tip the drained rice in with the seeds (it may spit as the water hits the hot pan). Stir the rice with the sizzling seeds and oil for a minute or so. Now pour in 400ml water, and add ¼ tsp fine salt. Stir gently, trying to make sure there are no bits of rice or seed stuck to the sides of the pan above the water.

Bring up to a gentle simmer, put the lid on the pan and turn the heat down as low as possible. Cook, without lifting the lid, for 30 minutes. Then take the pan off the heat and let it stand for 10 minutes.

Remove the lid and give the rice and seeds a stir with a fork. If there's a little excess liquid still in the pan, drain it off. Serve scattered with chopped parsley.

Swaps

Grains Give the same seedy treatment to wholegrain brown or red rice.

Brown rice with onions

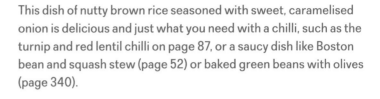

Serves 4

200g wholegrain basmati rice

2 tbsp olive or rapeseed oil

2 large onions, halved and sliced

Sea salt and black pepper

This dish of nutty brown rice seasoned with sweet, caramelised onion is delicious and just what you need with a chilli, such as the turnip and red lentil chilli on page 87, or a saucy dish like Boston bean and squash stew (page 52) or baked green beans with olives (page 340).

Rinse the rice then put it into a saucepan and cover with plenty of cold water. Add a good pinch of salt and bring to the boil. Reduce the heat to a simmer and cook until the rice is tender. This will probably be about 25 minutes but it depends on the brand of rice you're using (check the pack instructions); top up with more boiling water if necessary. Drain the cooked rice and return it to the warm saucepan.

Meanwhile, heat the oil in a large, wide pan over a medium heat. Add the sliced onions with some salt and pepper. Give them a good stir to break up the rings. When they are sizzling nicely, turn the heat right down and cover the pan (if you don't have a lid for it, place a baking sheet over the top – anything to trap in the steam).

Sweat the onions gently for 20–30 minutes, taking off the lid and stirring them from time to time, until they are very soft and wilted and reduced to a fraction of their original volume. Then take off the lid, increase the heat and cook for another 10 minutes or so, stirring often, until the onions are golden brown and caramelised.

Take the onions off the heat. Tip the hot brown rice into the onion pan and stir well. Taste, add more salt and pepper if required, then serve.

Swaps

Grains You can make this with any kind of wholegrain rice – it doesn't have to be basmati.

Alliums Replace the caramelised onions with thinly sliced leeks – sweated down in 1 tbsp oil for 20 minutes or so, until silky and soft.

Brown rice with parsley and garlic

Serves 4

200g wholegrain rice

4 garlic cloves, peeled but left whole

A bunch of flat-leaf parsley (about 50g), leaves picked from the stems and roughly chopped

Juice of ½ lemon

3 tbsp extra virgin olive or rapeseed oil

Sea salt and black pepper

In this simple dish, the rice is simmered with whole garlic cloves, which give it a subtle flavour. The soft, mild garlic is then blitzed with parsley, lemon and a little oil to form a fresh green sauce for the rice.

Put the brown rice into a sieve and rinse under the cold tap, then tip into a saucepan. Add the whole garlic cloves. Cover the rice with plenty of cold water, put a lid on the pan, add salt and bring up to the boil. Reduce the heat to a simmer and cook until the rice is tender. This will probably be about 25 minutes but it depends on the variety of rice — top up with more boiling water if necessary.

When the rice is tender, take the pan off the heat. Fish the cooked garlic cloves out of the pan and set them aside. Drain the cooked rice, and return it to the warm saucepan.

Put the soft garlic cloves into a small blender (or mini processor), or into a tall jug and use a stick blender. Add the roughly chopped parsley, lemon juice, oil and some salt and pepper. Blitz to a coarse purée.

Tip the green purée back into the hot rice and stir it through gently — it's quite nice if it's not completely evenly mixed, so the rice is more green in some places than others. Taste and add more salt or pepper if needed, then serve.

Swaps

Grains/Spuds Try using pearled spelt in place of the rice. The green garlic sauce is also delicious tossed into hot new potatoes.
Herbs Use coriander or basil instead of the parsley.

Index

Acknowledgements

I have produced this book with the help of a top team of talented individuals, most of whom I have now known and worked with for a decade or more. That feels very special and I am hugely grateful to them all.

Nikki Duffy has been amazing, as ever. Without her inspiring ideas, thorough editing and recipe testing, and great gift for keeping the show on the road, this book would not just have been diminished; it would be non-existent!

My other long-time culinary collaborator, Gill Meller, has also devised and honed many lovely recipes with his usual flair and precision. Gill is carving out his own remarkable path these days, buoyed by the huge success of his first solo cookbook, *Gather* (everyone should have a copy). But I'm trying not to let him get away entirely because I value his creative input so highly.

Gill and I were ably assisted on our veg-packed photo shoots by Alex Heaton-Livingstone, and we are very grateful to the team at Trill Farm, and to Millers Farm Shop near Axminster, who supplied us with so much lovely seasonal veg.

Those shoots would come to nothing, of course, without the superb work of Simon Wheeler, who remains my favourite food photographer of all time. I know these recipes are delicious but it's Simon's skill that ensures they truly look that way too.

Two brilliant editors at Bloomsbury, Natalie Bellos and Lisa Pendreigh, have nurtured this book from the seed of an idea through to leafy fruition. And we would all have been lost without the consummate editing and organisational skills of project editor Janet Illsley. Pulling a volume like this together is no mean feat — it's a joy to be able to do it with such a charming and patient editorial team.

I continue to be delighted by the work of illustrator Mariko Jesse, whose beautiful, quirky drawings and collages have brought these pages to life in the most celebratory style. Lawrence Morton has, as ever, brilliantly woven all the visual elements and text together. My deepest thanks go to him for turning raw copy and piles of potential images into a book that is so appealing to look at and friendly to use. Production manager Arlene Alexander has done a fantastic job of ensuring the finished item looks as good as it does.

My River Cottage colleague Sarah Turner road-tested many of the recipes for me — serving them up to her husband and hungry teenage sons, who I consider to be a pretty demanding panel! Her precise, thorough and insightful feedback has helped make these dishes the best they can be.

The irreplaceable Jess Upton has worked on recipe testing too, as well as masterminding the many shoots, meetings and liaisons necessary to complete a project like this — all with her usual efficiency and unflappable good nature.

I'd like to thank Naomi Devlin, River Cottage teacher and author of *Food for a Happy Gut*, for offering her advice on the veg-enhancing, life-enhancing techniques of fermentation. Gelf Alderson and Ben Bulger, great chefs who lead the development of our menus at River Cottage, have also generously shared their veg knowledge and ideas throughout this project.

Also at River Cottage, my thanks go to Will Livingstone and his garden team, who grow some of the loveliest and tastiest veg on the planet; and to Lucy Brazier, Lucy Lomas, Josie Curran and the home team at RCHQ who do so much fantastic work behind the scenes. At Bloomsbury, thanks to Ellen Williams, Sarah Williams, Amanda Shipp and Lena Hall.

Thanks also to Fran Bernhardt and Natalie Ward for discussing so helpfully the vegan approach to vegetables. Their thoughts and suggestions have, I hope, helped make this book entirely suitable for my vegan readers.

As always, I am hugely grateful to my agent, Antony Topping — a supporter, adviser and sounding-board I could not imagine being without.

And thank you, as ever, to my family. To Mum, Dad and Soph for sharing their love, knowledge (and opinions!) of growing and cooking with me down the years. And to Marie, Oscar, Chloe, Freddie (who also took some great pictures for the book) and Louisa, thanks for making the kitchen and veg garden at home the loveliest places to be in the whole wide world.

Bloomsbury Publishing
An imprint of Bloomsbury Publishing Plc

50 Bedford Square
London
WC1B 3DP
UK

1385 Broadway
New York
NY 10018
USA

www.bloomsbury.com

BLOOMSBURY and the Diana logo are trademarks of Bloomsbury Publishing Plc

First published in Great Britain 2017

British Library Cataloguing-in-Publication Data
A catalogue record for this book is available from the British Library.

Library of Congress Cataloguing-in-Publication data has been applied for.

ISBN: HB: 978-1-4088-6900-0
             ePub: 978-1-4088-6901-7

2 4 6 8 10 9 7 5 3 1

Project editor: Janet Illsley
Designer: Lawrence Morton
Photographer and props styling: Simon Wheeler
Illustrator: Mariko Jesse
Indexer: Hilary Bird

Printed and bound in Italy by Graphicom

River Cottage HQ, situated in Devon's beautiful Axe Valley, is home to the River Cottage cookery school,
smallholding and kitchen garden. As well as being the base for a huge range of cookery, gardening and
foraging courses, HQ is the venue for events including team-building days, weddings and the River Cottage
Fairs and Festivals. See rivercottage.net for details of events throughout the year.